NOV. 23 1987   FINE PD 1/4/88

OAKTON COMMUNITY COLLEGE

DES PLAINES, ILLINOIS   60016

Lawyers' Ethics

Lawyers' Ethics
Contemporary Dilemmas

Edited by
Allan Gerson

Transaction Books
New Brunswick (U.S.A.) and London (U.K.)

Library of Congress Catalog Number: 78-62895
ISBN: 0-87855-293-6
Printed in the United States of America

Library of Congress Cataloging in Publication Data

Main entry under title:

Lawyer's ethics.

    Includes bibliographical references.
    1. Legal ethics—United States—Addresses, essays,
lectures. 2. Lawyers—United States—Addresses, essays,
lectures. I. Gerson, Allan.
KF306.A5L38   174'.3   78-62895
ISBN 0-87855-293-6

Contents

Introduction

The practicing attorney is often confronted with the dilemma of discordant obligations owed to himself, clients, and society. In choosing his course of conduct he has, unfortunately, precious little to guide him. The Code of Professional Responsibility is likely to be too general to be of direct value. An up-to-date, comprehensive textbook on the subject is non-existent. Nor is there any developed body of case law in the field; judicial regulation of the profession, at least until the very recent past, has been notoriously slack. To make matters worse, not only does the attorney faced with a significant ethical problem often have to deal with it in uncharted waters, but whatever course of action is taken is susceptible to misunderstanding by an unsympathetic public.

This book hopes to provide a clearer understanding of the role of lawyers in America today and of some of the major ethical problems they must confront. It first examines, in historical and sociological context, the general values of the legal profession and the influence exerted by it on our society. The opening essay, Alex de Tocqueville's classic portrayal of the lawyer class as the high priests of American meritocracy, raises several questions for the reader about themes which recur throughout the book. Does de Tocqueville's observation that the legal profession is the mainstay of America's democratic order remain true today? If so, are lawyers a retrogressive or progressive force in assuring that order is responsive to the challenges of the day? Does de Tocqueville's further observation that although not "all the members of the legal profession are at all times the friends of order and the opponents of innovation . . . most of them are usually so" retain validity?

Our second essay by Senator Sam Ervin explores the qualities of "integrity" and "character" as essential components of the lawyer's makeup. President Carter would add to these attributes a sense of dedication to public service. In his recent speech before the American Bar Association, which we reproduce as our third essay, the President castigates the legal profession for having alienated itself from the societal problems of America by succumbing to the lure of wealth. "No resources of talent and training in our own society," he charges, "are more wastefully or unevenly distributed than legal skills." The reader is asked to ponder whether the President protesteth too much. Should we expect the attorney to seek justice and thereby emulate the physician who "seeks health," or the minister who "seeks God"? Or, viewed in a different perspective, is it not the primary and respectable function of lawyers to sell their

vii

representational talents to the highest bidder? We join the debate on this issue by juxtaposing in the two following articles the American Bar Association's response to the President's speech against a rebuttal by the Counsel to the President.

To add historical depth to the debate, we then include Professor Jerold Auerbach's essay, "Access to the American Legal System in Historical Perspective." Auerbach suggests that the legal profession has failed to fulfill its responsibility to champion causes aimed at ameliorating pressing social grievances. He places a great portion of the blame on the fact that American legal education, both traditionally and presently, teaches fledgling lawyers to divorce process from results, and to blur the distinction between the expertise they provide and the social policies their actions help effectuate. Referring to his own legal education, he states: "Never was there a whisper of a suggestion that law related to history, to society, to justice." Professor Joseph Bishop takes issue with this thesis. Professor Alan Dershowitz, in the essay which follows, concurs in part. All would agree, however, that the issue is hardly unimportant and that, like it or not, the values inculcated in law students today are likely to later have an inordinate effect in shaping this country's public policy. To further probe what those values are and the degree to which legal education has evolved in the course of the last three decades, we conclude this section with Judge Jerome Frank's incisive essay on legal education published in 1949.

Part II examines the particular nature of the lawyer's work that has given rise to so much controversy. Perhaps at the core of the public's ambivalence about the legal profession is the suspicion that, as often as not, the lawyer is attempting to obfuscate the truth. The public asks whether lawyers, assumed to be "officers of the court," do not have a duty to aid the tribunal in its search for truth. The question has bothered not only the public. At present, it is a heated topic of controversy within the profession. As this book goes to press, the ABA is in the midst of a great internal debate as to what the lawyer should do when confronted with a perjurious client: stay in, pull out, or do something in between.

Part II begins with Judge John Sirica's essay on the art of legal advocacy, and a call for more young lawyers to join its ranks. Professor Monroe Freedman then opens the debate on whether the lawyer is, indeed, simply a "hired gun" at the client's command, and if so, whether he need feel embarrassed by such a role. A brilliant essay by Marian Neef and Stuart Nagel on the roots of the adversary system follows. Contrasting the Anglo-American adversary system with its inquisitorial counterpart in the civil law countries, Neef and Nagel demonstrate that there is no inherent rational basis for the adversary system of justice, but that it stems from the suspicions and anachronisms of a past where the victor in combat was seen as the choice of divine will. Neef and Nagel suggest that the judge's role, then and now, is fairly passive, limited to assuring that the fight be fairly fought. In the ensuing essay, Judge Marvin Frankel, formerly of the United States District Court for the Southern District of New York, reflects on whether "our adversary system rates truth too low among the values that institutions of justice are meant to serve." Indeed, he suggests that "[O]ur relatively low regard for truthseeking is perhaps the chief reason for the dubious esteem in which the legal profession is held." Professor Monroe Freedman disagrees and argues that truth-finding should not be the paramount value in our criminal justice system. Professor Richard Uviller concurs with Freedman but concentrates on demonstrating the practical difficulties in finding suitable alternatives, or major improvements, for the present adversary system of justice.

Whether Frankel is correct or not in his contention that too little emphasis is placed on truth-finding in our system, the fact remains that the lay public finds the de-emphasis on truth-finding as but another manifestation of lawyers' curious ethics. Another incident demonstrating the public's difficulty with the ethical conduct of lawyers is the 1974 Lake Pleasant, New York case. Here, two attorneys, aware of the location of unburied and decomposing bodies of a murderer's victims, refused to inform the police or relatives who were searching for them. The lawyers felt that to offer any information about the whereabouts of these bodies might prove injurious to the interests of their client, the murderer, who gave the attorneys the information in confidence. Four former students at the New England School of Law—T. Hobin, D. Jensen, M. Callahan, and R. Pitkow—debate the pros and cons of the attorneys' actions and examine the limits of the attorney-client privilege. The section then ends with reference to two current approaches—that of the State of Massachusetts, and that of the ABA—to the resolution of the dilemma posed when the attorney finds that his client has perjured himself.

Part III examines in detail an aspect of the "character" requirement discussed in Senator Ervin's essay by focusing on the Alger Hiss reinstatement controversy. The problem posed is that of the extent to which an attorney's "character," rather than his competence, should be a condition for the practice of law. The brief on behalf of Alger Hiss maintains that disbarment needs to be a preventive rather than punitive measure. The Supreme Judicial Court of Massachusetts agreed. Barry Brown, former Associate Counsel of the Massachusetts Bar Association's Grievance Committee, who argued for denial of Hiss' petition for readmission, scrutinizes that decision and skillfully probes the larger dimensions of the problem raised by the case.

Part IV, the concluding section, examines several areas of concern from special perspectives. Max Kampelman, a prominent Washington attorney, discusses the relation between politics and law in the nation's capital and ethical questions raised by the sale of "influence." Milton Gwirtzman, a noted attorney with considerable international experience, raises perplexing questions concerning the responsibilities of the American lawyer practicing abroad, a subject of increasing concern as Congress attempts to regulate illicit overseas business practices. Finally, Martin Norton, who is a practicing physician as well as an attorney, places our discussion in its broadest perspective in his analysis of the divergent approaches by the medical and legal professions to common ethical problems.

Part I

The Legal Profession's Role
in American Society

The United States:
A Unique Government of Lawyers

Alexis de Tocqueville

In visiting the Americans and studying their laws, we perceive that the authority they have entrusted to members of the legal profession, and the influence that these individuals exercise in the government, are together the most powerful existing security against the excesses of democracy. This effect seems to me to result from a general cause which should be investigated, for it may be reproduced elsewhere.

The members of the legal profession have taken a part in all the movements of political society in Europe for the last five hundred years. At one time they have been the instruments of the political authorities, and at another they have succeeded in converting the political authorities into their instruments. In the Middle Ages they afforded a powerful support to the crown, and since that period they have exerted themselves effectively to limit the royal prerogative. In England they have contracted a close alliance with the aristocracy; in France they have shown themselves its most dangerous enemies. Under all these circumstances, have the members of the legal profession been swayed by sudden and fleeting impulses? Or have they been more or less impelled by instincts which are natural to them, and which will always recur in history? I am incited to this investigation, for perhaps this particular class of men will play a prominent part in the political society that is soon to be created.

Men who have made a special study of the laws derive from this occupation certain habits of order, a taste for formalities, and a kind of instinctive regard for the regular connection of ideas, which naturally render them very hostile to the revolutionary spirit and the unreflecting passions of the multitude.

The special information that lawyers derive from their studies ensures them a separate rank in society, and they constitute a sort of privileged body in the scale of intellect. This notion of their superiority perpetually recurs to them in the practice of their profession: they are the masters of a science which is necessary, but which is not very generally known. They serve as arbiters between the citizens, and the habit of directing to their purpose the blind passions of parties in litigation inspires them with a certain contempt for the judgment of the multitude. Add to this that they naturally constitute *a body*—not by any previous understanding, or by an agreement that directs them to a common end, but because the analogy of their studies and the uniformity of their methods connect their minds as a common interest might unite their endeavors.

Some of the tastes and the habits of the aristocracy may consequently be discovered in the characters of lawyers. They participate in the same instinctive love of order and formalities; they entertain the same repugnance to the actions of the multitude, and the same secret contempt of the government of the people. I do not mean to say that the natural propensities of lawyers are sufficiently strong to sway them irresistibly, for they, like most other men, are governed by their private interests and especially by the interests of the moment.

In a state of society in which the members of the legal profession cannot hold that rank in the political world which they enjoy in private life, we may rest assured that they will be the foremost agents of revolution. But it must then be asked whether the cause that then induces them to innovate and destroy results from a permanent disposition, or from an accident. It is true that lawyers mainly contributed to the overthrow of the French monarchy in 1789, but it remains to be seen whether they acted thus because they had studied the laws, or because they were prohibited from making them.

Five hundred years ago the English nobles headed the people and spoke in their name; at the present time the aristocracy supports the throne and defends the royal prerogative. But notwithstanding this, aristocracy has its peculiar instincts and propensities. We must be careful not to confound isolated members of a body with the body itself. In all free governments, of whatever form they may be, members of the legal profession will be found in the front ranks of all parties. The same remark is also applicable to the aristocracy; almost all the democratic movements that have agitated the world have been directed by nobles. A privileged body can never satisfy the ambition of all its members: it has always more talents and more passions than it can find places to employ. A considerable number of individuals are usually to be met with who are inclined to attack those very privileges which they cannot soon enough turn to their own account.

I do not, then, assert that *all* the members of the legal profession are at *all* times the friends of order and the opponents of innovation, but merely that most of them are usually so. In a community in which lawyers are allowed to occupy, without opposition, that high station which naturally belongs to them, their general spirit will be eminently conservative and antidemocratic. When an aristocracy excludes the leaders of that profession from its ranks, it excites enemies who are the more formidable—as they are independent of the nobility by their labors, and feel themselves to be their equals in intelligence, though inferior in opulence and power. But whenever an aristocracy consents to impart some of its privileges to these same individuals, the two classes coalesce very readily and assume, as it were, family interests.

I am, in the like manner, inclined to believe that a monarch will always be able to convert legal practitioners into the most serviceable instruments of his authority. There is a far greater affinity between this class of persons and the executive power than there is between them and the people, though they have often aided to overturn the former. Similarly, there is a greater natural affinity between the nobles and the monarch than between the nobles and the people, although the higher orders of society have often, in concert with the lower classes, resisted the prerogative of the crown.

Lawyers are attached to public order beyond every other consideration, and the best security of public order is authority. It must neither be forgotten that if they prize freedom much, they generally value legality still more. They are less afraid of tyranny than of arbitrary power, and provided the legislature undertakes of itself to deprive men of their independence, they are not dissatisfied.

I am therefore convinced that the prince who—in the presence of an encroaching democracy—should endeavor to impair the judicial authority in his dominions, and to diminish the political influence of lawyers, would commit a great mistake: he would let slip the substance of authority to grasp the shadow. He would act more wisely in introducing lawyers into the government; and if he entrusted despotism to them under the form of violence, perhaps he would find it again in their hands under the external features of justice and law.

The government of democracy is favorable to the political power of lawyers, for when the wealthy, the noble, and the prince are excluded from the government, the lawyers take possession of it in their own right, as it were. They are the only men of information and sagacity, beyond the sphere of the people, who can be the object of the popular choice. If, then, they are led by their tastes towards the aristocracy and the prince, they are brought in contact with the people by their interests. They like the government of democracy, without participating in its propensities and without imitating its weaknesses; whence they derive a twofold authority from it and over it. The people in democratic states do not mistrust the members of the legal profession, because it is known that they are interested to serve the popular cause; the people listen to them without irritation, because they do not attribute to them any sinister designs. The lawyers do not, indeed, wish to overthrow the institutions of democracy, but they constantly endeavor to turn it away from its real direction by means that are foreign to its nature. Lawyers belong to the people by birth and interest, and to the aristocracy by habit and taste; they may be looked upon as the connecting link between the two great classes of society.

The profession of the law is the only aristocratic element that can be amalgamated—without violence—with the natural elements of democracy, and advantageously and permanently combined with them. I am not ignorant of the defects inherent in the character of this body of men, but without this admixture of lawyer-like sobriety with the democratic principle, I question whether democratic institutions could long be maintained. I cannot believe that a republic could hope to exist at the present time, if the influence of lawyers in public business did not increase in proportion to the power of the people.

This artistocratic character, which I hold to be common to the legal profession, is much more distinctly marked in the United States and in England than in any other country. This proceeds not only from the legal studies of the English and American lawyers, but from the nature of the law and the position which these interpreters of it occupy in the two countries. The English and the Americans have retained the law of precedents; that is to say, they continue to found their legal opinions and the decisions of their courts upon the opinions and decisions of their predecessors. In the mind of an English or American lawyer, a taste and a reverence for what is old is almost always united with a love of regular and lawful proceedings.

This predisposition has another effect upon the character of the legal profession and upon the general course of society. The English and American lawyers investigate what has been done; the French advocate inquires what should have been done. The former produce precedents, the latter reasons. A French observer is surprised to hear how often an English or an American lawyer quotes the opinions of others, and how little he alludes to his own, for the reverse occurs in France. There, the most trifling litigation is never conducted without the introduction of an entire system of ideas peculiar to the counsel employed; and the fundamental principles of law are discussed in order to obtain a rod of land by the decision of the court. This abnegation of his own opinion; this implicit deference to the opinion of his forefathers; this servitude of thought which he is obliged to profess, necessarily give him more timid habits and more conservative inclinations in England and America than in France.

The French codes are often difficult to comprehend, but they can be read by everyone; nothing, on the other hand, can be more obscure and strange to the uninitiated than a legislation founded upon precedents. The absolute need of legal aid that is felt in England and the United States, and the high opinion that is entertained of the ability of the legal profession, tend to separate it more and more from the people, and to erect it into a distinct class. The French lawyer is simply a man extensively acquainted with the statutes of his country, but the English or American laywer resembles the hierophants of Egypt. Like them, he is the sole interpreter of an occult science.

The position that lawyers occupy in England and America exercises no less influence upon their habits and opinions. The English aristocracy, which has taken care to attract to its sphere whatever is at all analogous to itself, has conferred a high degree of importance and authority upon the members of the legal profession. In English society, lawyers do not occupy the first rank, but they are contented with the station assigned to them: they constitute, as it were, the younger branch of the English aristocracy, and are attached to their elder brothers, although they do not enjoy all their privileges. The English lawyers consequently mingle the aristocratic tastes and ideas of the circles in which they move with the aristocratic interests of their profession.

And, indeed, the lawyer-like character that I am endeavoring to depict is most distinctly to be met with in England. There laws are esteemed not so much because they are good, but because they are old. And if it is necessary to modify them in any respect, to adapt them to the changes that time operates in society, recourse is made to the most inconceivable subtleties, in order to uphold the traditionary fabric, and to maintain that nothing has been done which does not square with the intentions and complete the labors of former generations. The very individuals who conduct these changes disclaim any desire for innovation, and would rather resort to absurd expedients than plead guilty to so great a crime. This spirit appertains more especially to the English lawyers. They appear indifferent to the real meaning of what they treat, and direct all their attention to the letter; they seem inclined to abandon reason and humanity, rather than swerve one tittle from the law. English legislation may be compared to the stock of an old tree, upon which lawyers have engrafted the most dissimilar shoots in the hope that—although their fruits may differ—their foliage at least will be confused with the venerable trunk that supports them all.

In America there are no nobles or literary men, and the people are apt to mistrust the wealthy; lawyers consequently form the highest political class and the most cultivated portion of society. They have nothing to gain by innovation, which adds a conservative interest to their natural taste for public order. If I were asked where I place the American aristocracy, I should reply without hesitation that it is not among the rich, who are united by no common tie, but that it occupies the judicial bench and the bar.

The more we reflect upon all that occurs in the United States, the more we shall be persuaded that the lawyers, as a body, form the most powerful (if not the only) counterpoise to the democratic element. In that country we easily perceive how the legal profession is qualified by its attributes, and even by its faults, to neutralize the vices inherent in popular government. When the American people are intoxicated by passion or carried away by the impetuosity of their ideas, they are checked and stopped by the almost invisible influence of their legal counselors. These secretly pit their aristocratic propensities against the nation's democratic instincts; their superstitious attachment to what is old against its love of novelty; their narrow views against its immense designs; and their habitual procrastination against its ardent impatience.

The courts of justice are the visible organs by which the legal profession is enabled to control the democracy. The judge is a lawyer who, independent of the taste for regularity and order that he has contracted in the study of law, derives an additional love of stability from the inalienability of his own functions. His legal attainments have already raised him to a distinguished rank among his fellows; his political power completes the distinction of his station, and gives him the instincts of the privileged classes.

Armed with the power of declaring the laws to be unconstitutional, the American magistrate perpetually interferes in political affairs. He cannot force the people to make laws, but at least he can oblige them not to disobey their own enactments and be inconsistent with themselves. I am aware that a secret tendency to diminish the judicial power exists in the United States. By most of the constitutions of the several states, the government can, upon the demand of the two houses of the legislature, remove judges from their station. Some other state constitutions make the members of the judiciary elective, and they are even subjected to frequent reelections. I venture to predict that these innovations will sooner or later be attended with fatal consequences; and that it will be found out, at some future period, that by thus lessening the independence of the judiciary, they have attacked not only the judicial power, but the democratic republic itself.

It must not be supposed, moreover, that the legal spirit is confined in the United States to the courts of justice; it extends far beyond them. As the lawyers form the only enlightened class whom the people do not mistrust, they are naturally called upon to occupy most of the public stations. They fill the legislative assemblies and are at the head of the administration; they consequently exercise a powerful influence upon both the formation of the law and its execution. The lawyers are obliged, however, to yield to the current of public opinion, which is too strong for them to resist. But it is easy to find indications of what they would do if they were free to act. The Americans, who have made so many innovations in their political laws, have introduced very sparing alterations in their civil laws, and with great difficulty, although many of these laws are repugnant to their social condition. The reason for this is that in matters of civil law, the majority are obliged to defer to the authority of the legal profession, and the American lawyers are disinclined to innovate when they are left to their own choice.

It is curious for a Frenchman to hear the complaints that are made in the United States against the stationary spirit of legal men, and their prejudices in favor of existing institutions.

The influence of legal habits extends beyond the precise limits I have pointed out. Scarcely any political question arises in the United States that is not resolved, sooner or later, into a judicial question. Hence, all parties are obliged to borrow, in their daily controversies, the ideas (and even the language) peculiar to judicial proceedings. As most public men are or have been legal practitioners, they introduce the customs and technicalities of their profession into the management of public affairs. The jury extends this habit to all classes. The language of the law thus becomes, in some measure, a vulgar tongue. The spirit of the law, which is produced in the schools and courts of justice, gradually penetrates beyond their walls into the bosom of society, where it descends to the lowest classes; at last the whole people contract the habits and the tastes of the judicial magistrate. The lawyers of the United States form a party which is but little feared and scarcely perceived, having no badge peculiar to itself. It adapts itself, with great flexibility, to the exigencies of the time, and accommodates itself, without resistance, to all the movements of the social body. But this party extends over the whole community, and penetrates into all the classes which compose it; it acts upon the country imperceptibly, but finally fashions it to suit its own purposes.

The Role of the Lawyer in America

Samuel J. Ervin, Jr.

It is our proud boast as Americans that our national and state constitutions were ordained to establish for our people governments of laws instead of governments of men; and it is my purpose to demonstrate that these governments of laws cannot operate effectively for the benefit of our people without the assistance of the lawyer.

Sir Thomas More envisioned his imaginary nation, Utopia, as a land in which justice was administered without laws and without lawyers. The unreality of Sir Thomas' vision is manifest. Justice cannot exist anywhere without lawyers to champion it and laws to enforce it.

It is obvious, moreover, that the republic which the Founding Fathers gave to America will vanish if America ceases to have a government of laws. Alexander Hamilton, who was a brilliant lawyer, explained why this is so:

> It has been frequently remarked with great propriety that a voluminous code of laws is one of the inconveniences necessarily connected with advantages of a free government. [1]

In saying this, Hamilton emphasized that a government of laws necessarily requires many laws to define and limit the powers of government and its officers, and many laws to elaborate the rights and the responsibilities of the people.

At the same time, he warned his contemporaries and subsequent generations of Americans that "the facility and excess of law making seem to be the diseases to which our governments are most liable"; [2] that "all the repealing, explaining, and amending laws, which fill and disgrace our voluminous codes (are) but so many monuments of deficient wisdom"; [3] and that the incessant multiplying and altering of laws will produce disastrous consequences. He described these consequences in these words:

> The internal effects of a mutable policy are still more calamitous. It poisons the blessings of liberty itself. It will be of little avail to the people if the laws are made by men of their own choice, if the laws be so voluminous that they cannot be read, or so incoherent that they cannot be understood; if they be repealed or revised before they are promulgated, or undergo such incessant

11

changes that no man who knows what the law is today can guess what it will be tomorrow. Law is defined to be a rule of action; but how can that be a rule, which is little known and less fixed?[4]

Our laws have multiplied a thousandfold since Alexander Hamilton's day. Many of them have been the inevitable results of the increasing complexities of society. But many of them, I believe, are unnecessary and harmful products of a mania which has harassed our land in recent years.

Whenever anything they deem undesirable from their particular points of view happens, some politically powerful groups of Americans cry out for the immediate enactment of new laws. Their legislators, federal and state, hastily respond by passing new laws, often without pausing to determine (1) whether the remedy for the supposed evil must be found in ethics or religion rather than in law, (2) whether the old laws are adequate to cope with the supposed evil, or (3) whether the new laws are designed to deal with the supposed evil in a just and rational way.

What has been said makes America's need for competent lawyers plain. After all, the laws prescribe rules of conduct for all public officials and private individuals in our land. These officials and individuals are bound at their peril to observe these rules of conduct, even though they may not know or understand the laws which prescribe them. This is so because a government of laws would collapse if ignorance of law were an accepted excuse for its violation.

These public officials and private individuals require competent lawyers to counsel them in respect to the legality of the actions they may contemplate taking in the future, or to act as their advocates in respect to actions they or others may have taken in the past.

What I have just said reveals in simple words the role of the lawyer in America. In executing his role, the lawyer engages in activities incident to the practice of law. He may advise his client in respect to his legal rights or responsibilities, draft the legal documents necessitated by his client's personal or business affairs, act as agent for his client in negotiating and consummating commercial transactions with others, or act as an advocate for his client in legal proceedings before courts or administrative tribunals. In doing any of these things, the lawyer owes his client complete and dedicated allegiance.

To protect prospective clients and the public against incompetent or unscrupulous lawyers, government requires every applicant for admission to the bar to demonstrate, in appropriate ways, that he has a fair knowledge of law and a trustworthy character. Moreover, it disbars from further practice lawyers who have shown themselves unworthy of possessing a law license by violating specified laws or ethical standards.

A lawyer performs his role in an acceptable manner if he discharges, with reasonable skill and fidelity, the obligations which his high calling imposes upon its practitioners. These obligations consist of his obligation to his client, he obligation to the court or administrative tribunal before which he appears, his obligation to society, and his obligation to himself. I will endeavor to delineate these obligations.

The lawyer is not obliged to accept as a client anyone who seeks his professional aid. But whenever he undertakes to perform any legal task for a client, he impliedly assures his client that he possesses reasonable legal knowledge and skill; that he is competent, or will in apt time make himself competent by study of the relevant facts and law to perform his undertaking in reasonable fashion; and that in performing his undertaking he will exercise his knowledge and skill with diligence and fidelity, solely in his client's interest.

If his undertaking requires him to act as an advocate for his client, he implicitly gives the additional assurance to his client that he is reasonably acquainted with the rules of practice of the court or administrative tribunal before which he is to appear. But he does not undertake that the client will prevail in his cause, or profess that he knows all the law or is incapable of error or mistake in applying it to the facts. As the Supreme Court remarked on one occasion, even the most skillful of the profession would hardly be able to come up to that high standard.[5]

The lawyer also owes to his client the duty to maintain inviolate his confidences and secrets, and to be intellectually honest in all dealings with him.

I cannot overmagnify the crucial importance of accuracy and diligence on the part of the lawyer. As Daniel Webster said so well:

> Accuracy and diligence are more necessary to a lawyer than great comprehension of mind, or brilliancy of talent. . . . If he would be a great lawyer, he must first consent to become a great drudge.

Some laymen criticize lawyers for defending persons the laymen believe guilty of the offenses charged. When criticized for appearing on behalf of an unworthy client, Phocion, a lawyer of ancient Greece, replied that "the good have no need of an advocate."[6] Accused persons who are deemed guilty or hated by the public stand in greatest need of an advocate, because it may be that they are innocent.

It is not the function of the lawyer to determine the guilt of persons charged with criminal offenses. Besides, no person is guilty in law until he has confessed his guilt or been convicted in open court. Hence, legal ethics adjudges rightly that "a lawyer has a right to defend a person accused of crime regardless of his personal opinion as to guilt. He is bound by all fair and honorable means to present every available defense to uphold due process of law."[7]

Justice Story and Thomas Erskine (the eminent English advocate) made significant remarks on this subject:

> *Justice Story:* He (the lawyer) may be required to defend against the arm of the government a party standing charged with some odious crime, real or imaginary. He is not at liberty to desert even the guilty wretch in his lowest estate; but he is bound to take care, that even here the law shall not be bent or broken to bring him to punishment. He will, at such times, from love of the law, as well as from compassion, freely give of his talents to the cause, and never surrender the victim until the judgment of his peers has convicted him upon legal evidence.[8]

> *Thomas Erskine:* If the advocate refuses to defend from what he may think of the charge or of the defense, he assumes the character of the judge; nay, he assumes it before the hour of judgment; and in proportion to his rank or reputation, puts the heavy influence of, perhaps, a mistaken opinion into the scale against the accused.[9]

The client retains the lawyer's talents, but not his conscience. Hence, a lawyer is never justified in doing an illegal or unethical act to serve a client.

The law entrusts to the lawyer an indispensable part in the operation of our adversary system of justice. As a consequence, the law imposes upon him an obligation to aid courts and administrative tribunals with their efforts to make the system accomplish its objective, in a way that inspires public confidence. To this end, he must display respect for courts and administrative tribunals, defend them against unjust criticism, and act with decorum and dignity in his appearances before them. Moreover, he must exercise diligence in preparing the cause of his client for presentation to the court or administrative tribunal, and there present the relevant facts and law with fairness and candor.

A lawyer demeans himself and trifles with a court or administrative tribunal if he takes a position which is not worthy of serious notice. But he is justified in taking a position based on law, or a cogent argument that the law on which his adversary relies is unjust and ought to be modified or reversed. A lawyer does a grave disservice to his client and to the cause of justice itself if he accepts a retainer to try a case which he is too busy or too lazy to prepare for trial.

Society gives much to the lawyer. By prescribing for him arduous studies to fit him for admission to the bar, by granting to him authority to act as legal adviser, draftsman, and agent to others in connection with their personal and business affairs, and by committing to him the performance of an essential part in the administration of justice, society enables the lawyer to acquire a special competence in respect to many of its most important concerns.

As a consequence, society rightly expects that the lawyer will use his special competence to insure good government, to improve law and its administration, to promote the trust of the people in the legal profession and the administration of justice, to rid the legal profession of unworthy members, to make legal assistance available to the indigent, to defend hated individuals and unpopular causes in criminal proceedings, and to act in other respects as an upright, patriotic citizen.

The obligation of the lawyer to himself is to cherish and keep inviolate, in all his professional activities, that priceless element of good character which we call integrity. The famous theologian, Cotton Mather, had this obligation in mind when he admonished the lawyers of Massachusetts in 1710 "to keep constantly a court of chancery in your own breast."[10]

I have observed lawyers at work ever since that far distant day in August of 1919, when the Supreme Court of North Carolina granted me a license to practice law. In closing, I rejoice to bear witness that with rare exceptions they have performed in commendable fashion their obligations to clients, courts, administrative tribunals, society, and themselves.

Notes

1. A. Hamilton, The Federalist 78, at 495-496. (B.F. Right, ed. 1961).
2. *Id.*
3. *Id.*
4. A. Hamilton, The Federalist No. 62, at 411-12.
5. National Savings Bank v. Ward, 100 U.S. 195 (1879); *see also* Lord Chief Justice Tindal in Lanphier v. Phipos, 8 C&P 475 (1838).
6. Plutarch's Lives.
7. R.L. Wise, Legal Ethics 320 (2d ed. 1970).
8. J. Story, Miscellaneous Writings 521 (1852).
9. Stryker, For the Defense 217 (1949); Thomas Erskine (Lord Erskine) on the trial of Thomas Paine for publishing The Rights of Man (1792).
10. C. Mather, Bonifacius 127 (1966).

Attack on Lawyers and the Legal Profession

President Jimmy Carter

For the last half an hour I have been sitting in a room nearby listening to the report of the background of this tremendous organization, and also listening to the report of the future of the organization. And I have been touched by some of the struggles that you have experienced in your own history.

I would like to begin with a quote from a book published in 1852.

> Jarndyce and Jarndyce drones on. This scarecrow of a suit has, in the course of time, become so complicated that no man alive knows what it means— innumerable children have been born into the case; innumerable old people have died out of it; whole families have inherited legendary hatreds with the suit—there are not three Jarndyces left upon the earth, perhaps since old Tom Jarndyce in despair blew his brains out at a coffee house in Chancery, but Jarndyce and Jarndyce still drags its dreary length before the court.

This quotation comes from the novel *Bleak House*, and although Charles Dickens who, by the way, was a court reporter himself, was writing about a chancery suit in London long ago, he could have been writing about a modern antitrust suit in federal court. His subject was the same that should preoccupy you and me, lawyers, mayors, governors, and the president of the United States—that is, ensuring that our legal system serves the ends of justice without delay.

I am not a lawyer, but there is no question that has concerned me more throughout my adult life than that of human justice—striving to alleviate the inequalities, the unfairness, the chance differences of fortune that exist among people, and to help ensure that all people possess the basic material and political rights that they need for full participation in the life of our society.

I grew up in a community in Georgia that often did not provide simple justice for a majority of our citizens—because of the divisions of privilege between those who owned land and property and those who did not, the divisions of power between those who controlled the political system and

17

those who were controlled by it, and the wall of discrimination that separated blacks and whites.

As a governor and as a president, I have learned that, as Reinhold Niebuhr said, "It is the sad duty of politics to establish justice in a sinful world." I am trying now, as your president, to carry our nation's message of basic justice and human rights to other nations.

But I know that we cannot speak of human rights in other countries unless we are going to do our utmost to protect the rights of our own people here at home. Let me tell you about some of the things that concern me.

On the last day of the administration of Lyndon Johnson, the government filed an antitrust suit against a major computer company. Nine years have passed; three new presidential administrations have taken office; hundreds of millions of dollars have been spent on legal fees. But still the trial is not nearly over, and it has been speculated that the judge who has supervised it for the last nine years may die or retire before the trial is completed, in which case it would start all over again. Generations of computers have come and gone. There is not a single computer now being sold that was being sold when the case began—but still the case goes on.

I am worried about a legal system in which expensive talent on both sides produces interminable delay—especially when delay itself can often mean victory on one side. Justice should not be forced to obey the timetables of those who seek to avoid it.

As a public official, I have inspected many prisons, and I know that nearly all inmates are drawn from the ranks of the powerless and the poor. A child of privilege frequently receives the benefit of the doubt; a child of poverty seldom does.

In many courts, plea bargaining serves the convenience of the judge and the lawyers, not the ends of justice, because the courts simply lack the time to give everyone a fair trial.

We have the heaviest concentration of lawyers on earth—one for every 500 Americans—three times as many as are in England; four times as many as are in West Germany; twenty-one times as many as there are in Japan. We have more litigation; but I am not sure that we have more justice. No resources of talent and training in our own society (even including the medical) are more wastefully or unfairly distributed than legal skills.

Ninety percent of our lawyers serve ten percent of our people. We are "overlawyered" and under-represented.

Excessive litigation and legal feather-bedding are encouraged. Noncontested divorces become major legal confrontations in many states. Complete title searches on the same property are unnecessarily repeated with each sale. Routine automobile accident cases clog our courts, while no-fault automobile insurance is opposed.

The number of medical malpractice suits skyrockets. Mahatma Gandhi, who himself was a very successful lawyer, said of his profession, "Lawyers will as a rule advance quarrels rather than redress them." We do not serve justice when we encourage disputes, rather than resolve them.

In my own region of the country, perhaps even in yours, as well, lawyers of great influence and prestige led the fight against civil rights and economic justice. They were paid lavish fees by their states and heaped with honors for their efforts. They knew all the maneuvers, and for too long they kept the promises of the Constitution of the United States from coming true.

The basic right to vote, to hold a job, to own a home, to be informed of one's legal rights when arrested, to have legal counsel if an indigent—these rights have been denied for generations in our country, and are being recently won only after intense struggle.

I think about these things when I come to speak with you. What I think about most, however, is the enormous potential for good within an aroused legal profession, and how often that potential has not been and is not used. More than any other nation on earth, ours was created out of respect for the law. We had the first written constitution—it is the oldest. We proclaimed ours a government of laws, not of men; we put our faith in interpretations of the laws to resolve our most basic disputes.

None of us would change our system of laws and justice for any other in the world. From the beginning, it made the citizens the masters of the state and not the other way around, and it has extended increasing protection to the poor and the victims of discrimination.

It is because of the enormous power of the law, and the position of great influence and privilege which lawyers occupy within our society, that lawyers bear such a heavy obligation to serve the ends of true justice, and through dynamic effort—individually, and collectively through organizations such as this—search for those ends of justice. I know that you understand these obligations.

During the last generation, many of our most important advances toward racial integration and protection of our people against government and its abuse have been made through the courts.

I heard the comments a few minutes ago about Chief Justice Earl Warren, who has been an inspiration to all of us who serve in government. But let me mention briefly four challenges that we should face in order to improve justice in America.

First, in making criminal justice fairer, faster, more sensible, and more certain; second, in holding the law to the highest standards of impartiality, honesty, and fairness; third in ensuring that access to the legal systems does not depend on political influence or economic power; and fourth, in reducing our over-reliance on litigation, and speeding up those cases that are litigated.

Our starting point in ensuring justice is to reduce crime through measures that are effective and fair. There was encouraging progress in this direction last year, when the volume of crime fell, for the first time in many years, by four percent below the previous year's level. It is a welcome development, but it does not change the urgent need to control crime. States and local governments must take the lead in this effort, but the federal government must also do its part.

We should streamline the federal criminal code, which now contains many provisions which overlap, duplicate one another, are inconsistent, and need upgrading. With the leadership of Senator Eastland, Senator Kennedy, and the late Senator McClellan, a twelve-year effort recently culminated in the Senate passage of this new comprehensive criminal code. I hope the House will pass it this year without delay.

We are working with congressional leaders to reorganize the Law Enforcement Assistance Administration, to gear our funding system to our most pressing needs, to provide better support for state and local governments, and to concentrate our help on improving the criminal justice system and reducing crime. I will propose a consolidation and a reorganization of many of the functions now performed by more than 110 different federal agencies that have direct responsibility for law enforcement.

We can reduce the tremendous overload on our criminal justice system by removing such crimes as drunkenness and vagrancy from the courts, thereby freeing the courts to deal with serious offenses, and enabling us to treat these social illnesses in ways that offer a greater hope of success than conviction and incarceration.

I am supporting uniform sentencing standards for federal offenses, which will make the punishment for crimes more rational and fair, and will help ensure that the rich and the poor are treated alike, no matter what court might convict them.

Powerful white-collar criminals cheat consumers of millions of dollars; public officials who abuse their high rank damage the integrity of our nation in profound and long-lasting ways. But too often these big-shot crooks escape the full consequences of their acts. Justice must be blind to rank, power, and position. The Justice Department is now undertaking a major new effort on white-collar crime.

I have directed the Justice Department also to review our prison policy alternatives to incarceration, such as stationhouse citations, supervised release, work-release programs, and other community-based facilities.

I urge all judges and all lawyers to use your enormous influence to make these efforts a success.

Our second challenge is to see that our legal system lives up to its noblest tradition of honesty and impartiality, so that all people stand equal before the bar of justice.

One of the most important steps that we can take is to restore public confidence in our system of justice, to assure that government decisions are thoroughly impartial, and that personal interests and influence have no part. I have required all major appointees of mine, as a condition of accepting office, to disclose their personal financial interests. I have also required them to pledge that, after their term of public service is over, they will forgo all contacts with their former agency in government for one year.

Last year I proposed legislation to make these standards a permanent part of the American law. In its current form, this ethics legislation would extend similar standards to the legislative and judicial branches of our government. It has already passed the Senate and cleared the Rules Committee in the House, and is ready for floor action without delay.

Last week the House passed a bill I supported requiring organizations that do significant lobbying in Congress to disclose their activities to the public. Although lobbying is a constitutionally protected activity, the American people have a right to know what major forces are affecting the legislative process. It is time now for the Senate to follow the lead of the House and pass a lobby reform bill.

Law enforcement agencies must set a clear example in their respect for the law. Recently, as the number of undocumented aliens has grown, there has been a disturbing trend, particularly in your part of the country, toward routine police harassment of our Mexican-American citizens. I know that your own bar association has studied this problem.

Last month the Justice Department intervened in a harassment case in Texas where three policemen had been convicted for the death of a Mexican-American prisoner. In filing for a review of the one-year jail terms given to the convicted men, the Justice Department said, "The public perception of inequality and the belief that the life of a Mexican-American citizen has little value can only do damage to respect for the laws and belief in justice."

This kind of harassment must stop, and my administration, working with you, will do what it can to see that it does. Moreover, we have now submitted legislation to Congress which will stop the flow of illegal immigration, while fully protecting the rights of our Hispanic citizens.

The passage of the Omnibus Judgeship Act, now pending in a House-Senate conference committee, will provide a test for the concept of merit selection. The conferees have recently agreed that the president should set "standards and guidelines" governing the selection of district judges, and I intend to use this authority to encourage establishment of more merit panels and to open the selection process.

The passage of this act—which will create 152 federal judgeships—offers a unique opportunity to make our judiciary more fully representative of our population. We have an abominable record to date. Of the 525 federal judges, only twenty are black or Hispanic, and only six (about one percent), are women.

While the federal bench in Southern California has become more representative, this is not true elsewhere in the nation. My executive order on the Circuit Court Nominating Commission specifically requires special efforts to identify qualified minority and female candidates.

The third challenge is suggested by the American Bar Association's theme for this year: "Access to Justice." Too often the amount of justice that a person gets depends on the amount of money that he or she can pay. Access to justice must not depend on economic status, and it must not be thwarted by arbitrary procedural rules.

Overcoming these procedural barriers means that groups with distinct interests to defend—in civil rights, economic questions, environmental causes, and so forth—must be able to defend them fully. We are supporting efforts to broaden the use of class actions, and to expand the definitions of standing to sue. My fourth challenge is to make the adversary system less necessary for the daily lives of most Americans—and more efficient when it must be used. By resorting to litigation at the drop of a hat, by regarding the adversarial system as an end in itself, we have made justice more cumbersome, more expensive, and less equal than it ought to be. This is a phenomenon more and more widely recognized—I know—among members of the bar. One answer is to be sure that other pathways to justice do exist.

Many suggestions have already been made for making litigation less necessary, and my administration will work with you and other members of the bar to implement them. In the great numbers of cases there is no sound reason for a lawyer to be involved in land transfers or title searches. Simplified procedures and use of modern computer technology can save consumers needless legal fees.

We must eliminate from our judicial system cases which can be resolved in other ways. No-fault automobile insurance systems, adopted by many states, are a step in the right direction; national standards for no-fault insurance will have a much greater impact. We support no-fault divorce laws, like those passed when I was governor of Georgia and the ones passed here in California, that can reduce litigation that is unnecessary and also the bitterness that litigation brings. We must look for ways to reduce the tremendous burden of medical malpractice costs.

Delays in our courts because of the excessive litigation are matched by the interminable delays in many federal regulatory agencies. In trying to solve society's problems, our regulators have proposed unnecessarily detailed specifications, and written regulations in the kind of gobbledygook that could employ a generation of law school graduates just to interpret them.

I have pledged to reduce this regulatory burden for the first time on American citizens, and we have taken some steps toward change. A few weeks ago I signed an executive order which requires the heads of departments and agencies to personally approve the regulatory agenda of their organizations; that regulations be signed by the person who wrote them; that regulations be gone over rigorously in "sunset" reviews to terminate them when they have served their purpose; that they be simply written; and that they are the most cost-effective rules it is possible to devise.

We are reviewing suggestions for reducing litigation, including more arbitration, greater reliance on small claims courts, and experiments with alternative systems for resolving disputes such as the experimental arbitration systems now in existence in San Francisco, Philadelphia, and in other parts of our country.

But even with all of these steps, much litigation will, of course, still be necessary. There are a variety of steps that can be taken together, to make necessary litigation more efficient, and to reduce unnecessary delays.

I support legislation now in Congress to expand the functions and the jurisdiction of federal magistrates to reduce the burden on federal judges.

I support a speedy appeals act to reduce the delay between sentencing and appeal; and I have directed Attorney General Bell to study whether we can also apply strict time limits to civil trials and to regulatory proceedings.

Those of us—presidents and lawyers—who enjoy privilege, power, and influence in our society, can be called to a harsh account for the ways we are using this power. Our hierarchy of privilege in this nation, based not on birth but on social and economic status, tends to insulate some of us from the problems faced by the average American.

But if our nation is to thrive, if we are to fulfill the vision and promise of our founding fathers, if we are truly to serve the ends of justice, we must look beyond these comfortable insulations of privilege. I have too much respect for the potential of the law to believe that this leadership is not possible from you.

I hope that lawyers throughout the country will take up the challenges I have made today. I know you understand the responsibility to serve justice. You have dedicated your very lives to this task. This responsibility is older than our Constitution, older than the Bill of Rights, older even than the tradition of common law. It comes from the roots of our Western heritage, with the prophet Amos, who said, "Let justice roll down like waters, and righteousness like an ever-flowing stream."

The American Bar Association Responds

William B. Spann, Jr.

President Carter made some rather harsh statements last week (May 4) about the justice system, lawyers, and bar associations.

We agree with the president that much needs to be done to improve the workings of the justice system. Indeed, the existence of the American Bar Association is premised on this objective. But we disagree sharply with the implications of the president's remarks.

Is is clear that he has taken the popular course of attacking the professions at a time when our foreign allies are concerned over his policies, when we again appear headed for double-digit inflation, when challengers are appearing for the 1980 presidential nomination, and when his ratings in the polls are at a historic low.

Specifically, I am concerned over the charge that the organized bar has resisted innovation. I have been authorized by Chief Justice Warren Burger to say on his behalf that the ABA has cooperated fully in every innovation he has advocated since he became chief justice. There is much more to be done to improve our legal system—and heaven knows we have been late getting to some problems—but we are getting there. We are committed to getting there.

Second, I am disturbed by the simplistic nature of the president's statements. He has turned into slogans the serious and complex problems which judges and lawyers have been struggling with for years. For example, has he considered the human and financial costs of the abolition of plea bargaining?

Third, the president has flatly stated that people are "overlawyered" and under-represented. Again, a complicated problem has been reduced to a slogan. Some communities are underserved. Too many minor disputes are clogging the courts. The ABA has defined these and other problems, and spent considerable sums to solve them. Will President Carter, with the resources of the federal government at his fingertips, be able to speed up the process without either destroying the right of the people to be heard, or telling lawyers when and where to practice and for what fees? Will he limit access to law schools?

Fourth, President Carter seems to have again assumed that everyone disagreeing with him is immoral. I believe honest disagreement is possible

24

between people of good will on such things, for example, as *federal* no-fault legislation.

Last, the president has blamed lawyers for representing clients he finds reprehensible, such as those who resisted integration. The adversary system and every person's right to representation have been the Anglo-American tradition for at least 800 years. It is the tradition that has kept us free.

But the actions and beliefs of individual attorneys on behalf of their clients are often significantly different from those of the organized bar, which he disparages. For example, in 1963 the ABA proposed the establishment of the Lawyers' Committee for Civil Rights under Law, which met with the support and encouragement of President Kennedy. I am proud to have been a member of the executive committee of that group, which sent lawyers into Mississippi and many other states and cities elsewhere in the South and the nation to defend unjustly accused blacks. We did this with the consent and cooperation of local bar associations.

Frankly, we were surprised by the president's attack. We had not heard much from him since he was running for president and gave his views as a candidate to our annual meeting, and to the *American Bar Association Journal* (*see* 62 Am. Bar. Assoc. J. 1270 [1976]). As one can see from this material, the president has also been unable to accomplish all of his objectives. There are no instant solutions to the problems of decades for him or for us.

Since the lawyers of America live with the problems of the justice system every day of their professional lives, they are deeply aware of the need to unclog the courts, to improve the delivery of legal services to all citizens, and to help the elderly, the mentally disabled, and those in prison, to assert their legal rights. We want to get on with this work. We hope name calling will cease, so that the president, the judiciary, and the lawyers of America can do so in partnership.

The ABA invites and will welcome the president's support to obtain the objectives which we both seek—for example, an independent National Institute of Justice.

The President's Counsel Defends

To the Editor of the *Washington Post:*

Your lead editorial on May 7 displays some ambivalence about the president's recent speech on justice. "The question," you observe, "is not whether there is some considerable element of truth in what Mr. Carter says." But you conclude that he has not been specific enough, that ". . . the prescriptions have lost clarity."

In fact, the president's address is replete with specifics. In the area of criminal law, the president:

- called for House approval of the revised federal criminal code, and specifically endorsed the uniform sentencing provisions of the bill;

- noted that the administration is working closely with the Hill to reorganize the Law Enforcement Assistance Administration and to rationalize the agency's funding priorities;

- announced an intention to restructure the existing arrangement, in which some 110 federal agencies have varying degrees of responsibility for law enforcement;

- called on the states to remove offenses such as drunkenness and vagrancy from the reach of criminal law;

- supported the Justice Department's increased enforcement efforts aimed at white-collar crime;

- announced that he has directed the Justice Department to examine alternatives to incarceration.

These precise proposals are modest, measured, and—most important—fully consistent with the limited role that our system gives to federal efforts to control crime.

Second, the president challenged the bar to hold the law to high standards of impartiality, and specifically:

- called for House passage of ethics legislation that would limit potential conflicts of interest for federal officials, and help ensure that governmental decisions are impartial;

- called for Senate passage of a bill reforming lobbying activity;

26

- vowed to work with the states to eliminate official harassment of groups such as Mexican-Americans;

- announced his intention to use the expected passage of the Omnibus Judgeship Act—which will create 152 new federal judgeships—to expand the concept of merit selection now embodied in the president's Circuit Court Nominating Commission;

- also pledged to use passage of the act to increase the number of minority and female judges; the president aptly called the existing situation—twenty black or Hispanic judges and six women on a bench of 525—"abominable."

Third, the president addressed the theme of access to the legal system, noting that too often those with limited economic resources face difficulty in having legitimate claims heard. Here he:

- suggested that procedural barriers such as restrictions on class actions and the concept of legal standing be modified;

- noted that this administration has doubled the budget for the Legal Services Corporation;

- supported innovations such as prepaid legal plans and neighborhood justice centers;

- called on the bar to support competition and to limit increases in legal fees.

Finally, in urging that resort to the adversary system be made at once less necessary and more efficient, the president:

- recommended that title examinations be modernized through computer technology, so there will be less need to rely on lawyers to search title each time land is transferred;

- supported expanded use of the no-fault concept;

- noted that unwieldy government regulations often foster litigation, and pledged continuation of the effort to simplify agency directives;

- suggested that regulation should be abandoned where—as in the airline industry—competition can more effectively achieve public goals;

- supported legislation expanding the functions of federal magistrates, so that judicial resources can be used more economically;

- supported passage of a speedy appeals act in criminal cases, and announced that he has asked the attorney general to determine whether the same concept can be applied to civil trials and regulatory proceedings.

The *Post* may not agree with all of the president's proposals for improving our system of justice. But it is misleading in the extreme to suggest that his address lacked specificity. Frankly, some of us who reviewed it beforehand feared there might be too great an emphasis on specifics, to the detriment of the central theme of the speech: that individuals and groups occupying positions of privilege in this society are obliged to use their influence to advance social justice, not simply to uphold their own interests.

ROBERT J. LIPSHUTZ
Counsel to the President
May 1978

Access to the Legal System in Historical Perspective

Jerold S. Auerbach

In 1970, the Association of the Bar of the City of New York celebrated its centennial anniversary with a symposium, the published results of which appeared in a volume entitled *Is Law Dead?* In the introduction to that publication, Eugene V. Rostow noted that the idea of law as the compass of our social system was increasingly under question. If the death of law, like Mark Twain's death, is greatly exaggerated, historians want to know and to understand why the question was ever asked.

It seems to me that the answer to the question "Is law dead?" lies within the legal system itself. It is my contention that both the legal profession and the institutions of legal education have failed in at least two vital respects. First, they have failed to relate the legal process to the purpose of justice; and second, they have failed to understand how tenaciously the legal profession has aligned itself with privilege rather than justice. This alignment, the product of a century of historical development, has contributed to the sustained crisis of legal authority through which we recently lived.

It is the essence of the professionalization process to divorce law from politics, to elevate technique and craft over power, to search for neutral principals, and to deny ideological purpose. Lawyers and laymen alike must be persuaded that law embodies reason not will; and that it is a mysterious science inaccessible to the uninitiated. But if lawyers must believe this, historians need not. Professionalization has never been value-free. It is a process, an ideology, which has always served profoundly political objectives. Craft, as I understand it, is the central value of professionalism. Yet craft very often separates process from substance, and conceals the connections between law and policy. It defines the lawyer's role so as to disguise discretion and values under the cloak of technical proficiency. It sustains the illusion that law is scientific rather than political, and it ignores the fact that process can never be detached from purpose.

Legal education bears considerable responsibility for these disjunctions. For a century (or at least until the 1960s) it has remained largely frozen in its Langdellian mold. Then, with startling suddenness, some of its fundamental precepts were subjected to withering scrutiny, and young lawyers and law students discovered all sorts of hidden value judgments and political preferences lurking beneath the claim of value-free craftmanship. They rebelled against a professional and legal system which often elevated legal order above social justice. It has always been the proudest boast of law schools to train students to think like lawyers. This process entails a highly stylized mode of intellectual activity that rewards inductive reasoning, analytical precision, and verbal facility. Yet relentless doctrinal analysis of appellate opinions has always severely restricted the range and scope of professional inquiry. "Thinking like a lawyer" has always required the application of technical skills to problem solving within the confines of the adversary system. Justice, it has simply been assumed, emerged inevitably from the confrontation of skilled advocates in an adversary setting.

Law schools continue to proclaim their institutional neutrality, just as throughout the sixties they asserted their preference for technical competence unrelated to social goals. However, technical competence has always been related to social goals. In denying connections that were so apparent to so many law students a short time ago, law schools managed only to generate very deep cynicism about the values to which the legal profession was ostensibly committed. Process divorced from substance, as one young graduate of the sixties observed, represented a false equation between moral abdication and intellectual independence.

The recent confrontation between new professionals and an old profession can be illuminated by some historical understanding. It helps to consider that law is social, not scientific; that legal history is, after all, a chapter of social history, not a self-contained entity. Even lawyers' craft, applied to the most technical, professional issues, can be studied as an expression of particular values in a particular culture at a particular time. It has always appeared incongruous, to say the least, that lawyers who pride themselves on being generalists equipped to resolve any social problem (a conceit that American society all too eagerly encourages) should claim swift immunity as inscrutable specialists when anybody else wants to poke around into their professional activities. Lawyers are understandably predisposed to belittle differences that do not correlate with hard work, discipline, inductive reasoning skills, and academic achievement. The idea that the profession has traditionally been stratified along lines of race, religion, color, sex, or social origins is a very subversive idea in any system of equal justice. Acknowledgement that differentiation along such lines does in fact exist, and has existed for at least the last century, would cast very serious doubts on the fairness of the adversary process which is, after all, the cornerstone of the American legal system.

Yet the existence and the persistence of these divisions is beyond dispute. To understand them we need to go back to the turn of the century, when the corporate law firm emerged as a social institution which provided only those lawyers who possessed appropriate social, religious, and ethnic credentials with an opportunity to secure personal power for themselves and to shape the future of their profession. The corporate law firm was a fortress for certain social and ethnic groups. Its priorities were precisely the priorities of its corporate clientele. They shaped professional education, career patterns, professional ethics, mobility, and the availability and distribution of legal services. Indeed, these priorities still shape the very meaning of law and justice. Only lawyers who possessed considerable social capital could inhabit the law firm world of Wall Street, State Street, and LaSalle Street. They were born in the East to old American families of British lineage. They were college graduates, a distinct rarity, who tended to follow their fathers to business and professional careers. They molded the law firm to resemble the corporation. Both the law firm and the corporation restricted access to those who presented proper ethnic and social credentials.

According to folklore, the doors of access to the legal profession have always swung open to anybody who was ambitious. Lawyers might prefer a restricted guild, but in a democratic society, democratic realities required them to settle for less. But this is a half truth. It conceals the fact that although anybody might become an attorney, the doors to particular legal careers and to access to certain kinds of social and political power have always required keys that were distributed according to race, religion, sex, and ethnic origin. Myths notwithstanding, mobility was not a ladder whose rungs everybody could climb. Indeed, for those who did not come from the privileged groups, a career on Wall Street was more like scaling a high wall than climbing a ladder.

The law firm selection process was as discriminatory as the law school admissions process, and the two have often dovetailed. For a long time, law schools excluded women. The financial expense of four years in college (which became a prerequisite to admission) and three years in law school eliminated the impoverished, among whom minority group members were concentrated. The result has been that law schools, for at least the first half of this century, were especially open to male children of Northern European origins whose fathers were not day laborers. There are conspicuous examples to the contrary, but they are exceptions which prove the rule. Jewish law review editors, for example, were excluded from partnership in the prestigious corporate firms until after World War II. Blacks and women became token insiders only very recently. Other ethnic minority group members have barely begun to gain entry. Consequently, we have, as a matter of historical development, a situation in which Protestant partners in a small group of firms comprised the professional elite. Comprising it, they defined it. Defining it, they excluded non-whites, non-males, and non-Christians. Academic achievement was necessary, but insufficient for entry. Social origins, together with racial, sexual, and ethnic identity, determined both the possibility of academic achievement and the opportunity to reap its rewards in practice.

The Wall Street firm, and its counterpart in other cities, was the crucial link between corporate capitalism and social elitism in the legal profession. Stratification enabled relatively few lawyers (concentrated in professional associations) to legislate for the entire profession, and to speak on issues of professional and public consequence. Once, it was written that New England's Puritan ministers comprised a speaking aristocracy in the presence of a silent democracy. So it has been in the legal profession. A professional elite—defined as a group able to bias the terms of admission to suit the circle of the influential—had, as its paramount objective, to structure the legal profession (its education, ethics, discipline, and services) to serve certain political preferences at the expense of others. At the turn of the century these lawyers confronted choices between competing definitions of professional identity and obligation. Was the legal profession public or private? Should it be accessible or restricted? Were all citizens—regardless of social origin, politics, or income—entitled to adequate legal services?

These questions provoked a prolonged struggle for power within the legal profession which has not yet ended. The axis on which this struggle turned was ethnicity and class. At the turn of the century, the proportion of white Anglo-Saxon Protestants within the legal profession, and within American society, was diminishing. Changing immigration and demographic patterns swelled American cities and the legal profession with the foreign-born and their children. Native American lawyers were determined to repel a dual challenge; to their own ascendency in professional life, and to the economic institutions of industrial capitalism which they served. First, they consolidated their position within corporate law firms that became their special enclaves. Then, they moved into professional associations. Once these enclaves were secure, they worked hard to forge an identity between professional interest and their own political self-interest.

What does all of this have to do with present legal ethics? Is there some plausible connection between the past, which is the province of the historian, the present, and the future? I suggest that there are very real and strong connections. The problems which I have been alluding to have not been resolved, nor can they be resolved until their historical antecedents are understood; they are the products of history. Legal education is still haunted by Langdell's ghost. Too often, it ignores precisely those value considerations that lawyers, in their public policy roles, consistently confront and just as consistently evade. Ethical judgements still are framed within turn-of-the-century precepts, modified only slightly by the present Code of Professional Responsibility. The problem of minority-group admissions has not disappeared; only the identity of the victims of professional discrimination has changed. The debate over federal legal services echoed a much earlier debate over legal aid. In other words, the past occupies a conspicuous place in the professional present. I shall single out one or two issues of professional ethics in the sociohistorical context in order to illuminate this point.

Early in the twentieth century, elite lawyers were sharply criticized for their service to persons who were referred to by Theodore Roosevelt as "the malefactors of great wealth." Their response was the Canons of Ethics, which were adopted at the end of the first decade of this century. These new professional canons drew heavily on the *Essay on Professional Ethics* written by George Sharswood and published in 1854. Sharswood's essay was at best antiquated; at worst, irrelevant. He addressed it to a generation accustomed to moral exhortation and confident that its definitions of character, honor, and duty were eternal verities. Sharswood had urged high moral principle as the bedrock of professional dignity. In his world of the protected Philadelphia social elite, passivity and patience were the cardinal virtues. Like young maidens awaiting suitors, aspiring lawyers must await clients. Let business seek the young attorney, Sharswood had insisted. It might come too slowly for profit or fame; indeed, it might never come at all. But if the lawyer, as Sharswood wrote, cultivated habits of neatness, accuracy, punctuality, candor toward his client, and strict honor toward his adversary, it could be safely prophesied that his business would grow as fast as was good for him. Sharswood's safe prophecy may have comforted a young nineteenth century attorney in a homogeneous small town, apprenticed to an established practitioner with very few competitors. But advice to wait for business to seek out the attorney could hardly reassure the twentieth century new immigrant lawyer in a large city—where restricted law firms monopolized the most lucrative business, and thousands of attorneys scrambled for a share of the remainder. This attorney could draw scant comfort from Sharswood's confident assertion that some pre-ordained rule determined that his practice grow no faster than was good for him. He either hustled or he starved.

The new ABA Canons, which were quickly adopted at the state level, measured the social texture of the twentieth century urban practice against early nineteenth century memories. Emphasis on reputation as the key to professional dignity and success might be understandable in Sharswood's

Philadelphia, but it did not make much sense in a diverse heterogeneous urban community. A cluster of canons—pertaining to acquiring an interest in litigation, stirring litigation, and division of fees—almost exclusively affected the activities of struggling, metropolitan, solo attorneys who were drawn disproportionately from ethnic and religious minority groups. These canons did not apply to the conduct of the law firm members who drafted them. The canon—that prohibited lawyers from indicating publicly that they engaged in a specialty practice—equated the firm that was known to serve a roster of corporate clients with the solitary lawyer who might specialize in negligence work, and who depended upon constant client turnover for economic survival. The prohibition against advertising instructed lawyers that success flowed from their character and conduct, not from aggressive solicitation. The canon prohibiting solicitation discriminated against those lawyers in personal injury practice who bore the label "ambulance chasers." And although the canons reminded lawyers that their profession was committed to the administration of justice, and was not a mere money-grubbing trade, there was only one fee that was singled out for judicial scrutiny: the contingent fee of the negligence lawyer. This distinction suggested that the decisive question was who earned the fee, not the size of the fee earned.

What these canons did, in tandem, was to condemn the acquisitive urge, especially among those lawyers who earned the least money; to confine the lawyer to his office, awaiting a client who might wander in with a case which would assure fame and fortune; and to attribute success to good character. The lower the fee the lawyer earned, and the less discrete he was in pursuit of it, the more likely it was that his money-getting activities would be scrutinized and criticized. The canons, not accidentally, impeded those lawyers who worked in a highly competitive urban market with a transient clientele. They made more sense to an attorney in Sullivan & Cromwell, or in Fairfax County, Virginia, than to a personal injury lawyer on the Lower East Side of Manhattan.

The class and ethnic biases that appeared in the canons were nowhere more evident than in the special treatment reserved for contingent fees. Few other issues cut so deeply into the social mores of an industrial age. An alarming proliferation of accidents related to work and transportation generated human tragedies which a profit economy and its legal doctrines exacerbated. Accident victims and surviving members of their families were compelled to bear the full burden for the risks inherent in dangerous work—or in the dangers of crossing the street. Corporate profit was the primary social value. Legal doctrine impeded the opportunity of an accident victim to recover damages. Furthermore, legal services were available only to those who could afford to purchase them. The contingent fee was, therefore, a necessary financial inducement for the provision of legal services to personal injury victims. This was a gambler's chance. It assured profit to the counsellor, and counsel to the needy. It offered the victim his only chance of recompense, minus at least one-third of his recovery sum as the attorney's fee. In this diabolical game, a negligence lawyer could claim a sufficiently high percentage from his successful suits to compensate for his losses. The injured client had no such hope. Nevertheless, the contingent fee arrangement did make it possible for some people to secure otherwise unattainable legal services. But the costs to the legal system were high: enormous pressure to litigate, with predictable expense and delay, which served the employer's advantage; sustained public criticism of these delays and costs; and allegations of widespread ethical improprieties for ambulance chasing.

Consequently, when bar associations came to consider the adoption of Canons of Ethics, the propriety of contingent fees occupied a central place in their deliberations. Members of the ABA voted for court supervision of contingent fees, but not for other fees that lawyers earned. Curiously, court supervision was justified in the best interests of the personal injury victim—who was presumed to need protection from his attorney more than he needed monetary damages for his injury. Insistence upon court supervision of contingent fees to protect clients from their lawyers was especially incongruous at a time when other attorneys' fees were exempted from court supervision on the grounds of liberty of contract. There was no mention of the contribution of contingent fees to the enforcement of legitimate claims otherwise denied by the victim's poverty. Few lawyers complained about the cruel choice imposed upon an accident victim—who could either relinquish all hopes of recovery, or merely relinquish, to his attorney, one-third of the damages he collected.

The ethical crusade that produced the canons and the special concern for contingent fees concealed class and ethnic hostility. Jewish and Catholic new-immigrant lawyers, of lower class origin, were concentrated among the urban solo practitioners whose behavior was unethical after 1909— because Protestant lawyers said it was. There were—and still are—serious socioeconomic and occupational differences between the rule makers and those subject to the rules. Rules of ethical deviance were neither universal nor timeless. They were applied by particular lawyers to enhance their own status and prestige. Deviance was less an attribute of a particular act than a judgment by one group of lawyers about the inferiority of another.

To move ahead to more recent times: in 1964, amid growing criticism for neglect of its public responsibilities, the ABA re-examined professional ethics for the first time in more than half a century. At the request of its president, Lewis Powell, it established a special committee to consider changes to accommodate the canons to contemporary conditions. An additional spur to reconsideration—not publicly acknowledged by the ABA, but potentially much more unsettling—came from the Supreme Court: in a series of decisions that began in 1964, it chipped away at professional prerogatives which preserved the self-regulatory privileges of the bar, often at the expense of the public interest in expanded legal services. With the Office of Economic Opportunities generating its own pressure for expanded professional responsibility, the specter of group legal services, which the bar had tenaciously opposed for thirty years, increased professional unease. In the new Code of Professional Responsibility, approved in 1969, the ABA tried to balance the economic self-interest of the bar against a vast, neglected public, for whom legal services were unavailable. In some significant respects the Code went beyond the old canons in recognizing, for example, that every person should enjoy access to a lawyer's services. But even as it repudiated some of the more outmoded laissez-faire rules of the original canons, it remained committed to the very principles of individualized responsibility which had contributed substantially to the economically distorted allocation of legal services. ABA support for group legal services was, to say the least, minimal. Group services by salaried attorneys was prohibited under the new code, except insofar as Supreme Court decisions required them. In effect, the ABA did nothing more than to say that it would abide by the law of the land as interpreted by the Supreme Court. The presumption that the social obligations of the profession could be entirely discharged by the random results of individual efforts underlaid the new code, just as it had underlaid the old canons. Once again, the association went no further to assure the provision of legal services than the law required.

Beyond the inadequacy of services, another deficiency was (and still is) restricted information. The ABA has always operated under the presumption that secrecy is a virtue; that the less that is known about the nature of legal services, who provides them, how much they cost, and who is excluded, the better it will be—at least for the ABA, if not for the public. Lawyers, for example, were permitted to advertise their specialties in reputable law lists which the ABA would certify. These lists were circulated to banks, corporations, and insurance companies. But such information could not be communicated in the public media, which reached a much wider and much less privileged clientele. "Ethical" advertising has always been advertising directed at corporate clients. Persistent ABA efforts showed that anything else was deemed unethical. A professional double standard—sustained by rules which aid some in gaining access to the legal system and throw obstacles in the path of others—is still the professional legacy. It should, therefore, come as no surprise that the Justice Department has instituted antitrust proceedings against the ABA for its restrictions on advertising.

In analyzing the ethnic and class bias which has pervaded elite professional life in the twentieth century, my point is not that lawyers have been more prejudiced than other Americans; they have not been. But they have not been *less* prejudiced than other Americans. Bias in the legal profession has serious consequences, particularly in a society that depends so heavily on that profession to implement the principle of equal justice under law.

That legacy of prejudice poses fundamental questions. Is an adversary system of justice "just"—when the adversary process is skewed by the social origins, ethnic identity, and financial resources of attorney or client? Is there equal justice when the legal profession, the primary instrument of its attainment, is structured to reflect and reinforce social inequality? Should the morality of process and craft obliterate the social responsibility of lawyers? The bar, I think, must be judged by two standards, but not by a double standard: first, its sensitivity to the values and mores of the society in which it lives; and second, its implementation of the obligation to provide equal justice under law. In the United States, justice has historically been distributed according to race, ethnicity, sex, and wealth, rather than need. This is not equal justice. The professional elite bears a heavy and special responsibility for this maldistribution. Its members, absorbed with selective client caretaking for restricted clientele, have preserved social and economic inequality. Their efforts have crippled the capacity of the legal profession to provide equal justice or to fulfill those paramount public responsibilities which alone can justify professional independence and self-regulation.

If the practice of law is truly to become a public profession, rather than remain a private club, new values and voices are necessary. Justice should be defined not only by process, but by product. Is the result, measured by the interests of clients *and* the needs of society, fair? Legal services should exist by right to all citizens, not as a privilege to some. How do we assure this? Perhaps substantial federal subsidies, supplemented by an excess profit tax on corporate law firms, can make this possible. Compulsory tithing of lawyers' time might also help. But the prerequisite to any meaningful reform is public regulation of the legal profession in the public interest. Otherwise, equal justice under law will inevitably remain subservient to unequal justice under lawyers.

Against the Bar: A Critique of Professor Auerbach's Views

Joseph W. Bishop, Jr.

Unequal Justice is a philippic against the American Bar Association (with the exception of a few saints and martyrs like William Kunstler), particularly corporation lawyers. As Jerold Auerbach, a historian, sees it, these evil men and evil institutions have for more than a century generally conspired to serve and preserve "corporate capitalism," racism, privilege, and injustice.

There is, of course, nothing wrong with 140-proof polemics, so long as the stuff is plainly labeled. Auerbach honestly disclaims any intention to act as a "neutral observer" or to treat "truth ... as two sided." Although he frequently cites Abraham Lincoln, the lawyer of the "plain people" (and also of the big corporations, for, as Auerbach seems unaware, he had such clients as the Illinois Central and Rock-Island Railroads) as the antithesis of the lawyers he abhors, he would certainly be contemptuous of Lincoln's observation that "there are few things wholly evil or wholly good; almost everything is an inseparable compound of the two."

In a way this is a pity, for some of the indictments in *Unequal Justice* are valid, even if most of them have been made before and more convincingly. The American legal establishment for many decades did try, by fair means and foul, to exclude Jews and other newcomers from its upper levels. Most of its members did (and still do) share the American values, good and bad, of their day, including a belief (which still persists) in the efficiency of the profit motive. (All this is, of course, equally true of doctors, farmers, shopkeepers, and just about every other definable group in the population. The bar's special sin was that it spouted more cant about its noble ideals than any other trade except the clergy). Immigrants to the United States frequently did not get equal justice, although (as Auerbach does not point out) most of them, including those from the British Isles, got more of it than they had in the old country. Most serious of all his charges, it is still true that the legal profession has done a poor job of availing its services to people in the lower- and middle-income brackets at prices those people can afford.

One of Auerbach's major anathemas, to which he constantly returns, is legal education. His case is summed up in the Preface, where he describes his reasons for leaving the Columbia Law School (which he entered in

38

1957) after his first year. ". . . [N]ot only were Columbia Law School and Wall Street stations on the same subway line; they were stations on the same career line. The message was never explicitly conveyed but it was conveyed through the curriculum we studied . . . and the expected rewards for mastery of torts and contracts. Never was there a whisper of a suggestion that law related to choice, to history, to society, to justice."

As it happens, I began teaching law at Yale in 1957, and I therefore know that the latter statement was not true of Yale. Looking at the Columbia Law School catalogue for 1957-58, I found, sure enough, that torts and contracts were required for first-year students, as they were and are at virtually all law schools—for the same reasons that medical students are made to study anatomy. But so was the late professor Julius Goebel's *Development of Legal Institution;* its purpose was "to give the student a grounding in the history of the common law and to instruct him in the elements of historical method indispensable to a lawyer . . . (and) to emphasize the political, social, and economic facts that have determined the course of the law's development." Second- and third-year courses included jurisprudence (dealing, *inter alia*, with natural-law theory, sociological jurisprudence, and American legal realism), international law, Islamic law, Roman law, comparative law, and many other subject having no very obvious link with Wall Street.

Auerbach, who has a habit of gliding away from accounts of historical wrongs without any clear indication of whether they still exist, seems to believe that law-school curricula are to this day "weighted toward protection of the interests of the wealthy and powerful." The allegation is contradicted by contemporary law-school catalogues. The only courses that are commonly required are: torts, contracts, procedure, constitutional law, and criminal law—none of which has more to do with the interests of the wealthy and powerful than with those of other citizens. Every law school (of which I have knowledge) offers a wide variety of courses in such areas as urban problems, consumer protection, and welfare law.

He similarly misconceives the problem of admission of blacks and members of other minority groups to law schools and the bar as it exists today. There can be no doubt that many law schools, particularly in the South, long discriminated against blacks. Others, particularly the major schools, did not discriminate *against* blacks, but neither did they do anything to increase their enrollment. Today, however, a very large majority of law schools recruit and give substantial preferences to applicants from minority groups. Assertions that "nominally objective criteria of merit (meaning, presumably, the applicant's college record and score on the Law School Admission Test) are hardly unbiased" ignore or muddle the fact that the problem is not simply to get more black and

Chicano lawyers, but to get more *good* black and Chicano lawyers. Many law schools, including Yale, learned (or are learning) by painful experience that the problem is not solved, but is rather aggravated, by grabbing almost any minority-group applicant with a Bachelor's degree. Such practices, I think, do more to explain the fact that disproportionate numbers of blacks fail bar exams than does Professor Auerbach's accusation that bar examiners crudely and systematically discriminate against blacks. In virtually all jurisdictions, bar examinations are today graded blind; the examiners do not know the identity of the examinees whose papers they grade—a fact which Auerbach either does not know or chooses not to mention.

Auerbach tends generally to ignore whatever reforms have taken place in admission to law schools, to the bar, and to the big firms. In a piece on the Op Ed page of the *New York Times* (April 13, 1976) he describes "elite law firms as bastions of white, Protestant, male power," and adds that "minority-group members have been as unwelcome in Wall Street firms as in the board-rooms of the corporations they serve." Again, that *was* generally true twenty or thirty years ago—although with more exceptions than he cares to admit. But there are few, if any, Wall Street firms of which it is true today. On the evidence of law-school placement officers with whom I have talked, the big corporate firms in New York and other cities are quite willing, even eager, to hire good black graduates. Many of the latter are, however, more interested in public service, teaching, or practice in their own communities.

Unequal Justice: A Review

Alan Dershowitz

"How in God's name could so many lawyers get involved in something like this?" asked John Dean about Watergate. In this remarkable book about America's elite lawyers and their quest for power and profit, Jerold S. Auerbach—a Wellesley history professor and a former fellow in law and history at Harvard Law School—goes a long way toward explaining why lawyers have played such central roles in perpetuating so many injustices: ranging from racial and religious discrimination to McCarthyism and the denial of legal representation to the poor. This is not to deny that some lawyers have also played significant roles in helping to secure justice and equality, but that is a familiar story—celebrated in Law Day speeches, at bar association banquets, and in the authorized histories of the bench and bar.

Unequal Justice is an unauthorized history of the legal "four hundred," compiled by an outsider and employing as its primary source the words of the lawyers themselves (spoken with pride in prior generations, but anachronistically embarrassing to the modern ear). It reveals the hitherto unexplored dark side of the moon, which turns out to be much larger and uglier than the bright side that has been exposed to public view. Auerbach's basic view is that for every Abraham Lincoln and Clarence Darrow produced by the bar, there have been several John Mitchells—and that it is far more likely that the Mitchells have been more active in the American Bar Association than the Lincolns or Darrows.

Auerbach examines the development of the modern law firm during this century, but his major emphasis is on the social and religious bigotry of the elite bar—a bigotry that excluded all but a handful of blacks from the ABA, and all but a few "white" Jews from prestigious Wall Street firms, until quite recently. His point ". . . is not that lawyers have been more prejudiced than other Americans. It is, instead, that bias in the legal profession has had particularly serious consequences in a society that depends so heavily upon the legal profession to implement the privilege of equal justice under law . . ."

Auerbach relates how, in 1912, the ABA admitted three lawyers who, unbeknownst to the membership committee, were black. The executive committee immediately passed a resolution rescinding the admission under "the settled practice of the Association . . . to elect only white men as members." The membership chairman saw the issue as "a question of keeping pure the Anglo-Saxon race." But a lawyer-like compromise was reached, whereby the three duly elected black lawyers were permitted to retain their membership—provided that all future applicants were required to identify themselves by race. Thirty years later the situation had not changed much. In 1939, when distinguished federal Judge William Hastie (a black Harvard Law School graduate) was proposed for membership in the ABA, "a prominent civil liberties lawyer in the association questioned the wisdom of pressing for his admission at that time."

The bar's attempt to limit the number of Jewish lawyers—especially those with Eastern European backgrounds—was somewhat more subtle. Leaders of the bar (including future Chief Justices Harlan Stone and William Taft) made no bones about their dislike of Jewish and other immigrant lawyers who, in Stone's words, "exhibit racial tendencies toward study by memorization" and "a mind almost Oriental in its fidelity to the minutiae of the subject without regard to any controlling rule or reason." Others complained at the influx of Eastern European immigrants "with little inherited sense of fairness, justice, and honor as we understand them." Auerbach quotes Henry S. Drinker—who was chairman of the ABA Ethics Committee for many years, and whose treatise on legal ethics is still among the most widely relied upon by bar associations—on the ethics of "Russian Jew boys who came up out of the gutter (and) were merely following the methods their fathers had been using in selling shoestrings and other merchandise . . . ."

The attempt to equate Jewish "racial" traits with unethical behavior reached its nadir when President Wilson nominated Louis Brandeis to the Supreme Court. The leader of the ABA lined up solidly against the nomination. Six former ABA presidents, at the instigation of incumbent President Elihu Root, declared that Brandeis was "not a fit person to sit on the Court." Auerbach tells how former president and future Chief Justice Taft dipped his "pen in the vitriol, (dispatching) letter after letter of calumny to friends and family, berating Brandeis for his ethics, politics, and his religion." Numerous local bar association and individual elite lawyers alleged that Brandeis had a "defective standard of professional ethics." Brandeis's eventual confirmation only strengthened the resolve of the Anglo-Saxon legal establishment to preserve its hegemony. As James Bech, former solicitor general of the United States, wrote in 1922: "If the old American stock can be organized we can still avert the threatened decay of constitutionalism in this country."

Not surprisingly, the tack taken by the elite lawyers was to increase the power of the bar association to impose their own conception of legal ethics on all lawyers, practicing and prospective. This was far better designed to achieve the intended goal than an increase in educational requirements—which, as one bar association lawyer observed, might "keep our own possibly out." Accordingly, "character" committees sprung up throughout the country, charged with the function of screening prospective lawyers. It is not surprising that these committees—manned by the likes of Root, Drinker, and other lawyers with a distinct prejudice against immigrants—would disqualify a high percentage of "Russian Jew boys," blacks, and other ethnic undesirables.

Auerbach describes in detail the systematic and successful efforts of one state (Pennsylvania) to "cleanse" its bar; the number of Jewish applicants declined more than twenty percent after the establishment of screening mechanisms, and not a single black was admitted to practice between 1933 and 1943.

Those who made it past the character committees still had formidable obstacles to overcome. They had to align their professional—and all too often their personal and political—conduct with the ethical precepts that Drinker and others ordained to be the ethics of the bar. It is not surprising that lawyers who declared Brandeis's ethics to be "defective" and adopted the ethics of men like Drinker and Root would turn out canons that did not make it an unethical practice for a law firm to discriminate on grounds of race, religion, or sex—but did make it an unethical practice for an unknown lawyer to attempt to attract clients away from established firms by advertising or price cutting. The contingent fee, the only mechanism whereby poor accident victims could sue large corporations, was frowned upon and closely regulated by an elite bar more concerned with protecting its corporate clients than with assuring just compensation for indigent victims.

Auerbach, the historian, is at his best in reconstructing the past bigotries of the bar. However, his analysis of the contemporary legal scene is flawed by his failure to recognize real changes that have, in fact, occurred during the past decade. Bar associations are far less monolithic than they once were. While they still represent some of the most reactionary elements of the legal profession, a younger and more diverse group of lawyers—including minority-group members and women—are beginning to have some voice in formulating policies. The District of Columbia Bar and the New York City Association of the Bar (to mention two of the established legal associations most responsive to change) have taken considerable steps in the direction of promoting minority rights, consumer interests, and constitutional liberties.

In his zeal, Auerbach sometimes seems unwilling to give credit where credit is at least partially due; he views every liberalizing action taken by the established bar as designed to preserve its powers under "the stress of severe social turmoil," and interprets every refusal to embrace liberal trends as evidence of resurgent racism. But despite this weakness, *Unequal Justice* stands as a powerful and well-documented indictment of the elite bar's failure to live up to the trust that has been bestowed upon it by our system of justice.

Watergate revealed to the public that corruption and venality exist at every level of the legal profession; that they are not limited (as the established bar would have us believe) to Jewish, Italian, Irish, or black "street" lawyers; that they touch lawyers in the elite firms, lawyers in the Justice Department, and lawyers in the White House.

The ABA's characteristic response to Watergate has been to require law schools to offer compulsory courses in legal ethics. Unfortunately, many such courses will begin and end with the official ethics of the ABA. But if history has taught us anything, it is that the ABA should no more have exclusive responsibility for the formulation of legal ethics than the American Medical Association should have for medical ethics. *Unequal Justice* reminds us that—at bottom—the ABA is a lobby group for a particularly influential segment of an enormously powerful profession. Its primary goal is to maximize the prerogatives and profits of its members and their clients. The ABA is neither a government agency, nor the authorized representative of the legal profession. It is a voluntary organization that has historically excluded many of the best and most honorable lawyers. Even today—although it no longer discriminates on grounds of race, religion, or sex—a considerable number of lawyers, including some of the very best, have chosen not to be counted among its membership.

Auerbach's review of the failings of the elite bar during this century suggests that reform will not come by having law schools preach the ethics of the ABA. But reform will come by restructuring the legal profession so that its ethics no longer remain the nearly exclusive preserve of a lobby group—whose history is replete with bigotry, injustice, and the expansion of professional prerogatives at the expense of the citizenry. Legal ethics committees should include lawyers who are not members of the ABA, as well as nonlawyers (perhaps philosophers and consumers of the law) who can view legal ethics from a perspective broader than that of the entrepreneurs of the law. I, for one, propose to have my legal ethics students read *Unequal Justice* before they read the ABA's Code of Professional Responsibility.

Legal Education

Jerome Frank

The upper-court myth and legal rule magic are plainly related. for the perpetuation of that myth, and for the widespread dissemination of the belief in that magic, American legal education must take considerable blame. And if the addiction to such magic indicates a core of somewhat neurotic attitudes, the explanation of the faults of legal education in this respect is not far to seek. For contemporary law-school teaching got its basic mood at Harvard, some seventy years ago, from a brilliant neurotic, Christopher Columbus Langdell.[1]

When Langdell was himself a law student he was almost constantly in the law library. He served for several years as an assistant librarian. He slept, at times, on the library table. One of his friends found him one day absorbed in an ancient lawbook. "As he drew near," we are told, "Langdell looked up and said, in a tone of mingled exhilaration and regret, and with an emphatic gesture, 'Oh, if only I could have lived in the time of the Plantagenets!'"[2]

After graduation, he practiced as a lawyer in New York City for sixteen years. But he seldom tried a case or went into court. His clients were mostly other lawyers for whom, after much lucubration, he wrote briefs or prepared pleadings. He led a peculiarly secluded life. A biographer says of him, "In the almost inaccessible retirement of his office, and in the library of the Law Institute, he did the greater part of his work. He went little into company."

Is it any wonder that such a man had an obsessive and almost exclusive interest in books? The raw material of what he called "law," was to be discovered in a library and nowhere else; it consisted, as he himself said, solely of what could be found in print. Practicing law to Langdell meant chiefly the writing of briefs, and the examination of published "authorities." The lawyer-client relation, the numerous nonrational factors involved in a trial, the face-to-face appeals to the emotions of juries, the elements that make up what is loosely known as the "atmosphere" of a case—everything that is undisclosed in upper-court opinions was virtually unknown (and was therefore quite meaningless) to Langdell. Many of the realities of the life of the average lawyer were unreal to him.

What was almost exclusively real to him he translated into the law-school curriculum, when in 1870, at the age of fourty-four, he became a teacher at Harvard Law School, and, soon after, its dean. His pedagogic theory reflected the man. The actual varied experiences of the practicing lawyer were, to Langdell, improper material for the teacher and the student. They must, he insisted, shut their eyes to such data. They must devote themselves exclusively to what was discoverable in the library. The essence of his teaching philosophy he expressed thus: "First that law is a science; second, that all the available materials of that science are contained in printed books." This second proposition, it is said, was "intended to exclude the traditional methods of learning law by work in a lawyer's office, or attendance upon the proceedings of courts of justice."

Langdell declared that "the library is to us what the laboratory is to the chemist or the physicist and what the museum is to the naturalist. . . . The most essential feature of the [Harvard Law] School, that which distinguishes it most widely from all other schools of which I have any knowledge, is the library. . . . Without the library the School would lose its most important characteristics, and indeed its identity." In the same vein, the president of Harvard commented, not long after, "The Corporation recognizes that the library is the very heart of the Law School." "What qualifies a person to teach law," wrote Langdell, "is not experience in the work of a lawyer's office, not experience in dealing with men, not experience in the trial or argument of causes, not experience, in short, in using law, but experience in learning law. . . ." In *The Centennial History of Harvard Law School* (published in 1918), it was said, "If it be granted that law is to be taught as a science and in the scientific spirit, previous experience in practice becomes as unnecessary as is continuance in practice after teaching begins."

This philosophy of legal education was that of a man who cherished "inaccessible retirement." Inaccessibility, a nostalgia for the forgotten past, devotion to the hush and quiet of a library, the building of a pseudo-scientific system based solely upon book materials—of these Langdell compounded the Langdell method.

The neurotic, escapist character of Langdell soon stamped itself on the educational programs of our leading law schools. Unavoidably, their acceptance of the Langdell-Harvard method meant that most of the university law-school teachers were men who had never practiced or had practiced for only a brief interval. Indeed, in 1931, Adolf Berle, then a Columbia Law School professor, but himself an exception to the rule, said to me that ninety percent of the teachers in our leading law schools had never so much as ventured into a courtroom. There have been notable exceptions. I name, at random, former Dean (now Judge) Clark, Dean

Sturges, Douglas, Arnold, James at Yale; former Dean Pound, Dean Griswold, and Professor Morgan at Harvard; Professor Hinton at Chicago; Professors Michael, Wechsler and Hays at Columbia. Since 1931, the number of law teachers versed in courthouse ways has increased. Yet it is, I think, still true that at many law schools the majority of the professors have never met and advised a client, negotiated a settlement, drafted a complicated contract, consulted with witnesses, tried a case in a trial court, or assisted in such a trial, or even argued a case in an upper court.

The Langdell spirit choked American legal education. It tended to compel even the experienced practitioner, turned teacher, to belittle his experience at the bar. It tended to force him to place primary emphasis on the library, to regard a collection of books as the heart of the school. A school with such a heart is what one may well imagine. The men who teach there, however interested some of them may once have been in the actualities of law offices and courtrooms, feel obliged to pay but subordinate regard to these actualities. The books are the thing. The words, not the deeds. Or only those deeds which become words.

Langdell invented, and our leading law schools still employ, the so-called "case system." That is, the students are supposed to study cases. They do not. They study, almost entirely, upper-court opinions.[3] Any such opinion, however, is not a case, but a small fraction of a case—its tail end. The law students are like future horticulturists studying solely cut flowers; or like future architects studying merely pictures of buildings. They resemble prospective dog breeders who never see anything but stuffed dogs. (Perhaps there is a correlation between such stuffed-dog legal education and the overproduction of stuffed shirts in my profession.)

In such a school, that which is not in books has become "unscientific"; it may perhaps have truth, but is a lesser truth, relatively unreal; true reality is achieved by facts only when reported in books. To be sure, Dean Pound many years ago, spoke of "law in action." That awakened hopes. But has Harvard been showing its students "law in action"? The students have had the opportunity to read in books and law review articles about some very limited phases of "law" in action. But that, at most, is "law in action" in the library.

At Harvard's law school the students are given courses in evidence, practice, and pleading. Close by, courts are in action, and especially trial courts, where one can observe evidence in action, practice in action, pleading in action. Are the students urged to attend the courts frequently? Do they spend many days there? Are they accompanied there by their professors, who comment thereafter on what has been observed? Are the students familiar with the development of cases in those courts? Are they asked to speculate on the next move to be made in a trial—at a time when the results of that move depend on foresight and skill, instead of hindsight? Are the procedural possibilities of a real lawsuit shown to the students by their professors, together with the so-called "substantive law" formulae—or are the two split up into separate courses? Do they make any effort to watch, describe and interpret courts in action? I mention Harvard. I could as well refer to almost any of the leading university law schools.

"Law in action" was a happy phrase. It contained, to be sure, that miserably ambiguous word "law." Yet it was a pointer or guidepost; it seemed to indicate a new direction. But what university law school has followed the pointer? The phrase "law in action" has remained largely a phrase; at any rate, so far as legal pedagogy is concerned, the function of the phrase, psychologically, has been principally to substitute a new verbal formula for revised conduct. The contents of the bottle remained much the same; only the label was changed. One is reminded of the scene in the Gilbert and Sullivan opera where the policemen march around and around the stage, promising the distracted father that they will rescue his daughters from the pirates who have abducted them. "We go, we go," shout the policemen as they continue to march in circles. "But they don't go," exclaims the father despairingly.

In 1937, when I was still a practicing lawyer, I spoke at Harvard Law School to some six hundred law students. I talked about government and "economics." One of the Harvard professors had previously objected, urging me, instead, to talk about my experiences in litigation. I told the students of that suggestion, but said I had refused to comply with it, because, while what I might tell about litigation might be amusing to them, my remarks would be as remote from their knowledge as if I were talking about head hunting in the Solomon Islands. To test out the validity of that comment, I asked all those students who had ever been in a courtroom to raise their hands. Ten of the six hundred did so. I then asked which of those ten had visited a trial since he had been in law school. Five raised their hands. I then asked how many had been urged by their professors to attend trials. Not a single student raised his hand. I made similar experiments recently at both Columbia and Yale, with substantially the same results.

If it were not for a tradition which blinds us, would we not consider it ridiculous that, with litigation laboratories just around the corner, law schools confine their students to what they can learn about litigation in books? What would we say of a medical school where students were taught surgery solely from the printed page? No one, if he could do otherwise, would teach the art of playing golf by talking about golf to the prospective player and having the latter read a book relating to the subject. The same holds for toe dancing, swimming, automobile driving, cutting hair, or cooking wild ducks. Is legal practice more simple? Why should law teachers and their students be more hampered than golf teachers and their students? Who would learn golf from a golf instructor, contenting himself with sitting in the locker room, analyzing newspaper accounts of important golf matches that had been played by someone else several years before? Why should law teachers be like Tomlinson? " 'This I have read in a book,' he said, 'and that was told to me. And this I have thought that another man thought of a Prince in Muscovy.'"

Legal practice, I have said, is an art, a fairly difficult one. Why make its teaching more indirect, more roundabout, more baffling and difficult than teaching golf? But that is what the Langdell method has done. Legal teaching would be no "cinch" at best. The Langdell method has increased the difficulties, has made the task of the teacher as complicated as possible. Even the teacher who is a genius cannot overcome the obstacles. When I was at law school I sat next to a Chinese student who had learned his English in Spain. As a consequence, when he took his notes on what the American professors said, he took them in Spanish. On inquiry, I ascertained that he actually thought them in Chinese. University law teaching today is involved in a process not unlike that. It is supposed to teach men what they are to do in courtrooms and law offices. What the student sees is a reflection in a badly made mirror of a reflection in a badly made mirror of what is going on in the work-a-day life of lawyers. Why not smash the mirrors? Why not have the students directly observe the subject matter of their study, with the teachers acting as enlightened interpreters of what is thus observed?

As you will see in a moment, I am not advocating a plan for legal education which will produce mere legal technicians. It is imperative that lawyers be made who are considerably more than that. That "more" is alien to the Langdell spirit. That spirit, I grant, is somewhat weakened; the undiluted Langdell principles are nowhere in good repute today. But they are still the basic ingredients of legal pedagogy, so that whatever else is mixed with them, the dominant flavor is still Langdellian. Our leading law schools are still library-law schools, book-law schools. They are not, as they should be, *lawyer schools*.

Some eighteen years ago, Judge Crane of the New York Court of Appeals characterized the typical graduate of a university law school as follows:

> With the practical working of the law he has little or no familiarity. He may come to the bar almost ignorant of how the law should be applied and is applied in daily life. It is, therefore, not unusual to find the brightest student the most helpless practitioner, and the most learned surpassed in the profession by one who does not know half as much. Strange as it may seem, there were some advantages in the older methods of preparation for the bar. As you know, the law school is relatively a matter of recent growth.

Formerly, a student, working in the office of a practitioner, combined the study of law with its daily application to the troubles and business of clients. He had an opportunity of hearing the story at the beginning, of noticing how it was handled by his preceptor, of reading the papers prepared to obtain a remedy; he accompanied the lawyer to court and became acquainted with the manner of the presentaion of the case to the judge or to the jury. . . . You know much more law after coming out of a university [law school] than these former students ever knew, but you know less about the method of its application, and how to handle and use it.

Is that not a shocking state of affairs? Think of a medical school which would turn out graduates wholly ignorant of how medicine "should be applied and is applied in daily life." In this connection, it is important to note that, according to Flexner, in the best equipped medical schools, the student "makes and sees made thorough physical examinations, painstaking records, varied and thoroughgoing laboratory tests, at every stage in the study of the patient; the literature of the subject is utilized; at one and the same time medicine is practiced and studied—teachers and students mingling freely and naturally in both activities." In this manner, said Flexner, there has been

effected the fusion of bedside and laboratory procedures alike in the care of patients, in teaching, and in research. . . . From the standpoint of training, fragmentariness, if stimulative and formative, is desirable rather than otherwise. . . . The student must . . . acquire a vivid sense of the existence of breaks, gaps, and problems. The clinics I am now discussing carry him from the patient in the bed to the point beyond which at the moment neither clinical observation nor laboratory investigation can carry him. There he is left, in possession, it is to be hoped, of an acute realization of the relatively narrow limits of human knowledge and human skill, and of the pressing enigmas yet to be solved by intelligence and patience.[4]

Here is much that law schools should ponder carefully. The Langdell system is their albatross. They should cast it off.

* * *

It is a pleasure to report that many of the law schools today give marked emphasis to the role of lawyers as policy makers or policy advisers, and bring home to the students the need for embodying democratic ideals and values in the legal rules. But a law school which really means business about democratic ideals should interest itself mightily, as most of our schools do not, in the problem of thoroughly overhauling our trial methods, and in the inability of many litigants to obtain justice because of lack of money to meet the expense of obtaining crucial testimony.

Of course, the lawyer's interests should roam far beyond the courthouse aspect of government; yet, to say that is not to say that he should submerge his interest in that aspect. Without a doubt, the "full role of the lawyer in the community" compels recognition of "his impact on 'policy-advising' and 'policy-making'," and he should therefore "give imaginative consideration" to "the whole range of institutions. . . that can be created, improved, or rearranged for community values."[5] But in our democracy, prominent among the vaunted community values is the right to a fair trial; and a legal education which does not vigorously stimulate the interests of the future lawyers in that direction, while they are still youthfully idealistic, although it may deserve high praise for its general educational worth, is not a democratic education for lawyers. For, I ask once more, if lawyers do not cherish the values of which courts, peculiarly, should be the guardians, who will or can?

The schools should also concern themselves with the problem of the effect of judicial corruption. Of that problem, law students learn little or nothing. If one inquires why, he is told that dishonest judges and purchased or "fixed" decisions are "abnormal." That answer does not content me. I share the hope that all crooks will be driven from the bench; but that hope, alas, is not yet a reality—and probably will never be if the law schools maintain their present policy of failing to discuss the subject in classrooms. What would one say of an engineering school where students heard nothing of wind pressure? Such an obstacle to engineering is deplorable from an ideal point of view. But is it to be called "abnormal" and therefore ignored? Engineering students properly study frictionless engines; but they will do injury to mankind unless they are also taught much about friction. Should not law students be taught about judicial "friction"? What would be thought of a college course in city government in which no mention was made of "graft" and "pull"? How can we afford to have men practice law who have been educated to shut their eyes to the effect of those factors on decisions?[6]

Not of course, in order that they may learn how to use bribes or political pull,[7] but for these obvious reasons: (1) A lawyer should know which judges are corrupt, or susceptible to political influence, so that, when possible, he may keep his clients' cases from coming before those judges. (2) Lawyers should do what they can to help the public eliminate such blights on the judicial process. But lawyers engaged in practice before the courts find that a most perplexing problem. If some particular lawyers try to cause the removal of a judge they suspect of corruption, and if they fail, that judge probably will, in roundabout ways, visit his wrath on their clients. For that reason, practicing lawyers usually hesitate to initiate such removal proceedings. Moreover, most busy lawyers tend to lose a keen interest in reforms. Here is a problem, which, if it not be solved, should be discussed in the schools with the law students, who, still in their formative years, are generally rife with idealism.

It is objected that public reference to any judicial dishonesty may create the incorrect and unfair belief that many judges are dishonest. The answer is to say—as I do say unequivocally—that fortunately, most of the judiciary is honest, that but a very few scamps manage to get on the bench, and that the best way to avoid unfairness to the vast majority of judges is to oust the few rascals.

"Policy" teaching will be fruitless if "policy-minded" lawyers are not trained to protect policies when under fire in the trial courts. Let me give an illustration of the way such lawyer's know-how, or its lack, may vitally affect policies. In 1935-37, the constitutionality of the PWA statute was under attack in litigation in the federal courts. When I entered that litigation for the government, I found that the cases were on appeal. They had not been tried on evidence, because my booklawyer predecessor had "demurred" to the complaints, thereby admitting the truth of the allegations of fact made by the plaintiffs in those complaints. Those admitted allegations were to the effect that the PWA administrator, Harold Ickes, had, in dozens of ways, shockingly misused his powers under the statute. The solicitor general, Stanley Reed (now Mr. Justice Reed) and I agreed that, with those facts admitted, the defense of the statute's validity was in danger, since there would be such a bad "atmosphere" as to arouse marked hostility on the part of even the most liberal Justices when the cases were argued in the supreme court. Through considerable maneuvering, we managed to have the suits remanded, by several upper courts, to the lower courts for trial. We won those trials, obtaining findings of fact, based on the evidence, which flatly contradicted the plaintiff's factual allegations, thus completely dissipating the bad atmosphere. Then in the supreme court we were victorious. I strongly suspect that, but for those trial tactics, PWA and the valuable policy it represented would have been judicially destroyed.

* * *

To altogether too many law teachers, the comments of Anatole France are applicable:

> There are bookish souls for whom the universe is but paper and ink. The man whose body is animated by such a soul spends his life before his desk, without any care for the realities who graphic representation he studies so obstinately. He knows of the labors, sufferings, and hopes of men only what can be [found in books] sewn onto tapes and bound in morocco. . . . He has never looked out of the window. Such was the worthy Peignot, who collected other

people's opinions to make books out of them.... He conceived of passions as subjects for monographs, and knew that nations perish in a certain number of octavo pages.

Such an attitude, on the part of law teachers, means, I think, moral irresponsibility.[8] It induces in many a law student (when he emerges from school) a bitter, cynical, disillusionment like that described by Silone in the following passage:

> Don Paolo went back to his room to reflect on the peasants and their lives.... The idea occurred to him of using his remaining time at Pietrasecca to finish his essay on the agrarian question. He took his notebook from his bag and started reading the notes he had started.... He read them through, and was astonished and dismayed at their abstract character. All these quotations from masters and disciples on the agrarian question, all those plans and schemes, were the paper scenery in which he had hitherto lived. The country which was the subject of those notes of his was a paper country, with paper mountains, paper hills, fields, gardens, and meadows. The great events recorded in them were mostly paper events, paper battles, and paper victories. The peasants were paper peasants.

It is often said that it will do no harm to leave the law student ignorant of a large part of the facts in the legal world he will later enter, that he can learn those facts after his graduation. That argument comes to this: Have the student spend three long years being mis-educated, receiving erroneous impressions about the ways in which many courts and lawyers behave, because he will be able to dissipate those impressions subsequently.[9] Dr Brickner gave an apt reply to a similar argument: "It is a horrible thing to picture what is involved in the customary idea that ... we have about many an adolescent, 'Oh he is being disillusioned, he will soon be all right'—the idea that it is a customary thing for people to grow up in our society to have to go through a stage of disillusionment. That means we have been illusioned. What kind of education is it that has to be undone?" If, said Bentham, in his *Comment on the Commentaries*, "there be a case in which students stand in need of instruction, it is where the generality of books that come into their hands represent things in a different light from true ones. True it is, that after many errors and disappointments, observation and practice may let a beginner into the bottom of these mysteries; but what sort of an excuse is it to give for feeding him with falsehood, that some time or other he may chance to find it out?"

When Langdell counseled against having law teachers experienced "in dealing with men" or "in the trial and argument of causes," he said that properly equipped teachers should have "not the experience of the Roman advocate [court lawyer] or of the Roman praetor [magistrate] but the experience of the Roman jurisconsult." That reference to the "Roman jurisconsult" shows the defect of the Langdell method which still too much pervades legal education. For the jurisconsult was a man who seldom, if ever, tried a case or went to court. It was his business to give answers to legal questions based upon assumed states of fact. He did not bother about the means of convincing a court, through testimony, that those were the facts, or the method by which the court would reach that conclusion. Such matters were beneath the dignity of the jurisconsult; he left them to trial lawyers and judges.

Professor Max Rheinstein of Chicago, in a recent letter to me referring to my attempt to explain, by way of legal magic, the dominant law-school aversion to observation of trial courts, offered a supplemental explanation:

> To me, the reason seems to be rooted in history. In Rome, "legal" activities were divided up among three groups of men; the jurisconsults; the orators; and practical politicians, statesmen, and, during the late empire, bureaucratic officials. The jurisconsults busied themselves exclusively with the rules of law; the practical administration of justice remained outside of their field. Yet, their work has become the foundation of legal science ever since, not only in the countries of the so-called Civil but also in the Common Law or bit. The style of Common Law legal science was determined when Bracton[10] started out to collect, arrange, and expound the rules of the Common Law of his time in the very style of the Roman classics and the corpus juris.[11] All the law books since his time . . . have adhered to the pattern thus determined. Legal education built upon these books has been equally limited; from Pavia and Bologna[12] to Harvard, law schools have regarded it as their task to impart to their students a knowledge of the rules of law and hardly anything else. Of course, for practical work in the administration of justice such a training is far from being complete.

Rheinstein, commenting on my notions of a revised law-school curriculum, says that I am calling for the development of the "science of administration of justice." Change the word "science" to "art" and I agree. Instruction in such an art would include first-hand observation of all that courts, administrative agencies, and legislatures actually do. Such instruction would serve three purposes. First, it would aim to equip future lawyers to cope with courthouse realities, no matter how ugly and socially detrimental some of those realities are; for a lawyer cannot competently represent his clients if he is ignorant of the devices which his adversaries may utilize on behalf of their clients. Second, such instruction would stimulate the contrivance of specific practical means by which existing trial-court techniques can be improved, in order that justice may be judicially administered more in accord with democratic ideals. Third, it would train men to become trial judges.

A law school which turns its back on the observable happenings in the trial courts inevitable does what Langdell intended; it devotes itself basically to the *Rs*. It teaches students little about those elusive characteristics of the *Fs* on which I have been dwelling. And an *F*-less study of the judicial process necessarily yields a magical attitude towards the courts.

Notes

1. This chapter is based on several articles: Frank, *Why Not A Clinical Lawyer-School?* 81 U. Pa. L. Rev. 907 (1933); Frank, *What Constitutes a Good Legal Education,* 19 *Am. Bar Assoc. J.* 723 (1933); Frank, *A Plea for Lawyer-Schools,* 56 Yale L. J. 1303 (1947). More detailed descriptions of Harvard Law School under Langdell will be found in the first two articles.
2. Who reigned from 1154 to 1485.
3. "Non-legal" matter, now incorporated in many "case-books," seldom relates to the out-of-court activities of lawyers.
4. FLEXNER, MEDICAL EDUCATION 269-70 (1925).
5. McDougal, *The Law School of the Future,* 56 Yale L. Rev. 1345, 1348 (1947).
6. In the case of Root Refining Co. v. Universal Oil Products Co., decided in 1948—1969 F.2d 514—the court held that, in two earlier cases, the decisions had resulted from the bribery of a judge. That judge, on the bench for many years, had decided a multitude of cases. All those decisions are now, necessarily, under suspicion of having been purchased. It would be instructive to have law students track down those decisions to see which of them became precedents that lower courts were obliged to and did follow.
7. Professor Kantorowicz, in a much-quoted article, deplored the notion that law students should be told of the existence of dishonest judges; he said that such class-room discussions would amount to teaching the "art of bribing judges." Kantorowicz, *Some Rationalism About Realism,* 43 Yale L. J. 1240, 1252 (1934).
8. Their attitude recalls the story of Maxwell and Todhunter: Maxwell, having contrived an experiment which disclosed a new optical phenomenon, asked Todhunter to examine it. Todhunter refused. He explained that he had been teaching the subject of optics all his life, "and I do not want all my ideas upset by seeing it."
9. In 1840, when Prussia was under the Code of 1794 which had displaced the earlier Roman-derived "law," Savigny, at the University of Berlin, continued to base his legal teaching entirely on the Roman "Law." He said that there was no occasion for telling law students about the existing code, because, for "the needs of subsequent practice, [post-school] experience suffices."
10. Bracton was a 13th century English judge.
11. The collective title of the body of Roman "law" as promulgated by the Emperor Justinian in the sixth century.
12. Pavlia and Bologna were celebrated Italian law schools in the Middle Ages. In the twelfth century at Bologna a renaissance of "Roman law" began.

Part II

Lawyers and the Search for Truth: Conflict or Harmony?

The Art of Legal Advocacy: Duties and Obligations

John J. Sirica

The strength of America lies in individual liberty under law. Other countries have produced great artists, scientists, musicians, and other individuals of outstanding achievement. But no other system has produced the individual freedom which exists in America. And the reason for this solo achievement is that our system is founded upon and governed by the rule of law.

Due to the supremacy of the rule of law, the legal profession has, to a large extent, designed and constructed the political philosophy which has made this nation great. Moreover, the legal profession has created and preserved many of the individual freedoms we currently enjoy—through the efforts of many vigorous advocates who have defined, secured, and enforced them through the courts. At present, however, there is a very noticeable decline in both the number and ability of trial advocates, many attorneys having abandoned the courtroom for a less strenuous and more lucrative non-trial practice. The time has come, therefore, to make a plea for the renaissance of the trial lawyer; to encourage young lawyers and law students to study and master the art of advocacy. For it is only through a proficient and learned trial bar that our civil liberties will be protected and advanced.

Advocacy is not a skill that can be simply learned and applied. It is an art, and like any other art, its mastery can only be achieved by those who possess talent. Advocatory talent is not enough, however, to make a skillful advocate. The talent must be developed by learning the techniques of those who have mastered advocacy in the past, and by diligent practice of those techniques. Like painting and music, the art of advocacy has its virtuosi; Rufus Schultz, William Evans, Edwin Stanton, Daniel Webster, Luther Martin, and Max Doy are only a few. The more recently recognized masters include: William E. Lahey, Frank J. Hogan, Lloyd Paul Striker, John W. Davis, Archibald Cox, Edward Bennett Williams, James Saint Clair, and James Neil. These and many others have achieved the high standards which all advocates should strive for.

The training required to develop a good trial lawyer is long and arduous. It should, and I hope it does, begin in law school. But it will continue into actual practice, where some mistakes will be made. It takes time to learn such things as how to phrase a question, how to be propounded or put to a witness, when to pass up an objection (even though one has a good one), how to keep an adverse witness within the limits of inquiry or cross-examination, how to spot the opportune moment to terminate cross-examination, and how to avoid asking that one fatal question too many.

In achieving effective advocacy, there is simply no substitute for careful preparation. Trial lawyers must be able to present their client's case in a persuasive and convincing manner by presenting evidence and examining witnesses. To do so, the attorney must have thoroughly learned both the facts of the case and the relevant law. Careful preparation does not only insure that attorneys will logically approach the problems presented by litigation. it also serves to dispel their fear of making a mistake in the courtroom, thus enhancing their courtroom demeanor.

Though pretrial preparation can hardly be overemphasized, it comprises only about half of the foundation underlying masterful advocacy. The remaining groundwork consists of establishing a good rapport with the judge and jury, being able to think "on one's feet," and possessing a basic understanding of human nature. Of these elements, the most important is establishing a good rapport with the jury. Some elaboration is, therefore, warranted.

In order for an attorney to establish this advantage, he or she must utilize what I call "jury psychology." What I mean by this term is the ability to transpose oneself into the jury box and start thinking as a juror. From that point of view the strategy becomes evident. A juror is not responsive to a lawyer who gives the impression of being better or smarter than they are. Regardless of how intelligent and educated one might be, it is a fatal mistake for an attorney to do this. Good trial lawyers must be able to communicate on the level of the person on the street. A lawyer may eloquently plead for a client, but to be effective, the jurors must understand that plea and not be offended by it. Remember, they alone are the fact finders. Therefore, an attorney should talk to the jurors on their own level—with them but not at them.

Another aspect of "jury psychology" provides a very useful approach to direct and cross-examination of witnesses. It consists of asking oneself: "What questions would I want to ask the witnesses if I were a juror and had to decide the facts of this case?" After ascertaining which questions would be of interest to the jury, a lawyer should pose these to the witnesses, unless the expected response would weaken his or her client's case. A lawyer who lightens the jury's task by eliciting information which they deem important has won the respect of that jury, if not their benevolence. And, of course, this increases the likelihood of a lawyer's case prevailing.

Unfortunately, a lawyer fresh out of law school—regardless of an outstanding educational background—is no more equipped to try a case than the brightest graduating medical student is to perform a complicated surgical procedure. Both may know the theory perfectly, but neither has yet had the opportunity to develop their talent to the extent necessary to confidently handle the situation. In essence, then, the trial lawyer must have extensive training before he enters the courtroom—training which has only begun with graduation from law school.

Mr. Justice Robert Jackson, a great justice of the Supreme Court who was self-educated in the law, made a very astute observation regarding the weakness of the legal educational system in America:

> While the scholarship of the Bar has been improving, the art of advocacy has been declining. If the weakness of the apprentice system was to produce advocates without scholarship, the weakness of the law school system is to turn out scholars with no skill in advocacy.

I feel the law school graduates of today as a whole have a better knowledge and understanding of the law than any other group in the history of our nation. This has been, and will continue to be, extremely important to the operation and progress of our system of justice. These high standards must be maintained, and I am not suggesting that we discount the goal of scholarship in the law. What I do urge is the broadening of legal education to include programs which train law students to be advocates. Both faculty and students of all schools must accept the responsibility of seeing that talented young people pursue and master the fine art of advocacy. There is an immediate need to interweave more and further advanced clinical programs and moot court seminars into law school curricula. In addition, our bar associations and courts must sponsor and encourage programs aimed at giving students a taste of trial work, showing them the advocatory standards of excellence which must be met. Above all, greater enthusiasm, encouragement, and respect for the lawyer as a trial advocate must be engendered by all, including judges.

The legal profession has changed considerably since the late 1920s, when I started practicing law. At that time, the practice was on the verge of a great transition. As it changed, it became increasingly complex, broadening so much that it required skills of general practitioners that were beyond their capacities. Specialization was demanded of a large part of the legal profession, especially those practicing in large cities. Moreover, the practice of preventive law, like preventive medicine, became somewhat in vogue, as well as extremely lucrative. As a result of these changes, the incentive for young lawyers to practice trial advocacy has greatly diminished. In the 1920s and 30s, during less prosperous times, attorneys gladly accepted whatever legitimate business clients offered them; and if the case required going into court, they did so. At present, however, a capable lawyer in a fairly large city has the opportunity and choice of avoiding trial practice entirely, and regrettably, many do—some because they are afraid of it, lacking what they feel are professional skills, and others because they feel that it is not worthwhile.

I ask law students and attorneys to search their souls and ask themselves what their career objectives are. If they feel the motivation to become a champion of a good cause, however unpopular, they should not put the courtroom off limits. It is a wonderful and interesting place to work. Moreover, by becoming proficient advocates, they will be fulfilling their obligation to the profession and to society, by perpetuating the rule of law in America.

The Lawyer as a Hired Gun

Monroe H. Freedman

It is a singularly good thing, I think, that law students, and even some lawyers and law professors, are questioning with increasing frequency and intensity whether "professionalism" is incompatible with human decency—asking, that is, whether one can be a good lawyer and a good person at the same time. I have special interest in that question because at least one perceptive critic, Professor John T. Noonan, Jr., has drawn the inference from my book on lawyers' ethics[1] that I do not believe that a decent, honest person can practice criminal law or teach others to do so.[2]

Professor Noonan draws that inference, in substantial part, from my conclusion that a criminal defense lawyer will sometimes be compelled to knowingly present a client's perjury to the court, and to argue it in summation to the jury. I base that conclusion on such considerations as the Sixth Amendment right to counsel, the Fifth Amendment privilege against self-incrimination, and the obligation of confidentiality (under which the attorney induces the client to reveal all relevant information with assurances that the attorney will not act upon that information in a way that might injure the client). Thus, I might ask rhetorically whether Professor Noonan believes that a good person can induce another to rely upon assurances of confidentiality, and then betray those confidences. The difficulty is, of course, that the lawyer is frequently faced with conflicting moral obligations—here, either to participate knowingly in the presentation of perjury, or else to violate the client's trust which the lawyer has induced.[3]

In view of that kind of moral dilemma, a cynic might conclude that one cannot be a good lawyer and a good person at the same time. I do not believe, however, that one can properly be charged with immorality because one is presented with a moral dilemma. If that were so, the human condition would be one of guilt without realistic free will. On the contrary, I believe that in such circumstances, the only immorality lies in failing to address and to resolve the moral conflict in a conscientious and responsible manner.

At the same time that I discuss the issue of professionalism and personal moral responsibility, I will consider an integrally related question, one that is often expressed in terms of whether it is the lawyer or the client who

63

should exercise "control" in the relationship between them. As it is frequently put, is the lawyer just a "hired gun"—or must the lawyer "obey his own conscience and not that of his client?"[4]

Voicing a viewpoint prevalent in the profession, lawyers sometimes use the phrase "client control" (that is, control of the client by the lawyer) in expressing their professional pride in maintaining the proper professional relationship. In a law school commencement address titled "Professionalism in Lawyering," the chief judge of a federal court of appeals, Clement F. Haynsworth, stressed the importance of professional competence in handling a client's affairs; but Chief Judge Haynsworth went on to say that of even "greater moment" than competence on the part of a lawyer is the fact that

> [H]e serves his clients without being their servant. He serves to further the lawful and proper objective of the client, but the lawyer must never forget that he is the master. He is not there to do the client's bidding. It is for the lawyer to decide what is morally and legally right, and, as a professional, he cannot give in to a client's attempt to persuade him to take some other stand. . . . [T]he lawyer must serve the client's legal needs as the lawyer sees them, not as the client sees them. During my years of practice . . . I told [my clients] what would be done and firmly rejected suggestions that I do something else which I felt improper . . .[5]

Surely those are striking phrases to choose to describe the relationship of lawyer and client—the lawyer is "the master" who is "to decide what is morally . . . right," and who serves the client's needs, but only "as the lawyer sees them, not as the client sees them." Even more striking is the phrase once used by Charles Halpern, a sensitive and dedicated public interest lawyer. Between the lawyer and the client, he observed, it is the lawyer who turns "the whip hand."[6]

Thurman Arnold, who was a prominent practitioner and also a federal appellate court judge, held a philosophy similar to Judge Haynsworth's. As described with approval by former Supreme Court Justice Abe Fortas, Arnold did not permit a client to dictate or determine the strategy or substance of the representation, even if the client insisted that his prescription for the litigation was necessary to serve the larger cause to which he was committed."[7]

Critics of the legal profession argue not that such attitudes and practices are elitist and paternalistic, but rather that not enough lawyers abide by them.[8] In an article titled "Lawyers as Professionals: Some Moral Issues," Professor Richard Wasserstrom recalls John Dean's list of those involved in the Watergate cover-up. Dean had placed an asterisk next to the name of each of the lawyers on the list, because he had been struck by the fact that so many of those implicated were lawyers. Professor Wasserstrom concludes that the involvement of lawyers in Watergate was "natural, if not unavoidable"—the "likely, if not inevitable consequence of their legal acculturation." Indeed, on the basis of Wasserstrom's analysis, the only matter of wonder is why so many of those on John Dean's list were *not* lawyers. What could have possibly corrupted the non-lawyers and led them into the uniquely amoral and immoral world of the lawyers? "For at best," Wasserstrom asserts, "the lawyer's world is a simplified moral world; often it is an amoral one; and more than occasionally, perhaps, an overtly immoral one."[9]

Professor Wasserstrom holds that the core of the problem is professionalism and its concomitant, role-differentiated behavior. Role differentiation refers, in this context, to situations in which one's moral response will vary, depending upon whether one is acting in a personal capacity or in a professional, representative one. As Wasserstrom says, the "nature of role-differentiated behavior . . . often makes it both appropriate and desirable for the person in a particular role to put to one side considerations of various sorts—and especially various moral considerations—that would otherwise be relevant, if not decisive."[10]

An illustration of the "morally relevant considerations" Wasserstrom has in mind is the case of a client who desires to make a will, disinheriting her children because they opposed the war in Vietnam. Professor Wasserstrom suggests that the lawyer should consider refusing to draft the will because the client's reason is a "bad" one.[11] But is the lawyer's paternalism toward the client preferable—morally or otherwise—to the client's paternalism toward her children?

We might all be better served, says Wasserstrom, if lawyers were to see themselves less as subject to role-differentiated behavior, and more as subject to the demands of *the* moral point of view.[12] Is it really that simple? What, for example, of the lawyer whose moral judgement is that disobedient and unpatriotic children should be disinherited? Should that lawyer refuse to draft a will leaving bequests to children who opposed the war in Vietnam? If the response is that we would then have a desirable diversity, would it not be better to have that diversity as a reflection of the clients' viewpoints, rather than of the lawyers'?

In another illustration, Wasserstrom suggests that a lawyer should consider refusing to advise a wealthy client of a tax loophole legislated for only a few wealthy taxpayers.[13] If that case is to be generalized, it seems to mean that the legal profession can properly regard itself as an oligarchy, whose duty is to nullify decisions made by the duly elected representatives of the people.[14] That is, if the lawyers believe that particular clients (wealthy or poor) should not have been given certain rights, the lawyers are morally bound to circumvent the legislative process and forestall the judicial process by the simple device of keeping their clients in ignorance.

Nor is that a caricature of Wasserstrom's position. The role-differentiated amorality of the lawyer is valid, he says, "only if the enormous degree of trust and confidence in the institutions themselves [that is, in the legislative and judicial processes] is itself justified." And we are today, he asserts, "certainly entitled to be quite skeptical both of the fairness and of the capacity for self-correction of our larger institutional mechanisms, including the legal system."[15] If that is so, would it not be a non sequitur to suggest that we are justified in placing that same trust and confidence in the morality of lawyers, individually or collectively?

There is "something quite seductive," adds Wasserstrom, about being able to turn aside so many ostensibly difficult moral dilemmas with the reply that my job is not to judge my client's cause, but to represent his or her interest.[16] Surely, however, it is at least as seductive to be able to say, "My moral judgment—or my professional responsibility—requires that I be your master. Therefore, you will conduct yourself as I direct you to." A more positive view of role-differentiated behavior was provided in an article in the *New York Times* about the tennis star, Manuel Orantes:

> He has astounded fans by applauding his opponent's good shots and by purposely missing a point when he felt that a wrong call by a linesman has hurt his opponent.
>
> "I like to win," he said in an interview, "but I don't feel that I have won a match if the calls were wrong. I think if you're playing Davis Cup or for your country it might be different, but if I'm playing for myself I want to know I have really won."[17]

In other words, one's moral responsibilities will properly vary, depending, among other things, upon whether one has undertaken special obligations to one's teammates or to one's country.

Taking a different illustration, let us suppose that you are going about some pressing matter and your arm is suddenly seized by an old man with a long, gray beard, a wild look in his eye, and what appears to be an enormous dead bird hanging around his neck. He immediately launches into a bizarre tale of an improbable adventure at sea. If he is a stranger and you are alone on a poorly lighted street, you may well call the police. If he is a stranger but you decide that he is harmless, you may simply go on to your other responsibilities. If he is a friend or a member of your family, you may feel obligated to spend some time listening to the ancient mariner, or even confer with others as to how to care for him. If you are a psychiatric social worker, you may act in yet some other way, and that action may depend upon whether you are on duty at your place of employment, or hurrying so that you will not be late to a wedding—and in the latter case, your decision may vary depending upon whether the wedding is someone else's or your own.

Surely there can be no moral objection to those radically different courses of conduct, or to the fact that they are governed substantially by personal, social, and professional contexts (that is, by role-differentiation). One simply cannot be expected, in any rational moral system, to react to every stranger in the same way one may be obligated to respond to a member of one's family or to a friend.

In an interesting and thought-provoking article, Professor Charles Fried has analogized the lawyer to a friend—a "special-purpose" or "limited-purpose" friend "in regard to the legal system." The lawyer is seen to be "someone who enters into a personal relation with you—not an abstract relation as under the concept of justice." That means, Fried says, that "like a friend, [the lawyer] acts in your interests, not his own; or rather he adopts your interests as his own."[18]

The moral foundation of Fried's justification of that special-purpose friendship is the sense of self, the moral concepts of "personality, identity and liberty." He notes that social institutions are so complex that, without the assistance of an expert adviser, an ordinary layperson cannot exercise the personal autonomy to which he or she is morally and legally entitled within the system. "Without such an adviser, the law would impose constraints on the lay citizen (unequally at that) which it is not entitled to impose explicitly." The limited purpose of the lawyer's friendship, therefore, is "to preserve and foster the client's autonomy within the law."[19]

Similarly, Professor Sylvia A. Law has written:

> A lawyer has a special skill and power to enable individuals to know the options available to them in dealing with a particular problem, and to assist individuals in wending their way through bureaucratic, legislative or judicial channels to seek vindication for individual claims and interest. Hence lawyers have a special ability to enhance human autonomy and self-control. [She adds, however, that] far too often, professional attitude, rather than serving to enhance individual autonomy and self-control, serves to strip people of autonomy and power. Rather than encouraging clients and citizens to know and control their own options and lives, the legal profession discourages client participation and control of their own legal claims.[20]

The essence of Professor Fried's argument does not require the metaphor of friendship, other than as an analogy in justifying the lawyer's role-differentiation. It was inevitable, however, that Fried's critics would give the metaphor of friendship the same emphasis that Fried himself does. Perhaps inadvertently, therefore, they miss the essential point he makes, that human autonomy is a fundamental moral concept that must determine, in substantial part, the answers that we give to some of the most difficult issues regarding the lawyer's ethical role.

Thus, in a response to Fried, Professors Edward A. Dauer and Arthur Allen Leff make some perceptive and devastating comments about the limited-purpose logic of Fried's metaphor of friendship. At the same time, however, Dauer and Leff express their own views of the lawyer's role and character, views which I find to be both cynical and superficial. They describe an "invariant element" of the lawyer-client relationship in the following terms:

> The client comes to a lawyer to be aided when he feels he is being treated, or wishes to treat someone else, not as a whole other person, but (at least in part) as a threat or hindrance to the client's satisfaction in life. The client has fallen, or wishes to thrust someone else, into the impersonal hands of a just and angry bureaucracy. When one desires help in those processes whereby and wherein people are treated as means and not as ends, then one comes to lawyers, to us. Thus, if you feel the need for a trope to express what a lawyer largely is, perhaps this will do: a lawyer is a person who on behalf of some people treats other people the way bureaucracies treat all people—as non-people. Most lawyers are free-lance bureaucrats . . .[21]

Despite that caricature, Dauer and Leff manage to conclude that "a good lawyer can be a good person." They do so, however, by defining "a good person" in limited terms: "In our view the lawyer achieves his 'goodness' by being—professionally—no rottener than the generality of people acting, so to speak, as amateurs."[22] The best that can be said for that proposition, I believe, is that it is not likely to stop students with any moral sensitivity from continuing to ask whether it is indeed possible for a good lawyer to be a good person.

The most serious flaw in Professor Fried's friendship metaphor is that it is misleading when the moral focus is on the point at which the lawyer-client relationship begins. Friendship, like love, seems simply to happen, or to grow, often in stages we may not be immediately conscious of. Both in fact and in law, however, the relationship of lawyer and client is a contract, which is a significantly different relationship, formed in a significantly different way.[23]

Unlike friendship, a contract involves a deliberate choice by both parties at a particular time. Thus, when Professor Fried says that the lawyer's moral liberty "to take up what kind of practice he chooses and to take up or decline what clients he will is an aspect of the moral liberty of self to enter into personal relations freely,"[24] the issue of the morality of the decision to enter the relationship is blurred by the amorphous manner in which friendships are formed. Since entering a lawyer-client contract is a more deliberate, conscious decision, that decision can justifiably be subjected to a more searching moral scrutiny.

In short, a lawyer should indeed have the freedom to choose clients on any standard he or she deems appropriate. As Professor Fried points out, the choice of client is an aspect of the lawyer's free will, to be exercised within the realm of the lawyer's moral autonomy. That choice, therefore, cannot properly be coerced. Contrary to Fried's view, however, the choice of client can properly be subjected to the moral scrutiny and criticism of others, particularly critics who feel morally compelled to persuade the lawyer to use his or her professional training and skills in ways more consistent with personal, social, or professional ethics.[25]

As I have stressed elsewhere, once the lawyer has assumed responsibility to represent a client, the zealousness of that representation cannot be tempered by the lawyer's moral judgments of the client or of the client's cause.[26] That point is not only important in itself. It is one of the considerations that a lawyer should take into account in making the initial decision whether to enter into a particular lawyer-client relationship.[27]

In disagreeing with Professor Wasserstrom's criticism of role differentiation, I did not mean to suggest that role differentiation has not produced a degree of amorality, and even immorality, in the practice of many lawyers. The problem, as I see it, is expressed in the news item I quoted earlier regarding Manuel Orantes. Playing for himself, Mr. Orantes has earned an enviable reputation, not only for his athletic prowess, but also for his good sportsmanship—if you will, for his morality in his relations with his adversaries. Yet when he plays with teammates and for his country, he adopts different standards of conduct.

I think that Mr. Orantes is wrong, in a way that many lawyers frequently are wrong. I do not mean that in Davis Cup play he is not bound by special, voluntarily assumed obligations to others. On the contrary, he is bound by his role as teammate and countryman to accept the decision of his teammates—which may well be that each player should play to win, without relinquishing any advantage that the rules of the game and the calls of the judges allow. Where Orantes is wrong, however, is in preempting that decision, in assuming that their decision is that winning is all. Perhaps if he actually put the choice to them, Orantes' teammates would decide that they would prefer to achieve, for themselves and for their country, the kind of character and reputation for decency and fairness that Orantes has earned for himself. Perhaps they would not decide that way. The choice, however, is theirs, and it is a denial of their humanity to assume the less noble choice, and to act on that assumption without consultation.

In day-to-day law practice, the most common instances of amoral or immoral conduct by lawyers are those occasions on which we preempt our clients' moral judgments. These occur two ways. Most commonly, we assume that our function is to maximize the client's material or tactical position in every way that is legally permissible. Since our function is not to judge the client's cause, but to represent the client's interests, we tend to assume the worst regarding the client's desires. Much less frequently, I believe, we will decide that a particular course of conduct is morally preferable, even though not required legally, and will follow that course on the client's behalf. In either event, we fail in our responsibility to maximize the client's autonomy by providing the client with the fullest advice and counsel, legal and moral, so that the client can make the most informed choice possible.[28]

Let me give a commonplace illustration. Two experienced and conscientious lawyers (A and B) once asked me to help them to resolve an ethical problem. They represented a party, for whom they were negotiating a complex contract involving voluminous legal documents. The attorneys on the other side were insistent upon eliminating a particular guarantee provision, and A and B had been authorized by their client to forego the guarantee if the other side was adamant. The other lawyers had overlooked, however, that the same guarantee appeared elsewhere in the documents, where it was more broadly and unambiguously stated. Having agreed to eliminate the guarantee provision, with specific reference to a particular clause on a particular page, were A and B obligated to call the attention of opposing counsel to the similar clause on a different page? Or, on the contrary, were they obligated, as A put it, "to represent our client's interest, rather than to educate the lawyers on the other side?"

Each of the lawyers was satisfied that, if he were negotiating for himself, he would unquestionably point out the second guarantee clause to the other party. Moreover, each of them was probably more attentive to, and concerned about questions of professional responsibility than most lawyers. Each of them, that is, was highly sensitive to the question of personal responsibility in a professional system. Yet it had occurred to neither of them that their professional responsibility was not to resolve the issue between themselves, but rather to present the issue to the client for resolution.[29]

Notes

1. FREEDMAN, LAWYERS' ETHICS IN AN ADVERSARY SYSTEM (1975).
2. Noonan, *Book Review,* 29 Stan. L. Rev. 363 (1977). In fact, the title of this article derives directly from a challenge issued to me in the concluding paragraph of Professor Noonan's review of my book, urging that I write on "Personal Responsibility in a Professional System." *Id.,* at 270.
3. *See* FREEDMAN, *supra* note 1, ch. 3.
4. Noonan, *The Purposes of Advocacy and the Limits of Confidentiality,* 64 Mich. L. Rev. 1485, 1491 (1966) (quoting ABA Canons of Professional Ethics, Canon 15) (1908).
5. Haynsworth, *Professionalism in Lawyering,* 27 S.C.L. Rev. 627, 628 (1976).
6. *See* Comment, *The New Public Interest Lawyers,* 79 Yale L. J. 1069, 1123 (1970).
7. Fortas, *Thurman Arnold and the Theatre of the Law,* 79 Yale L. J. 988, 996 (1970).
8. *See, e.g.* AUERBACH, UNEQUAL JUSTICE (1976); GREEN, THE OTHER GOVERNMENT (1975).
9. 5 Human Rights 1, 2 (1975).
10. *Id.,* at 3.
11. *Id.,* at 7.

12. *Id.,* at 12.
13. *Id.,* at 7-8.
14. Wasserstrom acknowledges that concern, but finds it less than fully persuasive. *Id.,* at 10-13.
15. *Id.,* at 13.
16. *Id.,* at 9.
17. New York Times, Sept. 11, 1975, at 43, col. 8.
18. Fried, *The Lawyer as Friend: The Moral Foundations of the Lawyer-Client Relation,* 85 Yale L.J. 1060, 1071 (1976).
19. *Id.,* at 1068, 1073.
20. Law, *Afterword: The Purpose of Professional Education,* in LOOKING AT LAW SCHOOL, at 205, 212-13 (S. Gillers ed. 1977).
21. Dauer & Leff, *The Lawyer as Friend,* 86 Yale L. J. 573, 581 (1977).
22. *Id.,* at 582.
23. It is interesting to note that contract plays such a major role as a construct in political theory and in jurisprudence, but is overlooked in discussions of lawyer-client relations. Let me hasten to add, however, that I am not suggesting "the lawyer as contractor" as an all-purpose analogy. It is relevant to the question of the lawyer's personal moral responsibility in selecting (and rejecting) clients, but it may well be useless in other contexts.
24. Fried, *supra* note 18, at 1078.
25. Such criticism might be answered on the grounds that everyone is entitled to representation, but that response is not conclusive as long as there is, in fact, another lawyer who is willing to take the case.
26. Freedman, *supra* note 1, ch. 2.
27. *See* LAW, *supra* note 20, at 213-14. It is possible, of course, that a client will decide upon a course of conduct (not forseeable as a possibility at the outset of the lawyer-client relationship) that is so morally repugnant to the lawyer as to make it impossible to continue without a serious personal conflict of interest. In that event, the lawyer is permitted to withdraw, but only upon taking reasonable steps to avoid forseeable prejudice to the client's rights. *See* ABA Code of Professional Responsibility, DR 5-101(A); EC 5-2; DR 2-110(C) (1) (c); DR 2-110(A) (2).
28. *Cf.* ABA Code of Professional Responsibility, EC 7-7 *to* 7-12, 7-26; DR 7-101(A) (1), DR 7-101(B) (1).
29. That attitude does not appear to be the result of what Professor Wasserstrom refers to as the "acculturation" of legal training and practice. I have used that illustration and others like it as classroom problems early in the first semester of the first-year Contracts course; students who have had minimal exposure to the corrupting influence of law school (and no experience at all as practitioners) consistently assume that the lawyer's proper function is to preempt the client's moral decision. As indicated by that response, and by other student responses to problems of lawyer's ethics, law teachers have a moral role to perform as an essential part of their professional responsibilities. (*Cf.*) Freedman, *Professional Responsibility of the Civil Practitioner: Teaching Legal Ethics in the Contract Course,* 21 J. Legal Educ. 569 (1969).

The Adversary Nature of the American Legal System: A Historical Perspective[1]

Marion Neef and Stuart Nagel

Introduction

The purpose of this article is to examine the origins of the adversary nature of the American judicial system. After a brief description of the present American adversary judicial system, the authors will attempt to offer some ideas as to why the American judicial concept of adversary proceedings has taken root in this country, and whether such a system was inevitable in light of the history of our society. Finally, we will explore some of the reasons why the adversary system continues to flourish in America today.

The Adversary System of Justice in America

Under the American adversarial legal system, it is assumed that the fairest decision can be obtained when the two parties to the immediate conflict argue in open court according to carefully prescribed rules and procedures. The confrontation of witnesses in open court is at the heart of the American legal system,[3] since it is thought that the best result is obtained when the parties face each other as adversaries in a kind of constrained battle procedure.[4] The adversary theory of justice is premised on the assumption that the truth can best be discovered if each side strives as hard as it can, in a partisan spirit, to bring to the court's attention the evidence favorable to itself.[5]

Under the adversary system of the American courts, cross-examination is conducted by each party's attorney in a challenging manner. The witness is usually not allowed to testify in a smooth, narrative fashion; rather, he finds himself often interrupted and challenged by his opponent. The rationale for this type of procedure is that open confrontation of the witnesses insures that the judge will be made aware of all potential alternatives necessary for decision making. Those who favor the adversary method maintain that cross-examination is the most effective way to expose a witness who is not telling the truth.[6]

Under the adversary system, it is also assumed that the attorneys' arguments suspend the disposition of the case between the opposing interpretations of each party, thereby allowing the judge to make a proper, independent choice. At the same time, the presentation of each party's view aids the judge in exploring all the "peculiarities and nuances" of the case.[7] The attorneys are also supposed to help narrow the dispute and properly focus upon the problem, thus preventing a larger battle from developing from peripheral matters.[8]

The courts are not supposed to decide any disputes which are not brought to them by genuinely adverse parties.[9] Judges cannot rule on the legal aspects of matters which are not part of a specific controversy placed before them. Explicit rules exist to specify who the proper adversaries are, and only those who can prove to have an adverse interest in the matter can participate in the conflict.[10] The purpose of these rules is to insure that each trial which is brought to the courtroom will be a true contest between individual disputants. In the absence of this adverseness, the federal judiciary is helpless to supply an advisory opinion, or take on an independent investigatory role.[11]

In the ideal adversary system, the least skillful antagonist is expected to lose the dispute. The adversary system appears to embody the notion of individual initiative in its assumption that each man can completely carry out, with the aid of counsel, the preparation and presentation of his case. It is assumed that individual confrontation and cross-examination will reveal to the judge and jury who has the best case.

The judge in the adversary trial is often described as an umpire. His role is a neutral one. His duties are to interpret the law of the contest by which the parties can prove which one of them has the superior case, and to enforce the rules of procedure which regulate the progression of the courtroom battle, thereby insuring that it will be carried out fairly.[12] Nevertheless, the American judge is not impotent, and may exert great influence over the outcome of the dispute by controlling court procedure in a manner beneficial to the party believed to have the better case.

The adversary process is thus an intricate system of fact gathering and fact presentation, under which the opposing parties confront each other according to elaborate procedural rules. Each party is expected to discover all the facts pertinent to its own case, and expose any weaknesses in the other side's presentation. In this way, each side tries to establish a case and destroy its opponent's. If this ideal is accomplished, no fact is likely to be omitted from consideration, and false or irrelevant facts will not be allowed to stand.

Development of the Combat Model for the Adversary System

Trial by Ordeal

An important step in the evolution of the adversary system occurred when man began to take more of the responsibility for convicting other persons; a method for reaching that determination—trial by ordeal—was retained for a time.[37] Usually the accused was put in some sort of physical danger. If he came through unharmed, he was innocent. If he did not, it was taken to be a sign of guilt.[38]

Perhaps the ordeal by water is one of the oldest forms. It seems to have cut across the most cultures, and to have survived in usage for the longest period of time. Apparently it was frequently used in deciding the outcome of persons accused of witchcraft. The ordeal by water could be one of survival, or it could be a test to see whether the accused floated or sank upon plunging or being thrown into the water. In the Greek water ordeal, for example, sinking was proof of innocence, while coming to the top (or rejection by the water) was a certain sign of guilt.[39] Many other societies also adopted the rule that the innocent person would sink, while the guilty one would float. [40] Persons conducting an ordeal would pull to safety the innocent person—but the guilty one (who floated) was put to death for the crime which the gods decided he had committed.

The ordeal by fire was probably the next most frequently used. The accused might establish his innocence by walking on fire, swallowing fire, or passing through the flames unharmed. Later versions of the ordeal by fire involved the use of boiling liquids or hot irons; guilt or innocence might be established by the amount and extent of the injury they caused.[41]

Other ordeals involved the use of snakes, swords, poisons, or weights and balances.[42] In ancient Greece, for example, girls whose virginity was questioned were compelled to descend into a cavern in which a poisonous snake had been placed. If they were bitten by the snake, it indicated that they were no longer virgins.[43]

Ordeals were commonly used where evidence was especially conflicting and the judge or jury could not arrive at a decision.[44] In later periods, we can see that the combat or the ordeal was resorted to primarily when there was total lack of evidence. Among the Babylonians, for example, the ordeal was not used in judicial decisions except for those cases in which the truth could not be arrived at by the ordinary methods of discovery. Ancient Babylonian law demanded that the man charged with witchcraft "shall go to the river-god" and "shall leap into the holy river." If the river overwhelmed him, the accuser was entitled to take over the accused's property. However, if the river held him innocent and he was not drowned, the accuser was put to death—and the accused permitted to take *his* property.[45]

A significant development in the emergence of the present adversary system occurred . . . [when] William the Conqueror introduced trial by combat to the English legal system in the eleventh century. The combat was between the injured party and the accused, thus giving rise to a form of private war procedure to settle disputes.[47] The ordeal by combat was not as widespread as some of the other ordeals mentioned previously. While trial by combat retained much of the supernatural element of the earlier ordeals, it is significant that it began to be more of a test of men.

Under this system, if a criminal charge was made against someone, both the accuser and the accused were to fight the battle in person. On the other hand, when the claim involved a dispute over land, the plaintiff did not need to offer battle personally, but could send one of his men to do battle for him.[48] In theory, the man he sent was supposed to be a witness, but in practice he was a hired professional who made his living from fighting such battles.[49]

A ritual surrounded the battle in which the accuser swore to "prove by his body" that his side of the argument was the truthful one. According to Maitland, if he could not do this "before the stars appeared" that same night, he was a perjurer.[50] Apparently the object was not really to kill the opponent. In fact the adversaries were somewhat restricted in any effort to kill their opponents because of the weapons they were forced to use. Some were made specifically for this kind of battle, and apparently consisted of some kind of wood and bone, or wood and horn.[51]

Maitland says that the real purpose of the battle was to make one of the parties on his own cry "craven."[52] In effect, such vanquishment meant that the person confessed himself to be a perjurer. He usually had to pay a fine, and henceforth came to be known as a liar. On the other hand, if the battle involved a criminal case, the loser was "forthwith hanged or mutilated."[53]

It should be noted that most of the ordeals mentioned above were extensively regulated, and often an elaborate ritual accompanied them. The procedures governing them were specified in advance, and were known to the members of the society.[54]

Of course, a certain amount of magic nevertheless remained in these personal battles, as well as in other trials by ordeal which existed at this time for the purpose of determining guilt. There was probably a fine line between direct appeal to magical powers and weighing the truth of the accused by allowing him to do battle with his adversary. It might be argued that the methods used during this period differed little from the magical ordeals of fire and water, although we would contend that the triers of the accused increasingly began to assume more individual responsibility in deciding the ordeal's outcome. For example, ordeals began to take the form of administering an oath to the accused, listening to his story, and deciding whether he had made any "slip of the tongue" in presenting his case.[55]

Eventually, greater power came to be vested in the regulators of the ordeals. While ritual was retained in connection with the conflict-dispute settlement, authority in settling the matter began to be transferred from the gods and other divine powers to humans.

The Evolution of a More Rational Conflict Model

As people became more willing to assume greater responsibility for their decisions, skepticism naturally arose as to the efficacy of trials by ordeal and battle. Gradually, a more rational approach began to supplant the former modes of trial. Again, however, a transitional phase was needed, and thus, for some time both the magical and rational models existed side by side. With some reluctance, trials by magic, ordeals, and personal battles were increasingly replaced by trials before men.[56]

Settlements of Disputes in Greek Society

In early Greek society during the early modern legal period, no distinction was made between civil and criminal cases, and in civil suits the complainant had to institute the suit, as well as enforce the court's decision.[57] Criminal courts were probably not needed, since murder, which formed the basis of ancient criminal law, rarely occurred. It was branded as a sacrilege as well as a crime, and the murderer was thought to pollute the entire city. In certain cases feud revenge followed murders.[58] However, the cases which reached the courts were decided by juries.[59] First, the complainant had to submit his case to a public arbitrator.[60] The defendant also submitted his defense to the arbitrator, and both the complainant and the defendant paid him a small fee. The arbitrator then tried to reconcile the parties. If he could not accomplish this, he rendered his judgement for one or the other. Therefore, in early Greece the courtroom trial represented only those cases which could not be settled through negotiation, since the courts usually refused any cases which had not first been submitted to arbitration in the above manner.[61]

There appears to have been no confrontation of the parties once the case reached the courtroom. Each of the witnesses entered a sworn deposition to the court, always in written form. All the evidence was thus known to the court when the trial opened. These depositions were sealed in a special box and were opened when the court was ready to hear the case. The statements of each party were examined by a panel (chosen by a lot) and judgment was rendered on the basis of them.[62]

As society became more complex, however, procedure likewise became more complex. While at first no attorneys or special prosecutors had been used,[63] rhetors or orators began to present cases in front of the jury through oral testimony. At first such presentations were simply speeches read to the court, but subsequently an eloquent art of oration and persuasion developed. These special rhetor-pleaders were the forerunners of the modern lawyer.

In later Greek society evidence was ordinarily presented in writing, but the witness appeared and swore to it before the jurors. There was no cross-examination of the witness at all. Generally, all witnesses were males; women were allowed to testify only in certain murder cases.[65] It was assumed in Greece that slaves always lied, and therefore their testimony could only be admitted if it was accompanied by severe torture. Apparently, the Greeks believed that such torture elicited the truth from the slave. Many masters refused to allow their slaves to act as witnesses at trials. They were often severely injured during the eliciting of their testimony, and were afterwards no longer of any use as slaves.[66]

The jury voted secretly, without formally discussing the case. The outcome was determined by a simple majority.[67] After the jury rendered the verdict, the convicted person and his accuser were frequently allowed to name the particular fine or punishment that they each thought just and proper. The court then chose between the suggested penalties.[68] This, then, appeared to be a modification of the former "total" reconciliation sought between parties in earlier times.[69]

The Origins of Formalized Courtroom Procedure in Rome

The Roman legal system also represented a transitional phase between magic and human responsibility in dispute settlement. The early Roman legal system was not only a relationship between man and man, but between man and the gods, as well. Crime was taken to be a disturbance of the relationship with the gods, and the legal system was designed to restore that relationship. The priests declared what was to be right and wrong, and also decided on what days the court might meet. In early Rome, the assistance of a priest was needed in all legal matters, just as the assistance of a lawyer is needed in America today. Only the priests knew the "formulas" by which court matters had to be handled. Therefore, in Rome, the priests were among the first consultants to give legal opinions. They recorded current laws in their personal books, which were jealously guarded from the public, By about 300 A.D., however, the first public instruction was offered in the law, and from this date the public lawyer began to replace the priest.[70] This time the procedure of Roman law grew increasingly more complex. Lawyers were advising clients and pleading for them in court. However, the parties rarely engaged in direct confrontation with each other in the courtroom.[71] Testimony proceeded somewhat along the lines of the Greek court described above; slaves, as a matter of course, were tortured on the witness stand.[72]

In the Roman republic, all of the participants had to follow specific procedure, and any deviation might invalidate the trial.[73] The defendant had to deposit his own bail as security for his subsequent appearances at the court.[74] The dispute was then turned over to one of a list of persons qualified to act as judges. Almost any magistrate might act as a judge in the courtroom, but only senators and equites were eligible for jury service.[75] When jurors were needed, they were drawn from the list of those eligible, but either the defendant or the plaintiff could object to the selection of certain jurors at his trial.[76]

By this time in Rome, courtroom trials apparently were marked by great verbal displays. Sometimes a client had many lawyers on his side who all wanted to present an oration.[77] Almost any kind of presentation could be given to the court by the attorney. He could hold an injured child in his arms during the argument; he could display any kind of pictures he claimed to be part of the crime; and he could display the wounds of the client.[78] Almost any device was used by the attorney for distraction purposes.[79]

By the second century A.D., the magistrate had greater discretion in deciding cases.[80] By the end of the third century, the judgment of a magistrate responsible to the emperor was used in all cases.[81] The litigants could conduct their own case in front of the judge without lawyers if they wished, but few desired to do so. Interestingly, however, the judge had neither the right nor the means to execute his judgment. It was the successful litigant's task to bring that about, and he did not always have a direct means of doing so.[82]

In 322 A.D., a new idea began to pervade the administration of justice. Trials were no longer public and suits were submitted primarily in writing, without any personal activity on the part of the litigants.[83] The judicial hierarchy was parallel to that of the imperial officials, with the emperor at the top. Since the good will of the emperor and his judicial administrators could be trusted (because of the stability of the empire), it was thought that the formal procedures earlier employed could be dispensed with.[84] Therefore, by the fourth century A.D., the Romans, after having developed a highly sophisticated participatory judicial system (a system similar to our modern courtroom, except that there was no confrontation in open court), felt secure in abandoning this formal system. Instead, the resolution of issues was entrusted to officials of good will, who would exercise sound discretion in their determinations.

Developments in England's Courtroom Procedure

The Greek and Roman legal systems undoubtedly provided the background for the American legal system. However, Greek and Roman laws as affected by the peculiarities of the English experience provide the basis of the American system of jurisprudence.

When the Normans invaded, England was still largely in a local, tribal-law stage.[85] Disputes could be settled in several ways, but two of the most common forms used were ordeal and trial by compurgation. If the defendant had any standing in the community, he was probably allowed to attempt to clear himself by compurgation. Under this system, a certain number of "compurgators" swore that they believed the accused's oath to be true. Compurgators were similar to modern character witnesses, in that they did not testify to the facts involved in the accusation; rather they only attested to the defendant's reputation for truthfulness.[86] The more compurgators a defendant could find, the better his chances of a successful defense.[87]

The use of compurgation is thought to have been abandoned in criminal cases by an implied prohibition of the Assize of Clarendon in 1166.[88] However, it was retained for quite some time in the local courts of England.[89]

Usually, the accused was forced into the test of ordeal only if he were a stranger in the community, or for some reason lacked friends to swear for him. The ordeals commonly used in the twelfth century were by hot iron, hot water, or cold water. The accused person might be asked to carry a piece of hot iron for a certain distance, or to pull a stone out of a pot of boiling water. The hand which had consequently become inflamed was then bound up tightly and not examined until the third day after the ordeal. If the hand was not infected at that time, the person was declared innocent.[90] In trial by cold water, the accused, securely tied, was lowered into very cold water. If the person floated, he was guilty.[91]

As noted previously, the use of personal battle as a way to settle disputes was introduced into England by William the Conqueror,[92] who also transported to England the system of land tenure based on fighting.[93] The Normans, however, were also noted as administrators,[94] and they soon began to substitute feudal legal institutions for the more fragmented, tribal ones which they found to exist in England.[95] After the Norman invasion, the task of judging in the courts became one of the incidents of land tenure. It appears also that the Normans brought with them from the continent a form of jury system.[96] Central courts were gradually established in England for the adjudication of private disputes.[97]

One of the jury's functions during the twelfth century was to bring to the court's attention the cases it should try. Since communities were small, it was probable that any crimes committed would be known by such a group. This function is similar to the modern grand jury sytem, and stood in contrast to the former English system of accusation or "appeal," in which the wronged person brought the case to the attention of the court.[98] Notwithstanding the creation of a court system, the decision of guilt or innocence was still decided, for a time, by either the old ordeal methods or the newer personal battle methods introduced by the Normans.[99]

It has been pointed out that legal justice at this time usually rested on the general character of the contesting parties, rather than on the weighing of evidence in the particular case at hand. The court proceeding usually commenced with the plaintiff swearing his complaint under oath, after which the defendant, or accused, swore his denial. The main work of the men assembled to hear the dispute then revolved around deciding which of the parties should proceed to prove his case, and what method he should use in bringing forth such proof.[100]

It should be noted that the English jury system of the Middle Ages was not the democratic institution which is claimed to exist today. Jurors were freeholders. The great mass of Englishmen were not.[101] The English peasant was convicted not by his peers, but by his decided superiors. Originally, it was the practice of the emissaries of the king to rely on important freemen to give them information. This practice, which at first pertained only to administrative matters, was gradually extended to criminal matters. The judges then used the assemblage of freemen in their travels to give them information about criminal charges.[102]

During the thirteenth century, the body of men that decided the outcome of the dispute also originated the charges. Sometime during the middle of the fourteenth century, however, the practice of adding outside jurors was instituted in order to bring some fresh opinions into the jury trial.[103] At this time, the society was still relatively tight-knit and rural. Jurors could decide the dispute on the basis of what they personally knew about the case. In fact, for some time after the jury system was originated, to *not* have any personal knowledge of the case at hand was a ground for disqualification.[104]

Witnesses, separate from jurors, were not introduced into English trials until about 1500. If the regular jurors were not familiar with all of the details of a case, they were to investigate the matter for themselves outside of the courtroom, relying on gossip or hearsay, if necessary, to make a determination.[105] When the jury system first evolved, the defendant had few of the procedural safeguards which are taken for granted today in both the adversary and the inquisitorial systems.[106] There was no right to counsel of any kind.[107] The defendant did not even have the right to have a copy of the charges against him.[108] Confessions were often obtained by torture[109] and the defendant could be convicted on the basis of almost any kind of hearsay evidence.[110]

In the twelfth century, during the reign of Henry II, many legal reforms were instituted.[111] Separate criminal and civil procedures were developed; the judge began to assume the role of a passive umpire.[112] Interestingly, during this period penalties for criminal actions were usually addressed in terms of monetary damages—that is, the offender was forced to pay the family or his victim a certain amount of compensation for causing the victim's death or injury.[112] In time, however, the state, rather than the wronged party, began to assume the responsibility of prosecuting criminal matters, viewing such offenses as breaches of the "King's peace," rather than offenses against the individual. The judge, then, assumed the role of umpire, ensuring that the more sophisticated courtroom battle was played by the appropriate rules.[114] The English model of jurisprudence had thus taken its basic form—that of a controlled battle, within the confines of a courtroom and before a jury. Adversary confrontation had evolved and become rooted in the English sytem; it was destined to form the basis of the American mode.

Transfer of the Adversary System to America

The Early Settlers

The early American settlers most probably brought with them those English procedures with which they had been familiar, and adapted and shaped them to make them more appropriate to their colonial situation.[148] Thus, English court procedure was used . . . as a basic model, but it was molded to fit the circumstances of the New World.

Actually, there was little need for the colonists to concern themselves with formal legal systems until the colonies began to develop economically in the 1700s. As in primitive societies, the first settlers were dependent on one another for life itself. Although some simple codes of law were adopted, much of the initial system operated along compromise lines, since (as in the primitive communities discussed earlier) the earlier colonies consisted of tightly-knit communities.[149] Local law predominated, at first, because of the geographical separation and social and political differences between the founders of the various colonies. A Pennsylvania statute, for example, provided for three "peace-makers" to act as arbitrators in the settlement of disputes, and the Dutch colonists also used arbitration extensively.[150] On the other hand, from 1681 until the 1830s there were various unsuccessful attempts to establish courts with the chancery powers of the English courts.[151]

Considerable freedom of procedural action existed in the seventeenth century. The law and procedure of the early colonies varied widely, depending upon each colony's location, the social class from which its leaders came, and the amount and kind of contact which its leaders had with the English law.[152] Colonies such as Massachusetts, for example, chose to use relatively simple procedural laws, while others (such as Maryland) did not.[153] Also contributing to the early diversity of legal procedure was the variation in dates of settlement. In any event, court structure was virtually autonomous in each colony.[154]

Obviously, the colonists drew upon their previous backgrounds in developing legal procedures. However, most of the new settlers had very limited contact with the legal institutions of England, and their experiences were frequently too fragmented to allow them to transfer an accurate picture of the English system to their New World environment. It is thought that Blackstone's *Commentaries* was instrumental in preventing the kind of chaotic divergence in procedure that might have developed (as a result of the independent establishment of the various colonies).[155]

Many of the colonists settled in America because of certain ideals which they believed were not compatible with the English customs and procedures they had left behind. Thus, many persons were hostile to the reception of English law and courtroom procedure, simply because it was *English*. This hostility intensified around the time of the Revolution, and, for a while, retarded the transfer of some of the English procedures to America.[156]

Assertion of Individualism

The American settlers rewarded self-reliance. The harsh environment of the early colonies tended to encourage it and to generate individual expectations of material improvement.[157] The early Americans brought a belief in individual self-control over individual direction to their formation of legal procedures. Thus, the settlers came to America amidst a spirit of conscious self-effort to guide individual affairs. They were primarily opposed to legal procedures which seemed to direct the individual. The law of England, as the colonists knew it, was burdened with much formalism. It was based on ideals of an organized society of the Middle Ages, and thus did not reflect the needs and the ideas of people who were settling the new frontier. While the English law of the time came from an "era of organization," the colonists represented the beginning of a new "era of individualism."[158] There was much distrust of central authority, and the judiciary was particularly a target of this mistrust.[159] Any move toward centralization of legal proceedings was resisted. Instead, it was assumed that each person of ordinary intelligence would be able to plead his own cause in the courts.[160] Thus, various procedures had to be reshaped—as settlements began to take on the trappings of the competitive, self-asserting individualism which was to flourish in America, and the settlers began to prune away restrictions on free individual activity they felt were not applicable to their society.[161]

Developing Economic Interests

Many of the people who journeyed to America were motivated by the desire to develop individual monetary enterprises in the New World. The development of commercial enterprises was not undertaken immediately, of course, since the first settlers were preoccupied with establishing a new society and an agriculture to support themselves. As these needs were met, commercialism and trading increased. During the beginning of the rise of commercialism, arguments ensued as to the best legal procedures to be employed. Some argued that Americans should establish their own novel kind of legal procedure, while others argued that they should build upon already-existing methods.[162] While much debate existed during the early period of the American colonies with respect to the type of legal system which should be developed for the new country, the rapid economic growth of the country probably necessitated resort to a more technical legal system.

In England, the old aristocracy had held the dominant position of power. In the colonies a new class of entrepreneurs arose, demanding a more rational system of law, a system which would embody definite procedures and rules and allow the common man even more individual control of the proceedings. Because of its entrepreneurial spirit and preoccupation with monetary investments, the middle class demanded more rigorous rules and needed a greater degree of "predictability" from its courts. They wanted to be confident that they could invest their available money, and that rules would not be capriciously changed by judges who considered themselves representatives of the King.

Many of the emerging middle class who came to America believed they had been abused by the aristocratic government of England.[163] They were therefore most intent in preventing the formation of another aristocracy; the adversary system appeared to be a good method for protecting the citizenry against this. Since the adversary system restricted a judge's role to that of a passive arbiter, it was also looked upon as a good way to prevent judges from becoming an arm of the state.

For various reasons, then, the framers of the Constitution included provisions that would strengthen the adversary system as they wished. Included were such provisions as due process, right to trial by jury, habeas corpus, the right to counsel, the right to bail, the privilege against self-incrimination, and others. Many writers have noted that the founding fathers thought that these provisions would guarantee the adversary system. [164] However, it should be pointed out that the framers appeared to have been concerned with protecting the commercial interests of middle class merchants and industrialists, rather than providing protection and safeguards for the lower classes of society.[165]

Why the Adversary System Flourished in America

The Myth that Such a System is the "Best" System

Certain writers have argued that the American adversary system did not flourish in fact, but only *appeared* to have flourished. Burns, for example, suggests that by 1900 the realities of law enforcement in America consisted of two systems: one system on the books, and the other predicated on an informal process, based largely on the power of the district attorney.[166] Burns also suggests that after 1900 the Supreme Court, in its efforts to reform what it *thought* was an adversary system, applied corrective measures which may have actually caused some of the problems which it sought to correct.[167]

The reason for the retention of the adversary system, as usually stated by those who think it to be the best, is that the fairest decision is obtained when the parties argue in the manner it prescribes. Thus, for many people the adversary system is not merely a battle of wits; it is the best means of discovering the "truth."

Macauley defends the adversary system when he states that the fairest decision is obtained "when two men argue, as unfairly as possible, for then it is certain that no important consideration will altogether escape notice."[168] Certainly, the Supreme Court has used language to indicate its faith in the truth-evoking nature of the system.[169] And the ABA said (as recently as 1971) that "[t]he adversary system is the hallmark of arriving at justice," and "[c]ross-examination is an effective means to expose false or inaccurate testimony."[170]

Factors Cited as Operating Overtly to Cause Retention of the Combat System

Various theories have been advanced to explain the entrenchment of the adversary system in the United States. They are: (1) the fight theory; (2) the sporting, or game theory; (3) the laissez-faire theory; and (4) the ritual theory.

The Fight Theory. It is contended that an adversary courtroom trial is merely a substitute for the earlier personal battles designed to settle disputes.[171] Mayers, for example, says the trial is a public duel between the parties, with the judge acting as referee to enforce the rules of the contest and the jury acting as umpire to announce the victor (the judge assuming this role, of course, if there is no jury).[172] To some writers, modern courtroom techniques are analogous to the blood battles of the past. One writer has noted that the clank of armor has been replaced by the clank of leg braces, as skilled attorneys dramatically drag "the blood across the courtroom floor."[173] Some writers have implied that perhaps the courtroom is symbolic of America's continued fascination with the notion of war. Thus, the lawyer becomes an active, partisan warrior for his client. His armaments against the enemy are his skills of examination, cross-examination, and verbal disputation.[174]

While we would caution against carrying the battle or fight analogies too far, we did note earlier that the courtroom confrontation of today is still structured along conflict lines. American courts are limited to deciding disputes which are brought by individual adversaries. Judges cannot determine the legal aspects of any matter which is not part of a specific controversy placed before them, and the parties must be genuinely adverse.[175] The plaintiff must bring his own battle to the courtroom, and the matter is to be one of individual concern. The court settles a combat only where it has been properly brought before it.

Once the parties have gained access to the courtroom, they are to confront each other and argue in a keenly partisan spirit, in order to bring to the court's attention evidence favorable to their own side of the matter. Witnesses tell their story in a combative atmosphere, in which they are continually challenged by the opponent. Supposedly, bitter partisanship brings out the truth, and individual combat is to bring about clarity of the issues.

The Game Theory. The adversary system has been compared to a sport or game. Wigmore said that the common law originated in a community of sports and games, which (he theorized) led to the notion of the system as "legalized gambling."[176] James Marshall spoke of a theory of the trial in which the parties engage in a verbal duel of the sporting variety. As their spears and lances, the duelers of today use " 'make believe' assumptions of As Ifs . . . ."[177]

Often, attorneys themselves characterize the courtroom procedure in terms of some sort of a sport.[178] And certainly, many people have commented that murder trials evoke the same kind of popular interest that one might find on the eve of a championship football game, or at the outset of the world series in baseball.[179] The adversary fight system allows today's newspaper readers to enjoy the battle or game of the courtroom arena—much like the Romans enjoyed the direct confrontation of the gladiators. Though we still are a combative people, we are civilized enough to forego the spilling of blood during the combat.

There are several points of interest to the game theory. First, its proponents refer to those trials which generate public enthusiasm because of the unique or spectacular nature of the proceedings. It is likely that similar trials would generate the same amount of public enthusiasm and betting in other kinds of legal systems. A spectacular murder trial is likely to stimulate intense public interest in countries which have the inquisitorial system, though the rules of their trials are different. Also, it should be noted that in this country, similar enthusiasm has been generated not only by courtroom trials, but also by investigatory hearings. The Senate Watergate hearings, which did not proceed along the lines of an aggressive battle, provide a timely example. It seems, then, that public interest relates to factors either apart from or in addition to the *procedures* which are employed.

In addition, those who speak of the game theory refer primarily to participants other than the accused. The courtroom scene is viewed as a game either in terms of the attorneys or the onlookers. It is probable that litigants view the situation as anything *but* a game or sport. Carrying the metaphor to an extreme, the litigants would probably have to be called the pawns of the game.

The Laissez-faire Theory. In *Courts on Trial,* Jerome Frank suggests that our retention of the fighting theory of justice, embodied in the adversary system, is related to our laissez-faire heritage.[180] The laissez-faire notion is predicated on the belief of uncontrolled competition which leads to unbridled individualism. It assumes that when each individual strives to promote his own self-interest, the end result will be the most desirable distribution of resources.

When transferred to the courtroom, of course, this theory supposes that each man can competently carry out (with the aid of counsel) the preparation and presentation of his case through the use of "individual enterprise" techniques. Thus, at the base of the adversary proceeding, we encounter the old laissez-faire notion that each party will (or indeed *can*) bring out all of the evidence favorable to its own side, and that if the accused is innocent (if his is the best case) he can act to "out-produce" the presentation made by his competitors. In an ideal adversary system, the less skillful antagonist is expected to lose the dispute—the proper outcome under the laissez-faire notion.

As noted previously,[181] the middle class has historically believed that the adversary system was capable of producing the more stable conditions and rules needed so that, in the conduct of their business, they might know "where they stand." In addition, the middle classes retain some of the notion that everyone must fend for themselves. This may well represent a "carryover" into the courtroom of the individual enterprise system.[182]

The Ritual Theory. The judicial fact-finding process, "a highly ritualized trial by battle by wits," is not used in any other area of human activity—in science, in scholarship, in business—where a need also exists to determine facts or to verify data. This in part suggests that the adversary process is retained not because of its reliability on fact-finding, but because its ceremonialism is effective in "winning consent for difficult societal decisions."[183]

Other writers who discuss the American need for ritual point out some of the symbolic uses which the system has.[184] Certainly, the courtroom remains the symbol of continuing stability. It may well be that while the adversary system is an integral part of the American capitalist economic order, its support lies largely in the psychological realm.[185]

It is plausible that while the adversary system originated for specific purposes, it has continued mainly because of its increasingly ritualized aspects. What arose during an era of extreme individualism may be sustained in quite a different era, partly due to the force of inertia—but largely because the procedures used have become so ritualized and encumbered with formal terminology, that they are hard for the layman to understand, let alone change.[186]

Conclusion

This article has surveyed the origins of the adversary nature of the American legal system. . . . We have seen that the adversary method is not the inevitable way in which legal disputes must be settled. Nor has it been adopted by the majority of legal systems. . . . It seems clear that adversary procedures have changed over time to reflect the relative strength of social classes within the society. We can see, for example, that when the aristocratic class was dominant, social order was preferred to law. The emergence of the middle clas, however, brought about the demand for law in preference to social order—not only for the purpose of limiting the powers of the aristocracy, but also for stabilizing conditions and rules so that the middle class entrepreneurs could safely invest their available money in commercial enterprises. Furthermore, the middle class admired the adversary system because it represented the individualized enterprise upon which their entrepreneurial lives were founded. They thus carried into the courtroom the idea that everyone should take care of themselves.

Thus, the adversary nature of the American legal system evolved during an age of rugged individualism, in which "legal man" was equated with "economic man"—a man of prudence, who stands or falls by his own claim of defense and is presumed to have intended the natural and probable consequences of his acts. While society has subsequently undergone extensive economic and social changes, the American adversary system has not changed much, and still retains its essential characteristic of the conflict between the parties.

Notes

1. This article is based on a larger study which the authors are conducting.
2. Omitted.
3. 5 WIGMORE, EVIDENCE § 1367, at 29 (3d ed. 1940). U.S. Const., Amend. VI, el. 2 guarantees the accused in all criminal prosecutions the right to be confronted with the witnesses testifying against him.
4. FRANK, COURTS ON TRIAL: MYTH AND REALITY IN AMERICAN JUSTICE 80 (1949).
5. *Id.*
6. "[Cross-examination] is beyond any doubt the greatest legal engine ever invented for the discovery of truth. . . ." 5 Wigmore, *supra* note 3, § 1367, at 29. *See* Pointer v. Texas, 380 U.S. 400, 404 (1965); C. McCormick, Evidence § 19, at 43 (2d ed. 1972).
7. Report of the Joint Conference on Professional Responsibility of the Association of American Law Schools and the American Bar Association, 44 Am. Bar Assoc. J. 1159 (1959).
8. *See* Ewing v. United States, 135 F. 2d 633 (D.C. Cir. 1942); Attorney-General V. Hitchcock, 154 Eng. Rep. 38 (Ex. 1847); (*Cf.*) ABA Code of Professional Responsibility, DR 7-106 (c) (1) (1971); DOFFLER & REPPY, HANDBOOK OF COMMON LAW PLEADING 13-17 (1969).

9.   The courts are concerned as to whether

> [the] appellants [have] alleged such a personal stake in the outcome
> of the controversy as to assure that concrete adverseness which
> sharpens the presentation of issues upon which the court so largely
> depends for illumination of difficult constitutional questions.

Baker v. Carr, 369 U.S. 186, 204 (1962). *See also* U.S. Const., Art. III, § 2;
North Carolina v. Rice, 404 U.S. 244, 246 (1971); Association of Data Pro-
cessing Service Org. Inc. v. Camp, 397 U.S. 150, 151 (1970); Hall v. Beals,
396 U.S. 45, 48 (1969); Golden v. Zwickler, 394 U.S. 103, 110 (1969); Flast
v. Cohen, 392 U.S. 83, 96, 99 (1968).

10.   However, it can be noted that this concept of the "ideal" trial as a battle
between individual combatants has been tempered somewhat by the practice of allowing the participation of interest groups. Class actions where an
individual can bring suit as a representative party can be sustained in court:

> only if (1) the class is so numerous that joinder of all members is
> impracticable, (2) there are questions of law or fact common to the
> class, (3) the claims or defenses of the representative parties are typi-
> cal of the claims or defenses of the class, and (4) the representative
> parties will fairly and adequately protect the interests of the class.

Fed. R. Civ. P. 23(a). *See* 3B MOORE, FEDERAL PRACTICE, ch. 23 (2d. ed.
1969). *See also* Fed. R. Civ. P. 24, allowing parties to intervene in civil
actions; Fed. R. App. P. 29, concerning filing of a brief by an amicus curiae.
Given the time and expense involved in litigation today, it has become
extremely difficult for most individuals to successfully prosecute a case all
the way to the Supreme Court. Thus, organizational participation has
taken on a much more important role in providing the resources needed in
terms of money and expertise. *See, e.g.,* Sierra Club v. Morton, 405 U.S.
727 (1972). Usually, an individual is found who can remain with the suit
throughout the litigation, and the organization then supports his case. *See*
Vose, *Litigation as a Pressure Group Activity,* Annals 20 (1958), for a discussion of the use of interest group participation in court actions.

11.   The Supreme Court will not render advisory opinions. As enunciated in
the United States v. Fruehauf, 365 U.S. 146, 157 (1961):

> Such opinions, such advance expressions of legal judgment upon
> issues which remain unfocused because they are not pressed before
> the Court with that clear concreteness provided when a question
> emerges precisely framed and necessary for decision from a case of
> adversary argument exploring every aspect of a multi-faced situa-
> tion embracing conflicting and demanding interests, we have con-
> sistently refused to give. . .

See also Muskrat v. United States, 219 U.S. 346, 362 (1911); WRIGHT, LAW
OF FEDERAL COURTS 36-38 (2d ed. 1970).

12.   ABA Code of Judicial Conduct, Canon 3.

13-36. Omitted.

37.   It should be noted, however, that the ordeal is not locked into a particular
period of history, but in fact has existed in various forms over great periods

of time. Throughout history we have seen lapses into the ordeal method of dispute settlement, as in the Salem witch trials in the seventeenth century.

38. *See* Lowell, *The Judicial Use of Torture,* 11 Harv. L. Rev. 220, 221-22 (1897).

39. *Id.*

40. The thought was, apparently, that the river would not accept the guilty into its water.

41. Lowell, *supra* note 38. Sometimes merely scalding was taken to be a sign of proof, or in the case of the hot iron, the person might be forced to carry it for a certain distance without dropping it. An additional test might involve the extent of the burns which resulted to the accused from carrying the iron.

42. Lowell, *supra* note 38.

43. GOITEIN, PRIMITIVE ORDEAL AND MODERN LAW 148 (1923).

44. Lowell, *supra* note 38, at 221-22. Students of history might, quite rightly, question the futility of such judicial tests of torture. But, as Lowell indicates

> [the particular ordeal employed and] the severity of the ordeal itself . . . depended in part on the known character of the accused, and the amount of evidence against him; so that the result of the test was apt to accord with the previous opinions of the people.

Lowell, *supra* note 38, at 221-22.

45. DRIVER & MILES, THE BABYLONIAN LAWS 63 (1952). Apparently the early Germanic peoples used the water ordeal in which the person was innocent if he sank to the bottom. Roman actions, too, had the ordeal as their forerunner. Roman ordeals, however, were relatively few in number and emphasized the wagering, or gambling aspect of the outcome.

46. Omitted.

47. This practice was established by William I in criminal proceedings between an accuser of one race against an accused of another. REEVES, HISTORY OF ENGLISH LAW 33-34 (2d ed. 1787); Thayer, *The Older Modes of Trial,* 5 Harv. L. Rev. 45, 65 (1891). According to Thayer, the earliest reference to the use of trial by battle arose at the conclusion of the case of Bishop Wulfstan v. Abbot Walter in 1077. *Id.,* at 66.

48. BLACKSTONE, COMMENTARIES, at 337-41. Blackstone presents an illustrative account of the last trial by battle waged in the court of common pleas at Westminster in 1571 as reported by James Dyer. This account contains the reasoning underlying the use of servants to do battle:

> When the tenant in a writ of right pleads the general issue, viz. that he hath more right to hold, than the demandant hath to recover; and offers to prove it by the body of his champion, which tender is accepted by the demandant; the tenant in the first place must produce his champion, who, by throwing down his glove as a gage or pledge, thus *wages* or stipulates battel with the champion of the demandant; who, by taking up the gage or glove, stipulates on his part to accept the challenge. The reason why it is waged by champions, and not by the parties themselves, in civil actions, is because, if any party to the suit dies, the suit must abate and be at an end for the present; and therefore no judgement could be given for the land in question, if either of the parties were slain in battel and also that no person might claim an exemption from this trial, as was allowed in criminal cases, where the battel was waged in person.

49. 2 Pollock & Maitland.
50. F. Maitland and F. Montague, A Sketch of English Legal History 50 (1975).
51. *Id.*
52. 2 Pollock & Maitland.
53. 2 Pollock & Maitland.
54. According to Goitein, the formalities of the ordeal were numerous, and its very formalism was used to provide the element of risk that was the essential nature of the ordeal. Goitein, *supra* note 43, at 65. He moreover states, "Indeed, all the highly specialized stages of legal process are to be found in the ordeal, but as yet undifferentiated." Goitein, *supra* note 43, at 73.
55. Frank, *supra* note 4, at 45.
    It can be argued that deciding whether the person is telling the truth under oath in the courtroom of today still retains an element of magic, since the person who swears falsely risks "supernatural vengeance." Many other elements of magic and of trial by ordeal and by battle are also retained in some form in the modern courtrooms. For one such interesting discussion of the vestiges of earlier methods, *see* Frank, *supra* note 4, at 41-45.
56. Frank, *supra* note 4, at 45. The author notes that at first, trials by ordeal and by battle were considered to be fairer to the accused than a jury trial would be. After all, it was argued, a man who engaged himself in trial by battle had voluntarily submitted to that solution of his case; and the ordeal allowed the accused to demonstrate his innocence by supernatural means rather than relying on the mere testimony of fallible humans. Frank, *supra* note 4, at 45-46.
57. BONNER, LAWYERS AND LITIGANTS IN ANCIENT ATHENS 108 (1927); DURANT, THE LIFE OF GREECE 258 (1939).
58. Bonner, *supra* note 57, at 29-30; Durant, *supra* note 57, at 258.
59. These juries were drawn from all the citizens of Greece, and every person was supposed to serve as a juror every third year. Durant, *supra* note 57, at 259-60.
60. These public arbitrators were chosen by lot from all citizens over the age of 60. Durant, *supra* note 57, at 260.
61. The right to bring suit against another man was limited to freemen, although such freemen constituted only a fraction of the total population. Slaves could bring suit only if they could find a patron citizen to bring it for them. Durant, *supra* note 57, at 262.
62. Durant, *supra* note 57, at 260. Durant notes that any plaintiff who received less than a fifth of the jurors' votes was subject to a lashing or to a monetary penalty, apparently since it was believed that he had wasted the court's time in bringing a frivolous case. Durant, *supra* note 57, at 260.
63. There were no official prosecutor in Athens. Any citizen could prosecute someone else as a criminal. However, homicide cases were classified as private suits, and only close relatives of the victim could initiate the proceedings, although the penalties for the action were imposed by the state as in other public suits. Bonner, *supra* note 57, at 59-60.
64. Bonner, *supra* note 57, at 204-05.
65. Bonner, *supra* note 57, at 54.
66. Bonner states that "the statement frequently found in modern handbooks that slaves were competent to testify in homicide courts is due to a misinterpretation of a passage in one of Antiphon's speeches." Bonner, *supra* note

57, at 58. *See also* Bonner, *Evidence in the Areopagus,* 7 Classical Philology 450 (1912).

67. Bonner, *supra* note 57, at 56. Note that the process described here varied somewhat, depending on the particular period of Greek history we examine and what location in Greece we are discussing.

68. While slaves were punished physically and severely "in body" for their offences, freemen were punished "in property" by the assessment of fines. Durant, *supra* note 57, at 261.

69. *See supra,* at 128.

70. Sherman, *The Study of Law in Roman Law Schools,* 17 Yale L. J. 499, 501, 503-04 (1908).

71. BUCKLAND & MCNAIR, ROMAN LAW AND COMMON LAW 324 (1936). A party to an action was allowed to be present at a proceeding but he did not take part or give evidence. His only involvement in the trial was in a limited procedure similar to our system of discovery by interrogatories. *See id.,* at 321, for a discussion concerning the application of this procedure.

72. Lowell, *supra* note 38, at 220.

73. Gaius, a Roman jurist, says, for example:

> [A] man who sued another for cutting his vines, and in his action called them vines, irreparably lost his right because he ought to have called them trees, as the enactment of the Twelve Tables, which confers the action concerning the cutting of vines, speaks generally of trees and not particularly of vines.

IV GAIUS, INSTITUTES OF ROMAN LAW § 11, at 455 (4th rev.ed., Poste transl; Whittuck Ed. 1904).

74. JOLOWICZ, HISTORICAL INTRODUCTION TO THE STUDY OF ROMAN LAW 183-84 (2d ed. 1961); Scott, *Practice in the Courts of Ancient Rome,* 24 Case and Com. 687, 694 (1918).

75. Jolowicz, *supra* note 74, at 181, n. 1. As part of the emergence of the equites (cavalrymen) as a separate class, they were given the right, hitherto confined to senators, of sitting as jurymen. For a considerable period of time this right was to be a course of contention between these two classes until a settlement was effectuated. Jolowicz, *supra* note 74, at 77-78.

76. Jolowicz, *supra* note 74, at 181. This is similar to the modern practice of challenging jurors. *See generally* Fed. R. Civ. P. 47; 28 U.S.C § 1870 (1970); Fed. R. Crim. P. 24.

77. FORSYTH, THE HISTORY OF LAWYERS 103 (1875). By the second century, lawyers were forced to compete for cases. They therefore employed various techniques to attract new clients, including hawking their wares in the streets and hiring "clappers" to applaud their speeches before the judge.

78. *See* DECLAREUIL, ROME THE LAW-GIVER 67 (1927), where it is stated that "[i]t is remarkable that Roman law never had any theory concerning the nature of evidence, so that none was either preferred or excluded . . . " In modern times, some amount of bodily demonstration is allowed in the discretion of the judge, where the use of such is not considered prejudicial and where it is "the best and most direct evidence of a material fact. . ." McCormick, *supra* note 6, § 215, at 535. *See, e.g.,* Dictz v. Aronson, 244 App. Div. 346, 279 N.Y.S. 66 (2d Dept. 1935).

79. The orator Quintilian writes that:

> [I]n the examination of witnesses [t]he first essential is to know your witness. For a timid witness may be terrorised, a fool outwitted, an

irascible man provoked, and vanity flattered. The shrewd and self-possessed witness on the other hand, must be dismissed at once as malicious and obstinate; or . . . if his past life admits of criticism, his credit may be overthrown by the scandalous charges that can be brought against him . . .

See THE INSTITUTIO ORATORIA OF QUINTILIAN 183 (Butler transl. 1921)

80. Levy, *Statute and Judge in Roman Criminal Law,* 13 Wash. L. Rev. 298-302. This development began with Augustus' seizure of power, after which a few high officials assumed jurisdiction over criminal matters. *Id.,* at 298.
81. *Id.,* at 298-302.
82. Declareuil, *supra* note 78, at 67.
83. Declareuil, *supra* note 78, at 325.
84. Declareuil, *supra* note 78, at 322-23.
85. BERMAN & GREINER, THE NATURE AND FUNCTIONS OF LAW 479 (1966).
86. 2 Pollock & Maitland.
87. HALL, ALBION & POPE, A HISTORY OF ENGLAND AND THE EMPIRE-COMMONWEALTH 31 (4th ed. 1961).
88. ORFIELD, CRIMINAL PROCEDURE FROM ARREST TO APPEAL 345 (1947). An indictment jury was used as a substitute for the preliminary procedure and mode of proof of older forms of trial such as compurgation. For a discussion of compurgation as a predecessor to the jury system, *see* SAYLES, THE MEDIEVAL FOUNDATIONS OF ENGLAND 333, 334 (1961).
89. Orfield, *supra* note 88, at 345. *See* HOLDSWORTH, A HISTORY OF ENGLISH LAW 304 (7th rev. ed. 1956). Holdsworth found no evidence of the use of compurgation in Roman law; however, he says it was common with the barbarian tribes who overran the Roman empire, and was subsequently adopted by the church. *See also* WALSH, A HISTORY OF ANGLO-AMERICAN LAW 79 (2d ed. 1932).
90. 1 Holdsworth, *supra* note 89, at 310.
91. 1 Holdsworth, *supra* note 89, at 310.
92. 1 Pollock & Maitland.
93. For discussions of William's methods of confiscation and distribution of land *see* MAITLAND, THE CONSTITUTIONAL HISTORY OF ENGLAND 154 (1980).
94. One author has stated: "The Normans were neither swashbuckling invaders nor mere colonizers, but supreme administrators." METCALFE, GENERAL PRINCIPLES OF ENGLISH LAW 8 (1967).
95. Berman & Greiner, *supra* note 85, at 480. Berman and Greiner imply that the first changes which the Normans made were primarily procedural, rather than substantive ones. The change was one of extending administrative procedure "into the fabric of local and tribal life." *See* Berman & Greiner, *supra* note 85, at 480. Among the obvious changes during the reign of William the Conqueror were the introduction of feudalism, trial by battle, and centralization of the government.
96. Maitland says that "in its origin, trial by jury was rather French than English, rather royal than popular, rather the livery of conquest than a badge of freedom . . ." Maitland & Montague, *supra* note 50, at 46. It should be pointed out, perhaps, that the great concern for a rational, fair trial really did not crystallize in England until after the ordeals by combat were introduced. It can be noted that most of the original trials by magic had involved disputes between the lower classes of society, whereas the trials by combat involved primarily disputes between members of the upper classes over land rights (the mainstay asset of feudal lords).

97. 1 Reeves, *supra* note 47, at 49.
98. Maitland & Montague, *supra* note 50, at 58-59. For a discussion of the origins and history of the grand jury, *see* FORSYTH, TRIAL BY JURY (1895); 1 Holdsworth, *supra* note 89; 1 Pollock & Maitland, *supra* note 2; Morse, *A Survey of the Grand Jury System,* 10 Ore. L. Rev. 101, 102-18 (1930).
99. The ordeal was declared unacceptable in 1213, whereas the personal battle was not formally abolished until 1819, after it had fallen into neglect by the public anyway. Apparently long before it was legally ended, "[e]ven the devout began to question whether God settled fine points of land law through the relative merits of two husky professionals swinging pickaxes at each other . . ." Hall, *supra* note 87, at 71.
100. Apparently the assembled men left the burden of proof on the accused person rather than on the plaintiff. 1 Holdsworth, *supra* note 89, at 323.
101. Maitland & Montague, *supra* note 50, at 66.
102. Bonner, *supra* note 57, at 77. Not a great deal is known about how this loose assemblage of freemen, used as investigators, was gradually transformed into a formal body of jurors. Some scholars argue that the following phrase in the Magna Carta indicates that freemen in England were entitled to trial by jury in the thirteenth century.

     No Freeman shall be taken, or imprisoned, or be disseised of his Freehold, or Liberties, or free Customs, or be outlawed or exiled, or any otherwise destroyed; nor will we pass upon him, nor condemn him, but by lawful Judgement of his Peers, or by the Law of the Land.
103. WILLIAMS, THE PROOF OF GUILT: A STUDY OF THE ENGLISH CRIMINAL TRIAL 5 (1963).
104. During this time, jurors were held personally responsible for the "accuracy" of their verdicts, and they could be punished if a decision subsequently was found to be a "wrong" one. Maitland says it is possible that without this particular check, the jury system would not have lived through the sixteenth century. Maitland & Montague, *supra* note 50, at 65-66. However, as society grew increasingly complex, personal knowledge of the case came to disqualify rather than qualify a juror for hearing the case. Mayers says that "the development of many of our rules of evidence is closely bound up with the development of trial by jury . . ." MAYERS, THE AMERICAN LEGAL SYSTEM 103 (rev. ed. 1964). Juries of the earlier centuries were brought together only for the particular case in hand. They had no experience and were often illiterate. It was felt that irrelevant testimony needed to be filtered out for such jurors, since they were incapable of doing it for themselves; *Id.*
105. DEVLIN, TRIAL BY JURY 8 (1956); 1 Holdsworth, *supra* note 89, at 156-60.
106. Williams, *supra* note 103, at 4-10.
107. Maitland & Montague, *supra* note 50, at 94-95. The right to counsel in a criminal prosecution in the United States is guaranteed by the Sixth Amendment of the Constitution, which has been applied to the states through the Fourteenth Amendment. Gideon v. Wainwright, 372 U.S. 335 (1963).
108. In modern times, the Sixth Amendment of the Constitution guarantees the accused the right to be informed of the nature and cause of the accusation against him.
109. Maitland & Montague, *supra* note 50, at 118, discuss the use of torture in Star Chamber proceedings. In the United States, such practices are not allowed. *See, e.g.,* Spano v. New York, 360 U.S. 315 (1959).

110. Maitland & Montague, *supra* note 50, at 64, discuss the prevalence of the use of hearsay in English trials. Hearsay is generally not admitted today. *See generally,* 5 Wigmore, *supra* note 3, §§ 1360 *et seq.*

111. Henry II revitalized and reorganized the English government. With power greater than any English king had known, he suppressed the powers of the feudal lords, extended the jurisdiction of the king's court until it was described as the common law, initiated impartial and uniform administration of justice, and introduced the jury as a regular part of legal procedure.

112. *See* HANBURY, ENGLISH COURTS OF LAW 41-44 (2d ed. 1953).

113. *See* Walsh, *supra* note 89, at 300-01.

114. For a discussion of other aspects of the development of England's courtroom procedure, *see* Hanbury, *supra* note 112; 3 Holdsworth, *supra* note 13; JACKSON, THE MACHINERY OF JUSTICE IN ENGLAND (1967); STEPHEN, 1 A HISTORY OF THE CRIMINAL LAW OF ENGLAND (1883); Williams, *supra* note 103.

115.-147. [Omitted]

148. AUMANN, THE CHANGING AMERICAN LEGAL SYSTEM 5-8 (1940).

149. *See* POUND, THE FORMATIVE ERA OF AMERICAN LAW (1938), for a discussion of the beginnings of American law.

150. MORRIS, STUDIES IN THE HISTORY OF AMERICAN LAW 60-61 (1964). The widespread use of arbitration was found throughout the colonies, even in the late eighteenth century. *Id.,* at 61.

151. In this regard one author has written:

> Throughout the whole early history of Pennsylvania it appears that there was always a party which wanted Courts of Chancery, and sometimes succeeded in getting them . . . Before and immediately after the Revolution the same party was thwarted by the jealousy which the people felt for the exercise of unusual power . . .

Fisher, *The Administration of Equity Through Common Law Forms,* 1 L. Q. Rev. 455, 457 (1885).

152. *See* HASKINS, LAW AND AUTHORITY IN EARLY MASSACHUSETTS 3-8 (1960).

153. A thorough treatment of colonial legal beginnings up to the Revolution may be found in Aumann, *supra* note 148, at 3-16. Unfortunately, there is an absence of court reports in any quantity before the time of the Revolution. Pound, *supra* note 149, at 9.

154. Mayers, *supra* note 104, at 4.

155. Maitland says that Blackstone's *Commentaries* was largely responsible for the transfer of English law to America. Those who had defied the King "retained with marvelous tenacity" the laws as Blackstone detailed them. MAITLAND, READER 129-30 (Delany ed. 1957). Blackstone served as the foundation of legal education in early America and was considered the authoritative statement of English law. Aumann, *supra* note 148, at 30, n. 68. Of course, the main legal materials available to the colonists were based on Blackstone and Coke. Pound, *supra* note 149, at 8-9.

156. Pound, *supra* note 149, at 7. Pound states that the history of American law received a setback at the time of the Revolution, since most lawyers were conservative and therefore took the royalist side and "decimated the profession." Pound, *supra* note 149, at 7.

157. Auerbach, *Law and Social Change in the United States,* 6 U.C.L.A. L. Rev. 516, 522 (1959).

158. Pound, *supra* note 149, at 6.

159. Apparently, any move to centralize the judge's power in legal proceedings was "thwarted by the jealousy which the people felt for any exercise of unusual power . . ." Fisher, *supra* note 151, at 457.
160. Aumann, *supra* note 148, at 13. Aumann quotes William Duane, who advocated a system without lawyers in order to demolish the whole "farrago of finesse and intricacy" which has been imported into the colonies. Aumann, *supra* note 148, at 13-14, n. 52.
161. *See* Auerbach, *supra* note 157, at 522.
162. *See* Morris, *supra* note 150, at 15-16.
163. The many varying streams of migrants to the New World were stirred by numerous transgressions upon the human spirit, ranging from religious wars to political oppression. As Winston Churchill has noted:

    Though the general standard of living improved during the sixteenth century, a wide range of prices rose sixfold, and wages only twofold. Industry was oppressed by excessive Government regulation. The medieval system of craftsmen's guilds . . . made the entry of young apprentices harsh and difficult. The squirearchy, strong in its political alliance with the Crown, owned most of the land and ran all the local government. The march of enclosures, which they pursued, drove many English peasants off the land. The whole scheme of life seemed to have contracted and the framework of social organisation had hardened. There were many without advantage, hope, or livelihood under the new conditions. Colonies it was thought might help to solve these distressing problems.

    CHURCHILL, A HISTORY OF THE ENGLISH-SPEAKING PEOPLES, The New World 164-65 (1956).
164. Chambliss and Seidman state: "At the base of this system lies the notion of the criminal trial as an accusatory proceeding, guaranteed by the presumption of innocence." Chambliss & Seidman, *supra* note 17, at 423.

    Other writers have pointed to specific amendments designed to preserve the adversary "package". For a discussion of the framers' intention in regard to the Fifth Amendment, *see* LEVY, ORIGINS OF THE FIFTH AMENDMENT 432 (1968).
165. One historian has hypothesized that the Constitution was a product of economic interests of the "merchants, money lenders, security holders, manufacturers, shippers, capitalists and their professional associates" which overwhelmed the less influential "non-slaveholding farmers and debtors." BEARD, AN ECONOMIC INTERPRETATION OF THE CONSTITUTION OF THE UNITED STATES 12 (1913).
166. Burns, *Criminal Justice: Adversary or Inquest; Did Due Process Reform the Wrong System?* 2 Loyola U. of Chicago L. J. 249, 261 (1971).
167. *Id.*
168. Macauley, *supra* note 26, at 57 (omitted).
169. At the heart of the adversary system is the right to cross-examination, which is valuable "as a means of separating hearsay from knowledge, error from truth, opinion from fact, and inference from recollection. . . ." The Ottawa, 70 U.S. (3 Wall.) 268, 269 (1865). *See also* Pointer v. Texas, 380 U.S. 400, 404 (1965); *supra* note 6 (and accompanying text).
170. ABA Standards Relating to the Prosecution Function and the Defense Function, Approved Draft 1971, at 2-3.
171. Frank, *supra* note 4, at 80.

172. Mayers, *supra* note 104, at 101.
173. Gleisser, Juries and Justice 108 (1968).
174. Sigler, An Introduction to the Legal System 121 (1968).
175. *See id.,* at 190-93. *See also, supra* note 9 (and accompanying text).
176. 6 Wigmore, *supra* note 3, § 1845, at 374-75. *See also* 1 Wigmore, *supra* note 3, § 57, at 456; 8 Wigmore, Evidence § 2228, at 217; § 2251, at 298 (McNaughton rev. ed. 1961).
177. *See* Marshall, Law and Psychology 106 (1966).
178. Edward Bennett Williams, for example, calls the adversary system the "two wrestler" system. *See* Center for the Study of Democratic Institutions, 8 The Law: Interviews with Edward Bennett Williams and Bethuel M. Webster 10 (McDonald interviewer 1962).
179. Runyon, *The Hall-Mills Case,* in Trials and Tribulations 12 (1947). Runyon has observed that the same kind of conversational speculation is held among the population in talking of the probable result of each "sport." We assume that he is referring here to those few spectacular trials which may occur in any particular decade.
180. Frank, *supra* note 4, at 92.
181. *See supra,* at 157.
182. Roscoe Pound says, "Where, today, are the economically self-sufficient households and neighborhoods, where is the economically self-sufficient, versatile, restless, self-reliant man, freely making a place for himself by free self-assertion. . . ? Where, indeed, but in our legal thinking. . . ?" Pound, *The New Feudal System,* Ky. L. J. 1,6 (1930).
183. Murphy & Pritchett, Courts, Judges, and Politics: An Introduction to the Judicial Process 317 (1961).
184. Lerner points out "that [the] Constitution and Supreme Court are symbols of an ancient sureness and a comforting stability. . . ." Lerner, *Constitution and Court as Symbols,* 46 Yale L. J. 1290 (1937).
185. *Id..* While Lerner's thoughts are directed to the Supreme Court and the Constitution, his ideas seem equally applicable to our discussion of the adversary system.

The Search for Truth:
An Umpireal View

Marvin E. Frankel

What I have written for the Thirty-first Annual Benjamin N. Cardozo Lecture makes no pretense to be polished or finished wisdom. In the words of an imposingly great predecessor (Judge Charles E. Clark) beginning the fifth of these lectures in 1945, I propose "to suggest problems and raise doubts, rather than to resolve confusion; to disturb thought, rather than to dispense legal or moral truth."[1] Probably more rash than Judge Clark, I do not experience "trepidation"[2] for offering questions rather than answers; honest exploration in any province of the law is surely no dishonor to the questing spirit of Judge Cardozo.

My questions, briefly stated, have to do with some imperfections in our adversary system. My purposes are to recall some perennial problems, to touch upon one or two familiar ideas for improvement, and to sketch some tentative lines along which efforts to reform our law might proceed.

Because I plan to focus on recurrent criticisms of the activity to which my professional life is and has been devoted, I find it fortifying and prudent, if not heroic, to extend this introduction with a few deprecatory words. The business of the American trial courtroom seems to me in many ways to be instructive, creative, and sometimes even noble. As for the task of judging, it is nearly always a rich and satisfying challenge. The work produces fascinations and rewards that my imagination had failed to picture in advance. The trial court is a scene of drama, wit, humor, and humanity, along with the sorrows and the stretches of boredom. Even the periods of tedium are charged with the awareness of important stakes. There are daily choices that compel the judge to confront himself or herself, not less than those who will be affected, in stark and moving ways. There is power and there is, often more satisfying, the opportunity to forego the exercise of power.[3]

If I question the adequacy of our trial processes, it is not to serve the judges. It is to serve the ends of justice, for the furtherance of which all in our profession are commissioned. As is so often the case, Holmes said it better:

> I take it for granted that no hearer of mine will misinterpret what I have to say as the language of cynicism. . . . I trust that no one will understand me to

be speaking with disrespect of the law, because I criticize it so freely. I venerate the law, and especially our system of law, as one of the vastest products of the human mind. . . . But one may criticize even what one reveres. Law is the business to which my life is devoted, and I should show less than devotion if I did not do what in me lies to improve it. . . .[14]

The Judicial Perspective

My theme, to be elaborated at some length, is that our adversary system rates truth too low among the values that institutions of justice are meant to serve. Having worked for nine years at judging, and having evolved in that job the doubts and questions to be shared with you, I find it convenient to move into the subject with some initial reminders about our judges: who they are, how they come to be, and how their arena looks to them.

Except when we rely upon credentials even more questionable, we tend to select our trial judges from among people with substantial experience as trial lawyers. Most of us have had occasion to think of the analogy to the selection of former athletes as umpires for athletic contests. It may not press the comparison too hard to say it serves as a reminder that the "sporting theory"[5] continues to infuse much of the business of our trial courts. Reflective people have suggested, from time to time, that qualities of detachment and calm neutrality are not necessarily cultivated by long years of partisan combat.[6] Merely in passing, because it is not central to my theme, I question whether we are wise to have rejected totally the widespread practice in civil law countries of having career magistrates, selected when relatively young, to function in the role of impartial adjudicators. Reserving a fuller effort for another time, I wonder now whether we might benefit from some admixture of such magistrates to leaven or test our trial benches of elderly lawyers.

In any event, our more or less typical lawyer, selected as a trial judge, experiences a dramatic change in perspective as he moves to the other side of the bench. It is commonly said by judges that "[t]he basic purpose of a trial is the determination of truth. . . ."[7] Justice David W. Peck identified "truth and . . . the right result" as not merely basic, but "the sole objective of the judge. . . ."[8]

These are not questionable propositions as a matter of doctrine or logic. Trials occur because there are questions of fact. In principle, the paramount objective is the truth. Nevertheless, for the advocate turned judge this objective marks a sharp break with settled habits of partisanship. The novelty is quickly accepted because it has been seen for so long from the other side. But the novelty is palpable, and the change of role may be unsettling. Many judges, withdrawn from the fray, watch it with benign and detached affection, chuckling nostalgically now and then as the truth suffers injury or death in the process.[9] The shop talk in judges' lunchrooms include tales, often told with pleasure, of wily advocates who bested the facts and prevailed. For many other judges, however (probably a majority at one time or another), the habit of adversariness tends to be rechanneled, at least in some measure, into a combative yearning for truth. With perhaps a touch of the convert's zeal, they may suffer righteously when the truth is being blocked or mutilated, turn against former comrades in the arena, feel (and sometimes yield to) the urge to spring into the contest with brilliant questions that light the way.

However the trial judge reacts, in general or from time to time, the bench affords a changed and broadened view of the adversary process. "Many things look different from the bench. Being a judge is a different profession from being a lawyer."[10] In the strictest sense I can speak only for myself, but I believe many other trial judges would affirm that the differing perspective helps to arouse doubts about a process that there had been neither time nor impetus to question in the years at the bar. It becomes evident that the search for truth fails too much of the time. The rules and devices accounting for the failures come to seem less agreeable and less clearly worthy than they once did. The skills of the advocate seem less noble, and the place of the judge, which once looked so high, is lowered in consequence. There is, despite the years of professional weathering that went before the assumption of the judicial office, a measure of disillusionment.

The disillusionment is, as I indicated at the outset, only a modest element of the judicial experience. It is relevant here, however. It accounts for recurrent judicial expressions that seem critical of the bar, when they probably stem from more basic dissatisfactions. In any event, it is undoubtedly part of the genesis of this essay.

The Adversarial Posture

The preceding comments on the transition from bar to bench have touched explicitly upon the role of the advocate. That role is not, however, a matter of sharp and universally agreed definition. The conception from which this paper proceeds must now be outlined.

In a passage partially quoted above, presiding Justice David W. Peck said:

> The object of a lawsuit is to get at the truth and arrive at the right result. That is the sole objective of the judge, and counsel should never lose sight of that objective in thinking that the end purpose is to win for his side. Counsel exclusively bent on winning may find that he and the umpire are not in the same game.[11]

Earlier, stating his theme that court and counsel "complement" each other, Justice Peck said:

> Unfortunately, true understanding of the judicial process is not shared by all lawyers or judges. Instead of regarding themselves as occupying a reciprocal relationship in a common purpose, they are apt to think of themselves as representing opposite poles and exercising divergent functions. The lawyer is active, the judge passive. The lawyer partisan, the judge neutral. The lawyer imaginative, the judge reflective. [12]

Perhaps unfortunately, and certainly with deference, I find myself leaning toward the camp which the Justice criticized. The plainest thing about the advocate is that he is indeed partisan, and thus exercises a function sharply divergent from that of the judge. Whether or not the judge generally achieves or maintains neutrality, it is his assigned task to be nonpartisan and to promote, through trial, an objective search for the truth. The advocate in the trial courtroom is not engaged much more than half the time—and then only coincidentally—in the search for truth. The advocate's prime loyalty is to his client, not to truth as such. All of us remember some stirring and defiant declarations by advocates of their heroic, selfless devotion to the client—leaving the nation, all other men, and truth to fend for themselves. Recall Lord Broughams's familiar words:

> [A]n advocate, in the discharge of his duty, knows but one person in all the world, and that person is his client. To save that client by all means and expedients, and at all hazards and costs to other persons, and, among them, to himself, is his first and only duty; and in performing this duty he must not regard the alarm, the torments, the destruction which he may bring upon others. Separating the duty of a patriot from that of an advocate, he must go on reckless of consequences, though it should be his unhappy fate to involve his country in confusion. [13]

Neither the sentiment nor even the words sound archaic after a century and a half. They were invoked not longer than a few months ago by a thoughtful and humane scholar, answering criticisms that efforts of counsel for President Nixon might "involve his country in confusion." There are, I think, no comparable lyrics by lawyers to the truth.

This is a topic on which our profession has practiced some self-deception. We proclaim to each other and to the world that the clash of adversaries is a powerful means for hammering out the truth. Sometimes, less guardedly, we say it is "best calculated to getting out all the facts . . . ." [15] That the adversary technique is useful within limits none will doubt. That it is "best" we should all doubt, if we were able to be objective about the question. Despite our untested statements of self-congratulation, we know that others searching after facts—in history, geography, medicine, whatever—do not emulate our adversary system. We know that most countries of the world seek justice by different routes. What is much more to the point, we know that many of the rules and devices of adversary litigation, as we conduct it, are not geared for, but are often aptly suited to defeat the development of the truth.

We are unlikely to ever know how effectively the adversary technique would work toward truth—if that were the objective of the contestants. Employed by interested parties, the process often achieves truth only as a convenience, a by-product, or an accidental approximation. The business of the advocate, simply stated, is to win if possible without violating the law. (The phrase "if possible" is meant to modify what precedes it, but the danger of slippage is well known.) His is not the search for truth as such. To put that thought more exactly, the truth and victory are mutually incompatible for some considerable percentage of the attorneys trying cases at any given time.

Certainly, if one may speak the unspeakable, most defendants who go to trial in criminal cases are not desirous that the whole truth about the matters in controversy be exposed to scrutiny. This is not to question the presumption of innocence or the prosecution's burden of proof beyond a reasonable doubt. In any particular case, because we are unwilling to incur more than a minimal risk of convicting the innocent, these bedrock principles must prevail. The statistical fact remains that the preponderant majority of those brought to trial did substantially what they are charged with. While we undoubtedly convict some innocent people, a truth horrifying to confront, we also acquit a far larger number who are guilty, a fact we bear with much more equanimity.[16]

One reason we bear it so well is our awareness that, in the last analysis, truth is not the only goal. An exceedingly able criminal defense lawyer who regularly serves in our court makes a special point of this. I have heard him at once defy and cajole juries with the reminder that the question is not at all "guilt or innocence," but only whether guilt has been shown beyond a reasonable doubt. Whether that is always an astute tactic may be debated. Its doctrinal soundness is clear.

Whatever doctrine teaches, it is a fact of interest here that most criminal defense counsel are not at all bent upon full disclosure of the truth. To a lesser degree, but stemming from the same ethos, we know how fiercely prosecutors have resisted disclosure, how often they have winked at police lapses, how mixed has been their enthusiasm for the principle that they must seek justice, not merely convictions.[17] While the patterns of civil cases are different and variable, we may say that it is the rare case in which either side yearns to have the witnesses, or anyone, give *the whole truth*. And our techniques for developing evidence feature devices for blocking and limiting such unqualified revelations.

The devices are too familiar to warrant more than a fleeting reminder. To begin with, we leave most of the investigatory work to paid partisans, which is scarcely a guarantee of thorough and detached exploration. Our courts wait passively for what the parties will present, almost never knowing—often not suspecting—what the parties have chosen not to present. The ethical standards governing counsel command loyalty and zeal for the client, but not positive obligation at all to the truth. Counsel must not knowingly break the law or commit or countenance fraud. Within these unconfining limits, advocates freely employ time-honored tricks and stratagems to block or distort the truth.

As a matter of strict logic, in the run of cases where there are flatly contradictory assertions about matters of fact, one side must be correct, the other wrong. Where the question is "Did the defendant pass a red light?" or "Does the plaintiff have a scarred retina?" or "Was the accused warned of the reasons why anyone of sound mind would keep quiet and did he then proceed nevertheless like a suicidal idiot to destroy himself by talking?"—the "facts" are, or were, one way or the other. To be sure, honest people may honestly differ, and we mere lawyers cannot—actually must not—set ourselves up as judges of the facts. That is the great release from effective ethical inhibitions. We are not to pass judgment, but only to marshal our skills to present and test the witnesses and other evidence—the skills being to make the most of these for our side and the least for the opposition. What wins out, we sometimes tell ourselves and often tell others, is the truth. And, if worse comes to worst, in the end who really knows what is truth?

There is much in this of cant, hypocrisy, and convenient overlooking. As people, we know or powerfully suspect a good deal more than we are prepared as lawyers to admit or explore further. The clearest cases are those in which the advocate has been informed directly by a competent client, or has learned from evidence too clear to admit of genuine doubt, that the client's position rests upon falsehood. It is not possible to be certain, but I believe, from recollection and conversation, such cases are far from rare. Much more numerous are the cases in which we manage as counsel to avoid too much knowledge. The sharp eye of the cynical lawyer becomes at strategic moments a demurely averted and filmy gaze. It may be agreeable not to listen to the client's tape recordings of vital conversations that may contain embarrassments—for the ultimate goal of vindicating the client. Unfettered by the clear prohibitions actual "knowledge" of the truth might impose, lawyers may be effective and exuberant in employing the familiar skills: techniques that make a witness look unreliable, although the look stems only from counsel's artifice; cunning questions that stop short of discomfiting revelations; and complaisant experts for whom some shopping may have been necessary. The credo that frees counsel for such arts is not a doctrine of truth seeking.

The litigator's devices, let us be clear, have utility in testing dishonest witnesses, ferreting out falsehoods, and thus exposing the truth. But to a considerable degree these devices are like other potent weapons, equally lethal for heroes and villains. It is worth stressing, therefore, that the gladiator using the weapons in the courtroom is not primarily crusading after truth, but seeking to win. If this is banal, it is also overlooked too much, and, in any event, basic to my thesis.

Reverting to the time before trial, our unlovely practice of plea bargaining—substantially unique to the United States—reflects as one of its incidents the solemn duty of defense counsel to seek the acquittal of guilty people. Plea negotiations must begin, in principles governing all but some exotic cases, with the understanding that the defendant is guilty. Plea negotiations should not otherwise be happening. But the negotiations break down in many cases, most often because there is no mutually acceptable deal on the sentence, the key concern.[18] When that occurs, the defendant goes to trial, and the usual measures to prevent conviction are to be taken by his advocate. The general, seemingly principled view would hold his tendered plea and attendant discussions inadmissible at trial.[19] Does all this make sense? Is it comfortable? All of us in the law have explained patiently to laymen that "guilty" means not simply that "he did it"; it means nothing less than that he has been *"found-guilty-beyond-a-reasonable-doubt-by-a-unanimous-jury-in-accordance-with-law-after-a-fair-trial."* Despite the sarcastic hyphens, all of us mean that and live by it. But when a fair trial is as tortured and obstacle strewn as our adversary process, we make the system barely tolerable, if not widely admired, only by contriving that most of those who are theoretically eligible get no trial at all. The result suggests we might inquire how things work on the European continent, where the guilty plea, at least in technical strictness, is scarcely known, and the plea bargain seems to be truly nonexistent.

Our relatively low regard for truth seeking is perhaps the chief reason for the dubious esteem in which the legal profession is held. The temptation to quote poetical diatribes is great. Before fighting it off altogether, let us recall only Macaulay on Francis Bacon, purporting not to

> inquire . . . whether it be right that a man should, with a wig on his head, and band round his neck, do for a guinea what, without those appendages, he would think is wicked and infamous to do for an empire; whether it be right that, not merely believing but knowing a statement to be true, he should do all that can be done by sophistry, by rhetoric, by solemn asseveration, by indignant exclamation, by gesture, by play of features, by terrifying one honest witness, by perplexing another, to cause a jury to think that statement false.[20]

Less elegant than Macaulay, but also numbered among the laymen who do not honor us for our dealings with the truth, are many beneficiaries of such stratagems. One of the least edifying, but not uncommon, of trial happenings is the litigant exhibiting a special blend of triumph, scorn, complicity, and moral superiority when his false position has scored a point in artful cross-examination or some other feat of advocacy. This is a kind of fugitive scene, difficult to document in standard ways, but described here in the belief that courtroom habitues will confirm it from their own observations.

I am among those who believe the laity have ground to question our service in the quest for truth. The ranks of lawyers and judges joining in this rueful stance are vast. Many have sought over the years to raise our standards and our functioning, not merely our image. There has been success. Liberalized discovery has helped, though the struggles over that, including the well-founded fears of tampering with the evidence, highlight the hardy evils of adversary management. We have, on the whole, seemed to become better over time, occasional lapses notwithstanding. At any rate, the main object of this talk is not merely to bewail, but to participate in the ongoing effort to improve. Modest thoughts on that subject, respectively negative and positive, occupy the two sections that follow.

Two Unpromising Approaches

Two means for controlling adversary excesses in the trial process are intervention by the judge and better training and regulation of counsel. Both have been proposed, and attempted to some extent. The second method is receiving serious attention today, with high and persuasive sponsorship. Neither of the two approaches, at least as they have been formulated thus far, contemplates any basic changes in the existing standards and procedures. For this central reason, neither seems to me to hold much promise.

The Judge as Trial Director

> In a trial by jury in a federal court, the judge is not a mere moderator, but is the governor of the trial for the purpose of assuring its proper conduct and of determining questions of law.[21]

This observation has a clarion ring to the judicial ear. It is not inspiring to be a "mere" anything. The role of moderator is not heady. The invitation from the highest court to play a doughtier part is instantly attractive. It has proved, however, to be a siren's call. The "not a mere moderator" slogan is cited, as often as not, in cases reversing trial judges for being less "mere" or moderate than they should be.[22] The fountainhead case from which the quotation comes was itself such a decision. The reversals seem, even to a trial judge, to be warranted most of the time.

The fact is that our system does not allow much room for effective or just intervention by the trial judge in the adversary fight about the facts. The judge views the case from a peak of Olympian ignorance. His intrusions will in too many cases result from partial or skewed insights. He may expose the secrets one side chooses to keep, while never becoming aware of the other's. He runs a good chance of pursuing inspirations that better informed counsel have considered, explored, and abandoned after fuller study. He risks at a minimum the supplying of more confusion than guidance by his sporadic intrusions.

The ignorance and unpreparedness of the judge are intended axioms of the system. The "facts" are to be found and asserted by the contestants. The judge is not to have investigated or explored the evidence before the trial. No one is to have done it for him. The judicial counterpart in civil law countries, with the file of the investigating magistrate before him, is a deeply "alien" conception. (That this should be so is a matter for doubt, stirred again later on. The relevant point for the moment is that it *is* so.) Without an investigative file, the American trial judge is a blind and blundering intruder, acting in spasms—as sudden flashes of seeming light may lead or mislead him at odd times.

The ignorant and unprepared judge is, ideally, the properly bland figurehead in the adversary scheme of things. Because the parties and counsel control the gathering and presentation of evidence, we have made no fixed, routine, expected place for the judge's contributions. It is not a regular thing for the trial judge to present or meaningfully "comment upon" the evidence. As a result, his interruptions are just that—interruptions; occasional, unexpected, sporadic, unprogrammed, and unduly dramatic, because they are dissonant and out of character. The result—to focus upon the jury trial, the model for our system, including, of course, its rules of evidence—is that the judge's participation, whether in the form of questions or comments, is likely to have a disproportionate and distorting impact. The jury is likely to discern hints, a point of view, or a suggested direction, even if none is intended, and quite without regard to the judge's efforts to modulate and minimize his role. Whether the jury follows the seeming lead or recoils from it is not critical.[23] The point is that there has been a deviant influence, justified neither in adversary principles, nor the rational competence of the trial judge to exert it.

We should be candid, moreover, in recognizing that juries are probably correct (most of the time) if they glean a point of view from the judge's interpolations. Introspecting, I think I have usually put my penetrating questions to witnesses I thought were lying, exaggerating, or obscuring the facts. Less frequently, I have intruded to rescue a witness from questions that seemed to unfairly put the testimony in a bad light, or to confuse its import. Similar things appear in the reported decisions. The trial judge who takes over cross-examination seems to be hot on the scent after truth. Even the cold page conveys notes not wholly austere or detached. This would all be agreeable for a rational system of justice—if there were grounds to suppose that a judge was always, or nearly always, on the right track. But there are not such grounds. The apparatus is organized to equip the judge poorly for the position of attempted leadership. Within the confines of the adversary framework, the trial judge probably serves best as a relatively passive moderator.

This allows a scope far from trivial. The fair defining of the issues (sometimes, dubiously described as "commenting" upon the evidence), the initial attempt to formulate sound rules of law, the effort to be intelligible to juries, and the general regulation of procedures are challenging enough to ward off boredom. But the questioning of witnesses and the expression of points of view, at least while the system of trial remains fundamentally as it is, are not generally desirable. More importantly, of course, the system needs changing. But while that is postponed or ignored, the trial judge does best to conform.

These self-denying observations mark a point of retreat, or at least change, from views I cherished in earlier days on the bench. I started with a robust distaste for the image of the judge as umpire. I am not yet reconciled to it utterly. I still butt in, probably more than counsel would prefer, but far less than I used to. The reason is not growing modesty, a trait not necessarily strengthened by service as a judge. Quite to the contrary, experience has suggested that my interjections are not, on the whole, vitally necessary, useful, or principled. Reminded from time to time that I have not been duly prepared by advance exposure to or investigation of the facts, I am more likely of late to suggest lines of inquiry to counsel than to launch them independently. This, too, may change; it is where I stand now for the reasons stated.

The note of uncertainty is obviously justified, not least because I find myself uncomfortably at odds in this with some of our greatest trial judges. One in particular—Judge Charles E. Wyzanski, Jr.—dealt with the subject in a notable Cardozo Lecture. When he spoke in 1952, he offered a modest but variable formula for the trial judge's participation in jury trials, the variations to depend upon the nature of the case.[24] The experience and wisdom of the intervening years have led Judge Wyzanski in a direction opposite from mine, to the position that the trial judge ought to be considerably more active in criminal jury trials, as well as other things. His vivid reflection of the change was part of a recent lecture, in which he told about a federal charge of resisting an officer brought against a black man, in circumstances deemed severely questionable by Judge Wyzanski. He said:

> [T]he case was tried before me and a jury. In my charge to the jury, I made it perfectly plain that in my view the wrong persons had been indicted. The jury was unable to agree on a verdict.

> The case has recently come before another judge of the trial court; and Perkins was convicted. Now I am not saying, don't misunderstand me, that I was right and the other judge was wrong. I am merely pointing out the terrific significance of what Judge Shientag, a very able judge of New York . . . called

The Personality of the Judge. There is a terrific importance in the trial court, never equaled in any appellate court, of knowing who is the judge.[25]

To make certain Judge Wyzanski was expressing a belief that judges *should* act as he described, not merely that they do, I took the liberty of writing and asking. In a charming letter saying a number of important and poetical things, he assured me that the position outlined in his Cardozo Lecture has indeed changed, that the above quoted account now described his practice, and that he is "confessedly more activist today than[he] was a quarter of a century ago."[26] So there is, if it is needed, the highest kind of authority opposing my position.

Having strained to that agony of fairness, let me end this topic (for here and now) with the contention that the trial judge as a participant is likely to impair the adversary process as frequently as he improves it. What is more vital to my thesis is that the critical flaw of the system (the low place it assigns to truth telling and truth finding) is not cured to any perceptible degree by such participation.[27]

Education and Certification of Trial Lawyers

Led by the energetic Chief Justice of the United States, there is a substantial body of opinion favoring improved training and, probably, certification requirements for trial and appellate advocates. There are evident interconnections between that project and my theme.

Along with others, the Chief Justice has experienced "anxieties . . . concerning the quality of advocacy in our courts."[28] There is, he observes, an unfilled "need for skilled courtroom advocacy with a special emphasis on the administration of criminal justice."[29] Illustrating the deficiencies of the trial bar, he notes such points as:

1. Insufficient skill in "the seemingly simple but actually difficult art of asking questions. . . ."
2. Failure to learn "really . . . the art of cross-examination, including the high art of when not to cross-examine."
3. The tendency of inexperienced lawyers to "waste time making wooden objections to simple, acceptable questions, on uncontested factual matters."
4. The tendency, again in inexperienced lawyers, to be "unaware that 'inflammatory' exhibits such as weapons or bloody clothes should not be exposed to jurors' sight until they are offered in evidence."
5. Wasteful development of immaterial facts.[30]

More broadly, the Chief Justice is concerned with "the failure of lawyers to observe the rules of professional manners and profesisonal etiquette that are essential for effective trial advocacy."[31]

Turning to cures, Chief Justice Burger proposes better education and a licensing process. The law schools, he says, have been deficient, first, in teaching "the necessity of high standards of professional ethics, manners and etiquette as things basic to the lawyer's function."[32] Second, there is a lack of "adequate and systematic programs by which students may focus on the elementary skills of advocacy."[33] He joins those urging a reduction of the curriculum from three years to two, and then (for aspiring advocates), a clinical year in which they would "concentrate on what goes on in the courtrooms . . . under the guidance of practitioners along with professional teachers." Accentuating the practical, he stresses that "trial advocacy must be learned from trial advocates."[35] At the end of his program for reform, he sees that "[s]ome system of specialist certification is inevitable,"[36] and he urges broad collaboration to produce "a workable and enforceable certification of trial advocates."[37]

Chief Judge Kaufman of the Second Circuit has been thinking along the same lines. He sees advocates and judges as "partners" in the quest for justice, and believes that "the quality of justice dispensed by the courts is ultimately dependent on the quality of advocacy provided by the bar."[38] He, too, finds grave defects in this quality, summarizing them as "lack of experience, lack of competence, and lack of integrity."[39] He joins in the view that "[e]xperienced members of the bar are well suited to assist in teaching the art of advocacy."[40] He joins also in looking to certification as a likely means of improvement.[41] And, with characteristic decision, Chief Judge Kaufman has named a committee of lawyers and judges that has already forced out six drafts of implementing rules that would govern admission to federal district court bars. The rules would require, *inter alia,* some service as courtroom apprentice or observer following graduation from a law school program that included a "trial advocacy course." The prescribed course would be one "in which the students, under supervision of a member of the bar in simulated or actual litigation participate in various phases of trial work. Supervision must have been provided by lawyers who are familiar with litigation."[42]

Without altogether opposing the drive toward "clinical" training and certification, I am moved to deep skepticism. If, as I increasingly believe, the "art of advocacy" exhibits too much that is artful and not enough devotion to justice, how far should our law schools go in teaching it? Note, in the list of subjects offered illustratively by the Chief Justice, that the "arts" leading all the rest are those of "asking questions" and of "cross-examination, including the high art of when not to cross-examine." Consider to what a degree these arts consist in tailoring direct questions that will produce not the whole of the sprawling and unmanageable truth, but the portrayal that is most convenient and useful. All of us, as advocates, have sat in vital strategy sessions figuring out whether to ask a particular question, or how to ask it so that the answer would be a properly controlled flow or trickle, rather than a destructive geyser. Consider similarly the proportions to which truth seeking vies with obfuscation in the techniques of the cross-examiner. Recall, in the Chief Justice's own words, how much the adversary artist is "engaged in the destruction of adverse witnesses or undermining damaging evidence,"[43] all with habitual unconcern as to whether the "adverse witnesses" are truthful, or the enemy's evidence is causing deserved damage. Recall the last time you saw a negligence lawyer and a plaintiff or defendant physically going at each other, and ask how keen their professional schools would have been to claim credit for these performances. (It must be observed, at least parenthetically, that the Chief Justice expressed skepticism about the adversary system long ago. There is reason to infer that his proposals for improving advocates reflect a realistic estimate that the system we have, like it or not, is destined to endure for a while.[44])

While Chief Judge Kaufman complains, no doubt justly, about a portion of the Second Circuit's bar, who are said to file "late and oversized briefs . . . appendixes that ignore the . . . Rules . . ." and, in addition, perpetrate "miscitations, misstatements of fact, and missed points,"[45] I would submit that the professional skills of *appellate* advocacy are actually taught well and truly in our decent law schools. Over and over again, we see students handling themselves with grace and distinction in appellate moot courts. For the essential components of the appellate lawyer's work are intellectual: scholarship, professional skills of analysis, some rhetorical talent perhaps, and sound judgments of value and policy. All this, if it is to be effective, must be organized with candor, as well as artistry. These are matters fit for the precincts of a university. If Chief Judge Kaufman's clinical prescriptions were confined to the appellate level, they might augur a happy collaboration of the bar and the academy.

Trial advocacy is quite another thing. It is not taught well in the law schools when there is any attempt to teach it at all. The wiles, the stratagems, the dodges, the histrionics—the "arts"—are, in large measure, outside the bounds of scholarly discourse. They are too frequently outside of other bounds that should hedge a law school's proper work.

The legal academies have been well advised in resisting attempted controls like those in the draft changes of admissions rules for the federal courts. They should approach with maximum wariness the invitation to form teams with "experienced" non-academics for "courses in advocacy." The things in which advocates are experienced may or may not belong in the curriculum. The skills of advocates do not necessarily entail or include the ability to teach, or the promise of inspiring example.

As we contemplate, with justifiable pride, the recent splendor of our many great law schools, it remains useful to remember Veblen's scornful observation that "the law school belongs in the modern university no more than a school of fencing or dancing."[46] If that comment was ever justified, it has not been in recent years. Still, one may ask how much fencing and dancing might fairly be injected into the curriculum without adding merit to Veblen's disdain.

Instead of welcoming the opportunity to aid in the "certification" process, our legal scholars must eye this bandwagon from their accustomed postures of doubt and criticism. Broadly speaking, the law schools have done far too little close, intensive scrutiny of the adversary process, with a view to its improvement and modification in the public interest. The renewed exaltation of "advocacy" as the stuff of courses is a convenient challenge and opportunity. The main thing is for the law schools to see themselves as guides and teachers, not followers, of the profession. In that light, they must first determine for themselves how much of what advocates do is worth doing, and how much may be unworthy or evil for the public interest. There will be time enough after that to decide how and how far the law schools should seek to fashion "clinical legal education programs . . . looking to the training of advocates."

I would add only a few thoughts, at this point, on the troublesome topic of "ethics, manners and civility in the courtroom"[48] and, more broadly, on "integrity."[49] As to the aspects of these words directed mainly to etiquette, the problem seems to me, with all deference, to be essentially minor. A few celebrated cases have made headlines. For the most part, however, the manners of trial lawyers have seemed admirable to me, especially considering that we train them to be in combat in so much of their trial time. My own experience of nine years, for what it signifies, suggests that a judge quite lacking the air of command, but armed with our ancient traditions and a few marshals, rarely fails to find himself working in a safe and orderly place.[50]

As for the more basic matters of "ethics" and "integrity," only limited achievements may be expected from "courses in advocacy" or similar efforts to teach virtue. Our ethical rules being what they are, the effective "teaching" of them is not a program of great promise. It is the rules themselves, and the fundamental premises inspiring them that need reexamination.

As for the genuine concerns of thoughtful people like the Chief Justice and our Chief Judge, the need, I submit, is to reconsider our principles, not their teaching or application. In a system that so values winning and deplores losing—where lawyers are trained to fight for, not to judge, their clients; where we learn as advocates not to "know" inconvenient things— moral elegance is not to be expected. The morals of the arena and the morals of the marketplace, notwithstanding the aspirations of the extraordinary soul to whom these lectures are dedicated, tend powerfully to shape our conduct.

As for advocates specifically, the rule is essentially that they must not "knowingly" use "fraudulent, false, or perjured testimony"[51] or "[k]nowingly engage in other illegal conduct. . . ."[52] These are not sufficient rules for charting a high road to justice. The lawyer's capacity for ignorance is large. The proscriptions defining the "illegal" are narrow. The prohibitions, ethical or disciplinary, are under a canon telling the lawyer to *"represent a client zealously within the bounds of the law."*[53] And the proscription of fraud and illegality is under an italicized heading proclaiming the *"Duty of the Lawyer to the Adversary System of Justice,"*[54] not to the truth or to justice *simpliciter*.

Let us by all means stress ethics and seek to uplift ourselves. But let us not build our hopes for the system on a breed of lawyers and judges much better or worse than mere human beings. If we limit our fantasies in this respect, we will not expect that better rules of warfare are apt to produce peace and cooperative crusades for justice.

Some Proposals

Having argued that we are too much committed to contentiousness as a good in itself, and too little devoted to truth, I proceed to some prescriptions of a general nature for remedying these flaws. Simply stated, these prescriptions are that we should: (1) modify (not abandon) the adversary ideal; (2) make truth a paramount objective; and (3) impose upon the contestants a duty to pursue that objective.

Modifying the Adversary Ideal

We should begin, as a concerted professional task, to question the premise that adversariness is ultimately and invariably good. For most of us trained in American law, the superiority of the adversary process over any other is too plain to doubt or examine. The certainty is shared by people who are in other respects widely separated on the ideological spectrum. The august Code of Professional Responsibility, as has been mentioned, proclaims, in order, the "Duty of the Lawyer to a Client,"[55] and then the "Duty of the Lawyer to the Adversary System of Justice."[56] There is no announced "duty to the truth" or duty to the community." Public interest lawyers, while they otherwise test the law's bounds, profess a basic commitment "to the adversary system itself" as the means of giving "everyone affected by corporate and bureaucratic decisions . . . a voice in those decisions. . . ."[57] We may note similarly the earnest and idealistic scholar who brought the fury of the (not necessarily consistent) establishment upon himself when he wrote, reflecting upon experience as devoted defense counsel for poor people, that as an advocate you must (a) try to destroy a witness "whom you know to be telling the truth," (b) "put a witness on the stand when you know he will commit perjury," and (c) "give your client legal advice when you have reason to believe that the knowledge you gave him will tempt him to commit perjury."[58] The "policies" he found to justify these views included (as the first and most fundamental) the maintenance of "an adversary system based upon the presupposition that the most effective means of determining truth is to present to a judge and jury a clash between proponents of conflicting views."[59]

Our commitment to the adversary or "accusatorial" mode is buttressed by a corollary certainty that other, alien systems are inferior. We contrast our form of criminal procedure with the "inquisitorial" system, conjuring up visions of torture, secrecy, and dictatorial government. Confident of our superiority, we do not bother to find out how others work. It is not common knowledge among us that purely inquisitorial systems exist scarcely anywhere; that elements of our adversary approach exist probably everywhere; and that the evolving procedures of criminal justice, in Europe and elsewhere, are better described as "mixed" than as strictly accusatorial or strictly inquisitorial.[60]

In considering the possibility of change, we must open our minds to the variants and alternatives employed by other communities that also aspire to civilization. Without voting firmly, I raise the question whether the virginally ignorant judge is always to be preferred to one with an investigative file. We should be prepared to inquire whether our arts of examining and cross-examining, often geared to preventing excessive outpourings of facts, are inescapably preferable to safeguarded interrogation by an informed judicial officer.[61] It is permissible to keep asking (because nobody has satisfactorily answered) why our present system of confessions in the police station, versus no confessions at all, is better than an open and orderly procedure of having a judicial official question suspects.[62]

If the mention of such a question has not exhausted your tolerance, consider whether our study of foreign alternatives might suggest means for easing the unending tension surrounding the privilege against self-incrimination, as it frequently operates in criminal trials. It would be prudent at least to study closely whether our criminal defendant, privileged to stay suspiciously absent from the stand or to testify (subject to a perjury prosecution or "impeachment" by prior crimes), is surely better off than the European defendant. The latter cannot escape questioning both before and at trial, but he may refuse to answer, and is free to tell his story without either the oath or the impeachment pretext for using his criminal record against him.[63] Whether or not the defendant is better off, the question as to whether the balance we have struck is the best possible remains open.

To propose only one other topic for illustration, we need to determine whether our elaborate struggles over discovery, especially in criminal cases, are the incurable symptoms of pathology inherent in our rigid insistence that the parties control the evidence until it is all "prepared" and packaged for competitive manipulation at the trial. Central in the debates on discovery is the concern of the ungenerous that the evidence may be tainted or alchemized between the time it is discovered and the time it is produced or countered at the trial. The concern, though the debaters report it in differing degrees, is well founded. It is significant enough to warrant our exploring alternative arrangements abroad where investigation "freezes" the evidence (that is, preserves usable depositions and other forms of relatively contemporaneous evidence) for use at trial, thus serving both to inhibit spoilage, and to avoid pitfalls and surprises that may defeat justice.[64]

Such illustrative lines of study and comparison are tendered here only as the beginning of a suggested agenda. For myself, I plan to go back to law school with them by proposing their consideration as topics for seminars I shall be privileged to "give" (more aptly, to share) during the coming year. It is my hope that some of those who read this may wish to embark upon comparable efforts.

Making Truth the Paramount Objective

We should consider whether the paramount commitment of counsel concerning matters of fact should be to the discovery of truth, rather than to the advancement of the client's interest. This topic heading contains for me the most debatable and the least thoroughly considered of the thoughts offered here. It is a brief suggestion for a revolution, but with no apparatus of doctrine or program.

We should face the fact that the quality of "hired gun"[65] is close to the heart and substance of the litigating lawyer's role. As is true always of the mercenary warrior, the litigator has not won the highest esteem for his scars and his service. Apart from our image, in darker hours we have had to reckon with the knowledge that "selling" our stories rather than striving for the truth cannot always seem, because it is not, such noble work as befits the practitioner of a learned profession. The struggle to win, with its powerful pressures to subordinate the love of truth, is often only incidentally, or coincidentally (if at all) a service to the public interests.

We have been bemused through the ages by the hardy (and somewhat appealing) notion that we are to serve rather than judge the client. Among the implications of this theme are the ideas that lawyers are not to place themselves above others, and that clients must be equipped to decide for themselves whether or not they will follow the path of truth and justice. This means quite specifically (whether in *Anatomy of a Murder*[66] or in Dean Freedman's altruistic sense of commitment[67]) that the client must be armed for effective perjury as well as he would be if he were himself legally trained. To offer anything less is arrogant, elitist, and undemocratic.

It is impossible to guess how prevalent this view may be as a practical matter, or to what degree, if any, received canons of legal ethics give it sanction. My submission is, in any case, that it is a crass and pernicious idea, unworthy of a public profession. It is true that legal training is a source of power, for evil as well as good, and that a wicked lawyer is capable of specially skilled wrongdoing. It is likewise true that a physician or pharmacist knows homicidal devices hidden from the rest of us. Our goals must include means for limiting the numbers of crooked and malevolent people trained in the vital professions. We may be certain, notwithstanding our best efforts, that some lawyers and judges will abuse their trust. But this is no reason to encourage or facilitate wrongdoing by everyone.

Professional standards that place truth above the client's interests raise more perplexing questions. The privilege for client's confidences might come in for re-examination and possible modification. We have all been trained to know, without question, that this privilege is indispensable for effective representation. The client must know his confidences are safe, so that he can tell all and thus have fully knowledgeable advice. We may want to ask, nevertheless, whether it would be an excessive price for the client to be stuck with the truth, rather than having counsel allied with him for concealment and distortion. The full development of this thought is beyond my studies to date. Its implications may be unacceptable. I urge only that it is among the premises in need of examination.

If the lawyer is to be more of a truth seeker than combatant, troublesome questions of economics and professional organization may demand early confrontation. How and why should the client pay for loyalties divided between himself and the truth? Will we not stultify the energies and resources of the advocate by demanding that he judge the honesty of his cause along the way? Can we preserve the heroic lawyer, shielding his client against all the world—and against the state—while demanding that he honor a paramount commitment to the elusive and ambiguous truth? It is strongly arguable, in short, that a simplistic preference for the truth may not comport with more fundamental ideals—including, notably, the ideal that generally values individual freedom and dignity above order and efficiency in government.[68] Having stated such issues too broadly, I leave them in the hope that their refinement and study may seem worthy endeavors for the future.

A Duty to Pursue the Truth

The rules of professional responsibility should compel disclosures of material facts and forbid material omissions, rather than merely proscribe positive frauds. This final suggestion is meant to implement the broad and general proposition that precedes it. In an effort to be still more specific, I submit a draft of a new disciplinary rule that would supplement (or in large measure displace) existing Disciplinary Rule 7-102 of the Code of Professional Responsibility.[69] The draft says:

1. In his representation of a client, unless prevented from doing so by a privilege reasonably believed to apply, a lawyer shall:
   a. Report to the court and opposing counsel the existence of relevant

evidence or witnesses where the lawyer does not intend to offer such evidence or witnesses.

b. Prevent, or when prevention has proved unsuccessful, report to the court and opposing counsel the making of any untrue statement by client or witness or any omission to state a material fact necessary in order to make statements made, in the light of the circumstances under which they were made, not misleading.

c. Question witnesses with a purpose and design to elicit the whole truth, including particularly supplementary and qualifying matters that render evidence already given more accurate, intelligible, or fair than it otherwise would be.

2. In the construction and application of the rules in subdivision (1), a lawyer will be held to possess knowledge he actually has or, in the exercise of reasonable diligence, should have.

Key words in the draft—namely, in 1b—have been plagiarized, of course, from the Securities and Exchange Commission's Rule 10b-5.[70] That should serve not only for respectability; it should also answer, at least to some extent, the complaint that the draft would impose impossibly stringent standards. The morals we have evolved for business clients cannot be deemed unattainable by the legal profession.

Harder questions suggest themselves. The draft provisions for wholesale disclosure of evidence in litigation may be visionary or outrageous, or both. It certainly stretches out of existing shape our conception of the advocate retained to be partisan. As against the yielding up of everything, we are accustomed to strenuous debates about giving a supposedly laggard or less energetic party a share in his adversary's litigation property, safeguarded as "work product."[71] A lawyer must now surmount partisan loyalty, and disclose "information clearly establishing" frauds by his client or others.[72] But that is a far remove from any duty to turn over all the fruits of factual investigation,[73] as the draft proffered here would direct. It has lately come to be required that some approach to helpful disclosures be made by prosecutors in criminal cases; "the suppression by the prosecution of evidence favorable to an accused upon request violates due process where the evidence is material either to guilt or to punishment, irrespective of the good faith or bad faith of the prosecution."[74] One may be permitted, as a respectful subordinate, to note the awkward placement in the quoted passage of the words "upon request," and to imagine their careful insertion to keep the duty of disclosure within narrow bounds. But even that restricted rule is for the *public* lawyer. Can we, should we, adopt a far broader rule as a command to the bar generally?

That question touches once again the most sensitive nerve of all. A bar too tightly regulated, too conformist, too "governmental," is not acceptable to any of us. We speak often of lawyers as "officers of the court" and as "public" people. Yet our basic conception of the office is of one essentially private—private in political, economic, and ideological terms—and congruent with a system of private ownership, enterprise, and competition, however modified the system has come to be.[75] It is not necessary to recount the contributions of a legal profession thus conceived to the creation and maintenance of a relatively free society. It *is* necessary to acknowledge those contributions and to consider squarely whether, or how much, they are endangered by proposed reforms.

If we must choose between truth and liberty, the decision is not in doubt. If the choice seemed to me that clear and that stark, this essay would never have reached even the tentative form of its present submission. But I think the picture is quite unclear. I lean to the view that we can hope to preserve the benefits of a free, skeptical, contentious bar, while paying a lesser price in trickery and obfuscation.

Notes

1. Clark, *State Law in the Federal Courts: The Brooding Omnipresence of Erie v. Tompkins,* 55 Yale L. J. 267, 268-69 (1946).
2. *Id.,* at 268.
3. *(Cf.)* Bok, I, Too, Nicodemus 330 (1946).
4. Holmes, *The Path of the Law,* in Collected Legal Papers 167, 194 (1920). The quotation was used in a similar setting by Judge Jerome Frank. Frank, Courts on Trial 3 (1950). As will be seen, this lecture follows, in more pervasive respects, positions urged in that engaging and valuable book. That the positions have not prevailed might discourage people more impatient than those who believe in the possibility of law reform.
5. The phrase is undoubtedly a cliche when Roscoe Pound used it in a famous address in 1906. Pound, *The Causes of Popular Dissatisfaction with the Administration of Justice,* 29 ABA Rep. 395, 404 (1906). Like other cliches, it still tells an important story. It also shares with many cliches the quality of referring to a widely known, deeply troublesome problem which has become entombed in a phrase so that it does not seem to require much active attention as a live concern.
6. *See, e.g.,* Shientag, The Personality of the Judge 19 (1944) (3d Annual Benjamin N. Cardozo Lecture).
7. Tehan v. United States *ex. rel.* Shott, 382 U.S. 406, 416 (1966).
8. Peck, The Complement of Court and Counsel 9 (1954) (13th Annual Benjamin N. Cardozo Lecture).
9. As in the sentence just ended, this essay will be laced with general statements about matters of fact that are neither quantified nor tightly documented. These rest variously upon introspection, observation, reading, and conversations with fellow judges. They are believed to be accurate, but they are undoubtedly debatable in many instances.
10. Lummus, The Trial Judge 39 (1937). *See also* Medina, *Some Reflections on the Judicial Function: A Personal Viewpoint,* 38 Am. Bar Assoc. J. 107 (1952).
11. Peck, *supra* note 8, at 9.
12. *Id.,* at 7.

13. 2 Trial of Queen Caroline 8 (J. Nightingale ed. 1821).

14. Freedman, *The President's Advocate and the Public Interest,* N.Y. L. J., (Mar. 27, 1974), at 1, col. 1. Dean Freedman went on to explain that the system contemplates an equally single-minded "advocate on the other side, and an impartial judge over both." *Id.,* at 7, col. 2.

15. Peck, *supra* note 8, at 9.

16. One of our greatest jurists has observed:

> What bothers me is that almost never do we have a genuine issue of guilt or innocence today. The system has so changed that what we are doing in the courtroom is trying the conduct of the police and that of the prosecutor all along the line. Has there been a misstep at this point? At that point? You know very well that the man is guilty; there is no doubt about the proof. But you must ask, for example: Was there something technically wrong with the arrest? You're always trying something irrelevant. The case is determined on something that really hasn't anything to do with guilt or innocence. To the extent you are doing that to preserve other significant values, I think it is unobjectionable and must be accepted. But with a great many derailing factors there is either no moral justification or only a very minimal justification.

McDonald, *A Center Report: Criminal Justice,* The Center Magazine 69, 76 (Nov. 1968) (remarks of Judge Walter V. Schaefer).

17. Among the most recent and highly publicized examples of prosecutors subordinating truth and fairness to the lust after victory are the dismissals of indictments in the Wounded Knee and Ellsberg cases. United States v. Banks, 383 F. Supp. 389 (D.S.D. 1974); United States v. Russo, No. 9373-CD-WMB (C.D. Cal., May 11, 1973).

18. The discussion here applies quite generally, but not universally. "Sentence bargaining," probably a better label, is almost entirely unknown in the Southern District of New York. It happens with varying frequency in other federal courts—the Agnew case comes to mind, (*cf.*) Hoffman, *Plea Bargaining and the Role of the Judge,* 53 F. R. D. 499 (1971)—and appears to be widespread in the state courts of New York and elsewhere.

19. *See* ABA Project on Minimum Standards for Criminal Justice, Pleas of Guilty § 3.4 (Approved Draft) (1969).

20. 6 MACAULAY, THE WORKS OF LORD MACAULAY 135, 163 (Trevelyan Ed. 1900).

21. Quercia v. United States, 289 U.S. 466,469 (1933).

22. *E.g.,* United States v. Cisneros, 491 F.2d 1068,1072-74 (5th Cir. 1974); United States v. Wyatt, 442 F.2d 858,859-60 (D.C. Cir. 1971); Comer v. Smith's Transfer Corp., 212 F.2d 42, 47 (4th Cir. 1954); United States v. Brandt, 196 F. 2d 653,655 (2d Cir. 1952).

23. "Notwithstanding a summing up which was favourable to the accused, the jury returned a verdict of guilty." CROSS, THE ENGLISH SENTENCING SYSTEM 12 (1971). The sentence was not meant ironically. The extensive power of the English trial judge to express views on the jury's ultimate questions is well known and distinctly not emulated among us. *See, e.g.,* DEVLIN, TRIAL BY JURY 118-20 (1956).

24. Wyzanski, *A Trial Judge's Freedom and Responsibility,* 65 Harv. L. Rev. 1281,1283-93 (1952), proposing that the trial judge be generally passive in tort cases; more directive in commercial litigation, where judges are more likely to "have a specialized knowledge." *Id.,* at 1288; and forbearing again in criminal cases short of the point of sentencing.

25. Wyzanski, *An Activist Judge: Mea Maxima Culpa, Apologia Pro Vita Mea,* 7 Ga. L. Rev. 202,208 (1973).

26. Letter from Judge Charles E. Wyzanski, Jr., to Judge Marvin E. Frankel, June 11, 1973. For a broader argument favoring judicial activism, *see* Wyzanski, *Equal Justice Through Law,* 47 Tul. L. Rev. 951 (1973).

27. It is scarcely possible to leave this subject without at least a passing reference to Watergate and the work of Judge John J. Sirica. Having acknowledged that, I think it sufficient to say that nothing in the fantastic Washington trials alters what has been said here as it applies to the great bulk of cases. Whatever kind of law, if any, is made by great cases, the recent affirmance of the conviction of George Gordon Liddy was taken as an occasion to reaffirm that the trial judge usually does best to refrain from acting as interrogator. The unanimous court of appeals said, "Sound and accepted doctrine teaches that the trial judge should avoid extensive questioning of the witness and should rely on counsel to develop testimony for the jury's consideration." United States v. Liddy, No. 73-1565, at 21 (D.C. Cir., Nov. 8, 1974). Similarly, "Past decisions have stressed that in general the trial judge would do better to forego direct questioning, and the possible impact on his objectivity, since he has available the alternative of suggesting to counsel the questions he believes ought to be pursued." *Id.,* at 21, n. 31. The court went on to acknowledge that the case before it was one "of moment in both the daily press and history." *Id.,* at 25. Having determined in that setting that "[t]he impact of the extensive questioning by the trial judge was muted" (*id.,* at 22), the court concluded, "Assuming for discussion that the problems already noted reflect error by the trial judge, it must be ranked as harmless rather than prejudicial error." *Id.,* at 25.

28. Burger, *The Special Skills of Advocacy: Are Specialized Training and Certification of Advocates Essential to Our System of Justice?* 42 Fordham L. Rev. 227 (1973).

29. *Id.*

30. *Id.,* at 234-35.

31. *Id.,* at 235.

32. *Id.,* at 232.

33. *Id.*

34. *Id.*

35. *Id.*

36. *Id.,* at 238.

37. *Id.,* at 241.

38. Kaufman, *The Court Needs a Friend in Court,* 60 Am. Bar Assoc. J. 175 (1974).

39. *Id.,* at 176.

40. *Id.,* at 177.

41. *Id.,* at 178.

42. Proposed rule of admission to Fed. Dist. Cts. C(3) (2d Cir., Qualifications Comm., 6th Draft 1974).

43. Burger, *supra* note 28, at 236.

44. Judge Burger's initial statement—which criticized the adversary system of criminal justice and questioned the strength of some cornerstones of that system—became a kind of thesis around which the dialogue pivoted and developed:

> I raise the question, [Burger said] and I will overstate it to try to evoke a challenging response. I say that the adversary system is not the best

system of criminal justice, and that there is a better way. Many of us tend to think that while our adversary system may be inefficient, it is still the best that could have been devised. I challenge that proposition. The system is certainly inefficient and wasteful. I am not sure it is the best that could be devised. The American system, up to the time of the final verdict and appeal, puts all the emphasis on techniques, devices, mechanisms. It is the most elaborate system ever devised by a society. It is so elaborate that in many places it is breaking down. It is not working.

Judge Burger explained what he meant by techniques, devices, and mechanisms. They include the presumption that the accused is innocent; the use of juries and the consequent rules regarding evidence; the right of the defendant to remain silent; the placing of the burden of the proof on the prosecution. McDonald, *supra* note 16, at 69. Burger stated further:

> The British system and ours are both adversary in the highest sense of the word. Both are accusatory, very contentious. The reason why the British system works so much better is that only a highly trained professional trial lawyer—a barrister—is permitted to try a case in a court of general jurisdiction in important critical cases. There are only about two thousand barristers in all England but they can try a case in a fourth the time ours take. There is none of the inter-barrister wrangling or objections that we have. Also, British judges have greater power and greater professionalism. To become a judge in Britain a man must be a barrister first. Then he goes to the trial bench. And all the Appellate judges are drawn from the trial bench.
>
> I hope I am making it clear that I do not want simply an efficient system that convicts more people. My settlement point would be the British system, which though highly adversary, is handled entirely by skilled professionals. But beyond and apart from efficiency, I think the system in some of the Northern European countries is more humane. It is fairer across the board than it is in our country. I would suppose that a system of criminal justice ought to be judged by these three questions: Is it fair? Is it humane? Is it efficient? I put efficiency last.
>
> In our system, a trial is a traumatic experience for everybody involved—the judge, the prosecutor, the defense counsel, and most of all for the defendant, whether he be guilty or innocent. It is not anything like that in Holland or Denmark. The American system puts a premium on skill, adroitness, even trickery, on both sides.

    Id., at 75.

45. Kaufman, *supra* note 38, at 176.
46. VEBLEN, THE HIGHER LEARNING IN AMERICA 155 (1957)
47. Kaufman, *supra* note 38, at 177.
48. Burger, *supra* note 28, at 230.
49. Kaufman, *supra* note 38, at 176.
50. (*Cf.*) BOTEIN, TRIAL JUDGE 33 (1963); DORSEN & FRIEDMAN, DISORDER IN THE COURT 6-9 (1973).
51. ABA Code of Professional Responsibility, EC 7-26; DR 7-102 (A) (4),(5).
52. *Id.,* at DR 7-102 (A) (8).
53. *Id.,* at Canon 7.
54. *Id.,* (heading preceding EC 7-19).
55. *Id.,* (heading preceding EC 7-4).

56. *Id.,* (heading preceding EC 7-19).
57. Halpern & Cunningham, *Reflections on the New Public Interest Law,* 59 Geo. L. J. 1095,1109 (1971).
58. Freedman, *Professional Responsibility of the Criminal Defense Lawyer: The Three Hardest Questions,* 64 Mich. L. Rev. 1469 (1966).
59. *Id.,* at 1470. *See also id.,* at 1471,1477-78,1482.
60. Schaefer, The Suspect and Society 71 (1967); Damaska, *Evidentiary Barriers to Conviction and Two Models of Criminal Procedure: A Comparative Study,* 121 U.Pa. L. Rev. 506, 557-61,569-70 (1973).
61. *(Cf.)* Watts v. Indiana, 338 U.S. 49,54-55 (1949).
62. *See* Schaeffer, *supra* note 60; *(cf.)* Friendly, *The Fifth Amendment Tomorrow: The Case for Constitutional Change,* 37 U.Cin. L. Rev. 671,685,700-01,713-15 (1968).
63. *See* Damaska, *supra* note 60, at 527-28.
64. In the depths of the cold war, Mr. Justice Jackson reported a comparison that should be no more offensive in a time of even tremulous detente:

> [T]he Soviet Delegation objected to our practice on the ground that it is not fair to defendants. Under the Soviet System, when an indictment is filed every document and the statement of every witness which is expected to be used against the defendant must be filed with the court and made known to the defense. It was objected that under our system the accused does not know the statements of accusing witnesses nor the documents that may be used against him, that such evidence is first made known to him at the trial too late to prepare a defense, and that this tends to make the trial something of a game instead of a real inquest into guilt. It must be admitted that there is a great deal of truth in this criticism. We reached a compromise by which the Nurnberg indictment was more informative than in English or American practice but less so than in Soviet and French practice.

Bull, *Nurnberg Trial,* 7 F. R. D. 175,178 (n.d.) (quoting Justice Jackson, source not indicated).
65. *See* Packer & Erlich, New Directions in Legal Education 33 (1972).
66. Traver, Anatomy of a Murder (1958). For those who did not read or have forgotten it, the novel, by a state supreme court justice, involved an eventually successful homicide defense of impaired mental capacity with the defendant supplying the requisite "facts" after having been told in advance by counsel what type of facts would constitute the defense.
67. *See* text accompanying *supra* note 58. In Freedman, Lawyers' Ethics in an Adversary System, ch. 6 (forthcoming), Dean Freedman reports a changed view on this last of his "three hardest questions." He would under some circumstances (including the case in *Anatomy of a Murder*) condemn the lawyer's supplying of the legal knowledge to promote perjury. Exploring whether the dean's new position is workable would transcend even the wide leeway I arrogate in footnotes.
68. Two previous Cardozo lecturers have been among the line of careful thinkers cautioning against too single-minded a concern for truth. "While our adversary system of litigation may not prove to be the best means of ascertaining truth, its emphasis upon respect for human dignity at every step is not to be undermined lightly in a democratic state." Botein, *The Future of the Judicial Process,* 15 Record of N.Y.C. Bar Assoc. 152,166 (1960). *See also* Shawcross, *The Functions and Responsibilities of an Advocate,* 13 Record of N.Y.C. Bar Assoc. 483,498,500 (1958).

69. The affected portions of DR 7-102 are:

   A. In his representation of a client, a lawyer shall not:
      1. and 2. omitted
      3. Conceal or knowingly fail to disclose that which he is required by law to reveal.
      4. Knowingly use perjured testimony or false evidence.
      5. Knowingly make a false statement of law or fact.
      6. Participate in the creation or preservation of evidence when he knows or it is obvious that the evidence is false.
      7. Counsel or assist his client in conduct that the lawyer knows to be illegal or fraudulent.

   B. A lawyer who receives information clearly establishing that:
      1. His client has, in the course of the representation, perpetrated a fraud upon a person or tribunal shall promptly call upon his client to rectify the same, and if his client refuses or is unable to do so, he shall reveal the fraud to the affected person or tribunal.
      2. A person other than his client has perpetrated a fraud upon a tribunal shall promptly reveal the fraud to the tribunal.

70. 17 C. F. R. § 240, 10b-5) (1974).
71. *See* 4 MOORE, FEDERAL PRACTICE § 26.64 (2d ed. 1974).
72. ABA CODE OF PROFESSIONAL RESPONSIBILITY, DR 7-102(B).
73. *(Cf.)* American College of Trial Lawyers, Code of Trial Conduct, R. 15(b): A lawyer should not suppress any evidence that he or his client has a legal obligation to reveal or produce. He should not advise or cause a person to secrete himself or to leave the jurisdiction of a tribunal for the purpose of making himself unavailable as a witness therein. However, except when legally required, it is not his duty to disclose any evidence or the identity of any witness.
74. Brady v. Maryland, 373 U.S. 83,87 (1963).
75. *(Cf.)* Damaska, *supra* note 60, at 565-69,584-87.

Judge Frankel's Search for Truth

Monroe H. Freedman

The theme of Judge Marvin E. Frankel's Cardozo Lecture is that the adversary system rates truth too low among the values that institutions of justice are meant to serve. Accordingly, Judge Frankel takes up the challenging task of proposing how that system might be modified to raise the truth-seeking function to its rightful status in our hierarchy of values. His proposals, delivered with characteristic intellect, grace, and wit, are radical and, I believe, radically wrong.

Judge Frankel directs his criticism at the adversary system itself, and at the lawyer as committed adversary. Challenging the idea that the adversary system is the best method for determining the truth, Judge Frankel asserts that "we know that others searching after facts—in history, geography, medicine, whatever—do not emulate our adversary system."[1] I would question the accuracy of that proposition, at least in the breadth in which it is stated. Moreover, I think that to the extent that other disciplines do not follow a form of adversarial process, they suffer for it. Assume, for example, a historian bent upon determining whether Edward de Vere wrote the plays attributed to William Shakespeare, or whether Richard III ordered the murder of the princes in the tower, or even whether it was militarily justifiable for the United States to devastate Nagasaki with an atomic bomb. Obviously, the historian's inquiry would not be conducted in a courtroom, but the conscientious historian's search for truth would necessarily involve a careful evaluation of evidence marshalled by other historians, strongly committed to sharply differing views on those issues. In short, the process of historical research and judgment on disputed issues of history is—indeed, must be—essentially adversarial. In medicine, of course, there is typically less partisanship than in historical research, because there is less room for the play of political persuasion, and less room for personal interest and bias than in the typical automobile negligence case. Nevertheless, anyone about to make an important medical decision for oneself or one's family would be well advised to get a second opinion. And if the first opinion has come from a doctor who is generally inclined to perform radical surgery, the second opinion might well be solicited from a doctor who is generally skeptical about the desirability of surgery. According to one study, about nineteen percent of surgical operations are unnecessary.[2] A bit more "adversariness" in the decision-making process might well have saved a gall bladder here, or a uterus there.

Moreover, as Professor Black has recently reminded us, it is well established in our law that the extent of due process—meaning adversary procedures—properly varies depending upon the matter at stake in litigation.[3] In medical research, the situation is similar, and recent instances of dishonesty at the Sloan-Kettering Institute and at Harvard illustrate the increasing importance of adversariness in medical research.[4] Prior to World War II, apparently, the material rewards of biological research were small, "scientific chicanery" was extremely limited,[5] and adversariness was of minimal concern; but the stakes have risen since then. Now that publication of discoveries has become essential to professional advancement and to obtaining large grants of money, rigorous verification, as through replication by a skeptical colleague, has become a common requirement.[6]

Having started from what seems to me to be a faulty premise that adversariness is essentially inimical to truth, Judge Frankel concludes his proposals for change with a proposal for a fundamental revision of the Code of Professional Responsibility.[7] Specifically, Disciplinary Rule 7-102 currently forbids the lawyer from knowingly and actively participating in fraud in the course of representation.[8] Under Judge Frankel's proposed draft of Disciplinary Rule 7-102, however, an attorney would have an affirmative duty: (a) to report to the court and opposing counsel the existence of relevant evidence or witnesses where the lawyer does not intend to offer such evidence or witnesses; (b) to report to the court and opposing counsel any untrue statement, or any omission to state a material fact, even when committed by a client; and (c) to question witnesses "with a purpose and design to elicit the whole truth."[9] Moreover, in order to avoid the traditional sophistry used to evade responsibility in this area,[10] Judge Frankel provides that a lawyer "will be held to possess knowledge he actually has or, in the exercise or reasonable diligence, should have.[11]

To be fair to Judge Frankel—and, at the same time, as part of my attack on his thesis—I should note the repeated expressions of uncertainty with which Judge Frankel puts forth his own proposal. His article "makes no pretense to be polished or finished wisdom," but is intended "'to suggest problems and raise doubts, rather than to resolve confusion; to disturb thought, rather than to dispense legal or moral truth.'" In sum, his effort is only to "sketch" some "tentative lines" along which efforts to reform the adversary system "might" proceed.[12] Those substantial disclaimers are certainly disarming of criticism. At the same time, however, I trust that his audience will be particularly wary about adopting a view to which Judge Frankel has not yet succeeded in persuading himself.

Judge Frankel does not, of course, adopt the simplistic notion that a system for administering justice is concerned solely with truth seeking. Indeed, it is not even clear that Judge Frankel would make truth the paramount objective. His thesis is more modest—again, disarmingly so. It is not that truth has been denied its rightful place at the apex of our hierarchy of values, but only that it is now "too low" among the values that institutions of justice are meant to serve. One cannot fault Judge Frankel for failing to identify, in his initial and tentative effort, all of the values he might have in mind. However, before we proceed to think any more seriously about substantial modifications of our traditional—indeed, constitutional—system for administering justice, I think we ought to know just what values will be rearranged into what order of priorities.

For my own part, I think it is essential that any evaluation of the truth-seeking function of a trial be done in the context of our system of criminal justice[13] and, indeed, the nature of our society and form of government. We might begin, by way of contrast, with an understanding of the role of a criminal defense attorney in a totalitarian state. As expressed by law professors at the University of Havana, "'the first job of a revolutionary lawyer is not to argue that his client is innocent, but rather to determine if his client is guilty and, if so, to seek the sanction which will best rehabilitate him.'"[14] Similarly, a Bulgarian attorney began his defense in a treason trial by noting, "'In a Socialist state there is no division of duty between the judge, prosecutor, and defense counsel. . . . The defense must assist the prosecution to find the objective truth in a case.'"[15] In that case, the defense attorney ridiculed his client's defense, and the client was convicted and executed. Sometime later the verdict was found to have been erroneous, and the defendant was "rehabilitated."[16]

The emphasis in a free society is, of course, sharply different. Under our adversary system, the interests of the state are not absolute, or even paramount. The dignity of the individual is respected to the point that even when the citizen is known by the state to have committed a heinous offense, the individual is nevertheless accorded such rights as counsel, trial by jury, due process, and the privilege against self-incrimination. A trial is, in part, a search for truth; accordingly, those basic rights are most often characterized as procedural safeguards against error in the search for truth.

We are concerned, however, with far more than a search for truth, and the constitutional rights that are provided by our system of justice serve independent values that may well outweigh the truth-seeking value; a fact made manifest when we realize that those rights, far from furthering the search for truth, may well impede it. What more effective way is there to expose a defendant's guilt than to require self-incrimination, at least to the extent of compelling the defendant to take the stand and respond to interrogation before the jury? The defendant, however, is presumed innocent, the burden is on the prosecution to prove guilt beyond a reasonable doubt, and even the guilty accused has an "absolute constitutional right to remain silent" and to put the government to its proof.[17]

Thus, the defense lawyer's professional obligation may well be to advise the client to withhold the truth: "[A]ny lawyer worth his salt will tell the suspect in no uncertain terms to make no statement to police under any circumstances."[18] Similarly, the defense lawyer is obligated to prevent the introduction of some evidence that may be wholly reliable, such as a murder weapon seized in violation of the Fourth Amendment, or a truthful but involuntary confession. Justice White has observed that although law enforcement officials must be dedicated to "the ascertainment of the true facts, . . . defense counsel has no comparable obligation to ascertain or present the truth. Our system assigns him a different mission. . . . [W]e . . . insist that he defend his client whether he is innocent or guilty."[19] Such conduct by defense counsel does not constitute obstruction of justice. On the contrary, "as part of the duty imposed on the most honorable defense counsel, we countenance or require conduct which in many instances has little, if any, relation to the search for truth."[20] Indeed, Justice Harlan noted that "the lawyer in fulfilling his professional responsibilities of necessity may become an obstacle to truthfinding,"[21] and Chief Justice Warren has recognized that when the criminal defense attorney successfully obstructs efforts of the government to elicit truthful evidence in ways that violate constitutional rights, the attorney is "exercising . . . good professional judgment. . . . he is merely carrying out what he is sworn to do under his oath—to protect to the extent of his ability the rights of his client. In fulfilling this responsibility, the attorney plays a viatl role in the administration of criminal justice under our Constitution."[22]

Obviously, those eminent jurists would not lightly arrive at the conclusion that an officer of the court has a professional obligation to place obstacles in the path of truth. Their reasons go back to the nature of our system of criminal justice, and to the fundamentals of our system of government. Before we will permit the state to deprive any person of life, liberty, or property, we require that certain processes—which ensure regard for the dignity of the individual—be followed, irrespective of their impact on the determination of truth. By emphasizing that the adversary process has its foundations in respect for human dignity, I do not mean to deprecate the search for truth or to suggest that the adversary system is not concerned with it. On the contrary, truth is a basic value and the adversary system is one of the most efficient and fair methods designed for finding it. That system proceeds on the assumption that the best way to ascertain the truth is to present to an impartial judge or jury a confrontation between the proponents of conflicting views—assigning to each the task of marshalling and presenting the evidence for its side, in as thorough and persuasive a way as possible. The truth-seeking techniques used by the advocates on each side include investigation, pretrial discovery, cross-examination of opposing witnesses, and a marshalling of the evidence in summation. The judge or jury is given the strongest case that each side can present, and is in a position to make an informed, considered, and fair judgment. Nevertheless, the point that I now emphasize is that in a society that respects the dignity of the individual, truth seeking cannot be an absolute value. But it may be subordinated to other ends,[23] although that subordination may sometimes result in the distortion of the truth.

As indicated earlier, Judge Frankel is neither ignorant of nor insensitive to such concerns. In his Cardozo Lecture, however, he seems to me to give them substantially less than their due, pausing only to note briefly, near the end of his article, that it is "strongly arguable . . . that a simplistic preference for the truth may not comport with more fundamental ideals— including, notably, the ideal that generally values individual freedom and dignity above order and efficiency in government."[24]

One suspects that in minimizing his advertence to that critical aspect of the problem, the umpireal judge was back-sliding into a bit of lawyerly adversariness. For if we ask, as I think we must, just how strongly arguable is the case for the "more fundamental ideals," we will find either that we are being asked to sacrifice those ideals in some substantial measure (because the case for them is not sufficiently strong), or that Judge Frankel's proposal is wholly impractical (because regard for those ideals precludes a single-minded search for truth). Moreover, if the former be the case, then I think we would be compelled to turn our attention to some fearsome questions, thus far elided by Judge Frankel: precisely which parts of the Fourth, Fifth, and Sixth Amendments are we being asked to scrap? And how can the requisite amendments to the Bill of Rights be phrased, without doing irreparable damage to some of the most precious aspects of our form of government?

In sum, Judge Frankel has succeeded in what he set out to do: He has suggested problems, raised doubts, and disturbed thought. Moreover, he has done so in a way that charms and delights. However, as Judge Frankel warned us at the start of his article, his proposals for radical surgery on the adversary system neither resolve confusion nor dispense truth.

Notes

1. Frankel, THE SEARCH FOR TRUTH: AN UMPIREAL VIEW, 123 University of Pennsylvania Law Review 1031, 1036 (1975).
2. N.Y. Times, June 19, 1973, at 21, col. 1.
3. BLACK, CAPITAL PUNISHMENT 32-35 (1974).
4. Borek, *Cheating in Science*. In N.Y. Times, Jan. 22, 1975, at 35, col. 2. *See also* Levine, *Scientific Method and the Adversary Model: Some Preliminary Thoughts,* 29 Am. Psychologist 661,669-76 (1974).
5. *Id.*
6. *Id.*
7. Frankel, *supra* note 1, at 1057-59.
8. ABA Code of Professional Responsibility, DR 7-102. Even that proposition is not as unambiguous as it might appear on first reading. *See* FREEDMAN, LAWYERS' ETHICS IN AN ADVERSARY SYSTEM, ch. 3 (forthcoming).
9. All of the foregoing is subject to the qualifying phrase "unless prevented from doing so by a privilege reasonably believed to apply." Frankel, *supra* note 1, at 1057. I am not sure what that clause is intended to mean, but it could, of course, effectively nullify the entire proposal.
10. *See* FREEDMAN, *supra* note 8, ch. 5.

11. Frankel, *supra* note 1, at 1058.
12. *Id.,* at 1031.
13. Judge Frankel makes no apparent distinction in his article between criminal and civil cases, and several references in the article indicate clearly that his modifications of the system are intended to reach criminal as well as civil trials.
14. Berman, *The Cuban Popular Tribunals,* 69 Col. L. Rev. 1317, 1341 (1969).
15. N.Y. Times, Dec. 14, 1949, at 9, col. *cited* in KAPLAN CRIMINAL JUSTICE 264-65 (1973).
16. N.Y. Times, Apr. 4, 1956, at 1, col. 4.
17. Escobedo v. Illinois, 378 U.S. 478,491 (1964); Malloy v. Hogan, 378 U.S. 1,8 (1964).
18. Watts v. Indiana, 338 U.S. 49,59 (1949) (Jackson, J., concurring and dissenting).
19. United States v. Wade, 388 U.S. 218,256-57 (1967) (White, J., dissenting in part and concurring in part).
20. *Id.,* at 258.
21. Miranda v. Arizona, 384 U.S. 436,514 (1966) (Harlan, J., dissenting).
22. *Id.,* at 480-81 (opinion of the court).
23. *See* ABA PROJECT ON STANDARDS FOR CRIMINAL JUSTICE, STANDARDS RELATING TO THE ADMINISTRATION OF CRIMINAL JUSTICE 59-60 (1974). *(Cf.)* Tehan v. United States ex rel. Shott. 382 U.S. 406,416 (1966) (Stewart, J.):

> The basic purpose of a trial is the determination of truth.... By contrast, the Fifth Amendment's privilege against self-incrimination is not an adjunct to the ascertainment of truth. That privilege, like the guarantees of the Fourth Amendment, stands as a protection of quite different constitutional values. ... To recognize this is no more than to accord those values undiluted respect.

24. Frankel, *supra* note 1, at 1056-57.

The Advocate, The Truth, and Judicial
Hackles: A Reaction to Judge Frankel's Idea

H. Richard Uviller

Introduction

It must be distressing to preside over the rape of truth in the courtroom. At the altar of justice, before the judge's very eyes, the atrocity is perpetrated in a casual, routine manner, bespeaking long and regular usage. And the rapists are people who proclaim themselves honorable and devoted to the victim. Apart from the occasional nostalgic ex-litigator who relishes the spectacle, the judicial witness may be tempted, understandably enough, to take a more heroic role.

But if the judge breaks with customary passivity, vaulting the bench and riding to the rescue, his merciful mission often turns out to be a lame and embarrassing sortie. It's enough to raise a judicial hackle or two.

Judge Frankel's hackles are as stable as most, to my knowledge. Yet they are clearly ascending. Their rise invites us to revisit an old acquaintance: the adversary myth. Our beloved dialectic model of litigation offers much in the way of healthful mental exercise, he suggests, but the "truth" that emerges may be more synthetic than real. For the collision of opponents is better designed to find an athletic victor than to search for truth. Still, it seems to me that, properly directed and purged of obvious abuses, the juxtaposition of two contrary perspectives, the impact of challenge and counter-proof, often discloses to a neutral intelligence the most likely structure of truth. Thus, at least in those instances (which I may regard as more common than does Judge Frankel) where neither side knows with certainty the actual contours of a past occurrence, I conclude that the adversarial encounter, for all its hazards, serves as one of the better methods of reconstruction.

Venturing into the causes of Judge Frankel's dissatisfaction, and appraising his call for major surgery on the system, it may be well to keep systemic flaws separate from overlaid abuses from the start. For the essence of Judge Frankel's argument is that the design of the adversary system itself is responsible for the dangerously recurrent violation of truth, whereas it may be that the ills that trouble him are attributable to improper excesses of advocacy. And Judge Frankel, being as conservative as I in

130

such things, would probably reject radical surgery if lesser measures might relieve the condition.

Few would dispute Judge Frankel's theorem that truth often suffers in the courtroom. He rightly reminds us that in those relatively few cases (civil or criminal) that go to trial, one side or the other seeks—wittingly or unwittingly—to defeat truth. Indeed, it is likely that neither party is advancing the entire truth as some Omniscient Recorder might know it. And it may well be that if both lawyers told each other or the court (with ideally matched generosity) all that they knew or suspected concerning the facts, the result might bear a somewhat closer resemblance to the past event in issue. Further, if our judge could preside in the Southern District of Utopia, where trial lawyers, including criminal defense counsel, act as diligent investigators for their opponents, even finer details of truth might be supplied.

Insofar as Judge Frankel is disturbed by the penchant of terrestrial attorneys to argue contrary to, or independently of private belief, he has ample cause for discomfort. Few experienced and successful advocates do not count among their well-worn tools some devices to conceal at least a part of what they believe to be the factual truth. Many can recall instances in court in which they advanced factual propositions (the strict accuracy of which they had cause to doubt), or sought to discount or discredit evidence they had reason to think was true. And I venture that, at least among defense counsel in criminal cases, the concession causes little regret or chagrin. The adversary system, in which trial lawyers are trained and participate, serenely countenances such techniques—short of subornation of perjury. The rewards of victory are rarely marred by the victor's misgivings over whether the verdict actually spoke the truth. And for those lawyers who might pause over some tactical choice designed to dim the full glare of truth, several available maxims of self-justification offer to soothe his scruples.

I cannot grant a priori, however, that the prevalent ethic supporting such license inheres in the adversary system. While free sharing of the products of partisan investigation may not comport with the adversarial model—at least as applied to criminal defendants—the concealment or distortion of known facts is no necessary corollary of contention.

This is not to say that I, any more than Judge Frankel, believe that the remedy for such impropriety may be found in more intensive law school instruction on the subject of ethics. The notion that virtue and upright deportment at the bar can be taught to law students, like trusts or the Uniform Commericial Code, seems to me unrealistic and self-deluding. Nor (with due deference to the dignity of its proponents) can the faults of advocates in this regard be assigned to lack of skill. The judge is surely correct when he points out that the conventional skills of adversaries include the techniques of truth bending.

other respected judges have derived a contrary conclusion from their experiences. And at least some judges who try less complex, more hastily prepared cases report that their interventions usually have a healthy effect on the emergence of truth from the adversary fray. Yet my own inclination is with Judge Frankel's—to the effect that a trial judge is poorly positioned and informed to perceive or rescue truth in the midst of a trial. And his errors are costly, since his view of truth must align his formidable presence with one of the partisans. To many of us, imbued with the American model, such a fall from neutrality is a primal sin.

Thus, for what it is worth, I endorse Judge Frankel's assessment of (1) the frequency of adversarial liberties taken with truth in the American trial process; (2) the strange shape of an ethic which tolerates (if it does not encourage) the advocate's disregard for the facts as he knows them; and (3) the impotence of the commonly proposed methods of prevention and counteraction. To these endorsements, however, I must append a few misgivings.

The Advocates

First, and by way of a preliminary quibble, I dissent from the judge's inclusion of public prosecutors among his licensed truth defilers. To be sure, prosecutors sometimes conceal all or a portion of the evidence they have unearthed about a case; sometimes they sit quietly by as a helpful witness distorts the facts; in short the procecutor's conduct may mirror defense counsel's partisan assault on truth. But in every such deplorable instance, the prosecutor—unlike defense counsel—violates his ethical duty, and perhaps the law as well.[2] The Code of Professional Responsibility enjoins defense counsel to be faithful, resourceful, and relentless in the service of his client's interest. No such injunction directs the prosecutor; he has no client, no interest, save the interest of justice.[3] And the interest of justice is not a partisan cause. Jencks,[4] Brady,[5] Napue,[6] and a thousand other cases and codes urge the prosecutor to fully divulge harmful facts and foster truth. Moreover, I believe the consciences of most prosecutors are bent as the law would bend them: to exert all precautions against the calamity of an innocent person convicted of a crime. This ethic, of course, does not address the prosecutor's failure to prosecute someone he believes to be truly guilty (if that is part of the substance of Judge Frankel's accusation), but I submit that such inaction is of a different order of offense to truth. Without elaborate (and perhaps questionable) argument supporting that submission, I would simply aver that Judge Frankel's final reformulation of DR 7-102,[7] the embodiment of his point, has done no more than generally articulate and decree for the bar the ethical imperative currently controlling prosecutorial conduct in litigation.

I should also add, in a personal vein, that, having performed most of my courtroom services in the role of prosecutor, obedient (I hope) to the precepts advanced by Judge Frankel, I am tempted to declare that I see nothing onerous in calling upon the rest of the bar to live by the strictures familiar to me. "If I can do it, they can do it," and "we'd all be better off if everyone were as virtuous as me" are notions which fall readily to hand, despite the dictates of due modesty. Yet, I can not let arrogance win the day by default. And I am constrained by ordinary sense to acknowledge that the prosecutor's finest blossoms may not thrive in the garden of the defense. I must get on with my deeper misgivings concerning the judge's appealing thesis.

For me, the main difficulty in assimilating Judge Frankel's lesson has been my uncertainty as to whether I was hearing a simple and rather tired lament of the shortcomings of adversarial truth seeking, or a refreshed and invigorated proposal for basic restructure of our mode of determining facts in litigation. My perplexity stems, I think, from Judge Frankel's choice not to explore the refinements and implications of his thesis. For, while recognizing some of them, the judge has deferred treatment, labelling his efforts tentative, preliminary, and provocative only. I do not disparage the privilege of broad statement, or denigrate the value of a thoughtful report of experience from the judicial vantage. Indeed, I admire the courage of the judge to raise, for discussion, a familiar notion that would commonly pass without serious notice. I say only that in his humility, the judge has assigned to others the analytic task which will validate or destroy his suggestion.

Take, for example, the implication of his revision for the traditional American relationship between counsel and client. The canons Judge Frankel criticizes reflect our esteem for fidelity between the lay and professional partners. In his obedience to his client's cause, in his service of the client's interest, the lawyer is expected to eschew only the grossest personal or professional dishonor. The lawyer is employed not as a detached and judgmental intelligence, but as a weapon. In litigation, at least, the lawyer's performance and advice is to serve a partisan interest. Could we live with a system in which the lawyer's faith was divided, in which he felt a stronger obligation to enhance a result which conflicts with the interest of the party engaging his talent?

An early casualty of the proposed new purpose of the assistance of counsel for the defense (to borrow the language of the Sixth Amendment) would be the confidentiality assured by the lawyer-client privilege.[8] A lawyer, obedient to the Frankel tenet, could not promise his client that his

I cannot be so certain that Judge Frankel is right, however, when he also rejects the remedial role of the presiding judge.[1] He acknowledges that preliminary disclosures would not injure his cause. The lawyer, perparing for trial, would be bound to exert efforts to learn the true facts, and (however that truth may cut) to lay them fully before the court. And, ideally, defendants would know that they could enlist no lawyer to shade or obscure the truth. A public appreciation of this new ethic would doubtless improve the sagging repute of the bar. And such detached professional conduct might well improve the truth-detecting capability of the trial mechanism. But (at least according to the general assumption) the candor of a defendant to his lawyer would appreciably shrivel.

How grievous is this presumed consequence? I, for one, find it difficult to assess. In counselling, it may be that the lawyer requires and obtains complete and trusting disclosure from his client. Many lawyers report that, in at least the commercial context, it is comparatively easy to steer a basically honest client away from evil or over-reaching purposes. Concealment and distrust could only hamper these worthy professional purposes. Yet discussions of present counselling must contemplate litigation, however remotely, and to that extent suffer from the consequence of the Frankel impairment of secure confidence.

For defense counsel in criminal cases, I suspect, diminution of the privilege would have substantially less impact. Although some defense attorneys stoutly insist that they probe the client's guilt, and fashion the defense accordingly, I don't believe this mode of defense is the rule. Generally, I think, "truth" is simply not an operative factor to a defense lawyer. Few lawyers believe their clients tell them the unvarnished truth about the case (privilege or no), and few lawyers insist that they do so. The version of the facts requested and obtained is the defendant's "story." It may or may not be true, but the prime concerns of the lawyer are only two. First, is the story convincing? And second, does it adequately meet the more damaging aspects of the prosecution account (so far as may be learned in advance)? Of course, the lawyer should do nothing to "improve" the story in either respect. But he would be remiss if he failed to strike it here and there (in the supposed privacy of a client conference), to test its ring of truth on the anvil of prospective cross-examination. And it is not extraordinary for the story to change somewhat in the process, usually acquiring a clearer and more persuasive tone. However, we should not confuse the lawyer's activity here with truth seeking—although the revised "story" may be truer than the first, in the sense of a more complete and accurate rendition of recalled facts. Neither should the judge, nor others, suppose that the lawyer is here administering the first painful twist on truth—although he may be indirectly counselling truth-concealing wrinkles to a client who is alert for hints favoring the development of a winning defense.

In fairness, I submit, this essential and thoroughly professional preparatory conference can only be taken as having nothing whatever to do with truth. Aiming neither to enhance nor subvert it, and having little or no reliable basis for judging his impact on truth, counsel seeks only to explore the strengths and weaknesses of the story he must advance in court. The openness and fluidity of this preliminary conference may be impaired by weakening the protection of the attorney-client privilege. But, if my informants in the defense bar are to be credited, there is little to lose in the way of truth.

More disturbing than the possible harm to candor is the hint in Judge Frankel's proposal that defense counsel, in preparing *his* case for trial, is somehow obliged to simultaneously further the prosecution's investigation. Judge Frankel would make available to the court not only what the lawyer knows of the issue, but what diligent effort might discover as well. Does this not suggest that the defendant has acquired and paid for an agent for his prosecution, as well as the assistance of counsel for his defense? The proponent of this "double-agency" pauses only momentarily to wonder about the appropriate fee for uncertain fealty and diminished fervor. He leaves to others the description and evaluation of the fundamental alteration in the character of legal representation which his new ideology imports. For myself, though rectitude at the bar has a pleasanter odor than the morality of the mercenary warrior, I confess to a shiver of apprehension. Judge Frankel is, of course, right—usually truth is no friend of the criminal defendant. Thus, to convert the defendant's only champion into yet another member of the state's legions seems an unnecessary and offensive step.

It is beyond the scope of this piece to demonstrate it, but surely many within and without the bar feel that, apart from the romantic dimension, an important ingredient of individualism is interwoven in the sytem of loyal counsel. The confidences of the humblest citizen or the most depraved criminal are, in a criminal case, held defiantly inviolable—as a demonstration that the state must do its work against us, if it will, without our help. There are assuredly other societies that think very differently about the meaning of a criminal trial in the relationship between citizen and state. And the role of counsel reflects that difference of perception.[9]

But, for better or worse, our view of the lawyer's duty is bound to our history and cultural traditions. Much as we might all appreciate the incremental, professional honor Frankel's model promises, I fear we must live without it. For we cannot tolerate an affirmative duty of betrayal laid upon defense counsel, however, we might restrain his zeal by prohibition of this tactic or that.

The Judge

Moving from bar to bench, it is not altogether clear to me whether Judge Frankel, while developing his contention that a judge's intervention to save truth is frequently blundering argues at the same time for a better informed presiding officer. He seems to debit the adversary system by the degree of imposed judicial naivete. With some longing, our judge seems to dream of the dossier which informs his continental counterpart. If only our system provided such a document for the trial judge, the rueful effects of adversarial zeal might be neutralized by timely and intelligent intervention from the bench.

Even assuming that wisdom accompanies information, indulging the gentle assumption that informed judicial participation in an adversary proceeding may be helpful, we might still wonder how this informative dossier is to be compiled within the American structure. Our trial judges, after all, are not—and surely need not be—totally uninformed concerning the case on trial before them. Pleadings and pretrial proceedings may not convey tactical nuances of proof, but they must open a small hole in the judge's ignorance. And upon the slightest injury or show of curiosity, a judge can usually induce a trial brief, and one or two illuminating sidebar colloquies. Yet, such sophistication as the trial judge readily acquires evidently does not satisfy Judge Frankel's desire for informed participation. It is not so much the extent of the judge's knowledge, but the source of it that worries Judge Frankel. The passive judicial umpire is educated on the case by the adversaries—the very parties whose questionable commitment to the truth necessitates judicial participation in the first place.

But if a judicial demand for enlightenment cannot produce whole and undistorted information from knowledgeable counsel, where is the judge to look for the missing ingredients of his dossier? Judge Frankel seems to regard with interest the investigation conducted in European courts by a quasi-judicial figure. Here is the trustworthy file, free of partisan bias, an account of the facts adequate to equip the trial court for a truth-saving role in the adversary process. Whatever might be the appeal to an American judge of finding upon his bench a complete set of factual findings, attested by a neutral and adept colleague, Judge Frankel should cool his enthusiasm. For again, I believe it largely idle to attempt vital organ transplants between dissimilar organisms. And the system employing the "juge d'instruction"[10] or its equivalent is, from root to leaf, another genus. If we had an inquiring magistrate, who would be his investigators? The same police who gathered the evidence for the prosecutor's case? Or an independent and competitive body? What would be the defendant's part in the compilation of this all-important record? Adversarial? And, when all has been arranged for the production of the best and fairest dossier, have we simply created two full-fledged trials where we had one before?

Judge Frankel's notes suggest that one of the main attractions of the continental inquiry is the availability of the mind of the defendant himself as a source of evidence; in short, a drastic revision of our sacrosanct privilege against self-incrimination. The judge has come, by an unusual route, to this familiar scholarly doubt concerning the Fifth Amendment's service in the cause of justice. I am among those who have tried to take a tradition-free view of the principle of external proof. It is immensely difficult. And it hardly seems worth the candle for the marginal enlightenment it might provide to the trial judge contemplating a more intelligent intervention in the adjudicatory process.

The "Truth"

These disturbances—to the attorney-client relationship as we know it, and to the judicial role as it has developed in the American system—are relatively minor. What troubles me far more about the Frankel formulation is his unrefined employment of the concept of truth, as though he perceived it in bold silhouette. Judge Frankel certainly requires no instruction on the plural forms and multifaceted aspects of that beguiling concept. Yet he chooses to treat it as a flat fact. He has afforded little guidance to the sort of truth he alludes to, or the conditions in which he regards its place as paramount. At the risk of tedious discourse (an occupational hazard, after all), I feel called upon to parse some notions of truth which shift and slide under the smooth surface of the Frankel thesis.

To begin at the simplest level, factual truth should be distinguished from legal or consequential truth. Did the victim, moments before the defendant shot him, point a six-inch blade at the defendant and say, "I'll kill you," or did he show a two-inch knife and say, "Don't come step closer"? That is a simple issue of factual truth, and it is quite different from the question: did the defendant act in self-defense? Surely, Judge Frankel is primarily concerned with truth in the sense of a complete and accurate trial reconstruction of an objective occurrence. Or to be more precise, he would abjure any effort by counsel to limit or alter any admissible evidence which might etch, color, or erase any element of the factual picture. According to Frankel, therefore, counsel should not countenance testimony from his client that the victim "brandished a knife" if he has reason to believe that a fuller answer would disclose the two-inch blade and defensive utterance. But would Judge Frankel leave counsel free to argue all reasonable implications from a fact in evidence? May he, for example, assert the justification of self-defense suggested by the unaltered facts, although, from his sense of his client's temperament and experience, he strongly suspects that even the six-inch blade would not have unnerved the man?

Such questions raise the more fundamental problem to which I earlier adverted: how is defense counsel to know or recognize the truth? Judge

Frankel, I think, proceeds from the assumption that the shining truth is known or knowable by all diligent lawyers acting in good faith. But is it? Does the first "spontaneous" account of the accused stand thereafter as the truth against which counsel must measure later variations in the story? Why such faith in the naive rendition? Is it any more likely to be true than, say, the versions of the witnesses against him? And what if the spontaneous descriptions of two defense witnesses vary? Is Judge Frankel suggesting not only that counsel is obliged to ferret facts, but to judge credibility as well? Should a defense be shaped according to counsel's "sense" or "suspicion" of the true state of affairs?

A somewhat more subtle dichotomy might be discovered between what I shall term the ultimate and the instrumental facts. The ultimate truth may be that the defendant had drugs in his possession, but the police witness against him may be lying about how he acquired the contraband from the defendant. Does fidelity to the truth preclude counsel's efforts to discredit the police testimony, in order to obtain dismissal of the charge? I doubt whether Judge Frankel would argue the affirmative on this one. For the Constitution itself, at least as currently read by the Supreme Court, directs the release of the guilty defendant if the truth is that the evidence was unlawfully acquired. Or does the ultimate truth-defeating quality of the exclusionary rule argue against its retention, whatever other benefits it might claim in vitalizing the Bill of Rights?

To avoid that scorcher, let's take the same problem in an "ordinary" context. Suppose the lawyer is defending a man he believes committed the robbery charged, but also believes that one of the witnesses against him is "improving" the case by false testimony. Attacking that witness serves the instrumental truth, but may defeat the ultimate truth. Here Judge Frankel's proposition may encounter some difficulties. He cannot very well disparage counsel's efforts in good faith to keep the jury's evidence as truthful as possible. Yet if he approves defense attacks on the credibility of instrumental proof, he comes dangerously close to accepting the very adversarial tactics he elsewhere rejects. Moreover, to demonstrate falsity, counsel may have to resort to the "clever tricks" of cross-examination: leading questions, innuendo, and magnification of conflicts in trivial detail. For, off the TV tube, a well-woven falsehood does not become unravelled by a few open-ended and respectful inquiries.

One writer, praised by Judge Frankel as "a thoughtful and humane scholar," has taken the problem one step further. Monroe Freedman argues that to achieve an ultimate truth, and the acquittal of an innocent person, a lawyer may have to undermine the credibility of a witness he believes is telling an instrumental truth.[11] In Dean Freedman's example, an honest witness may give damning circumstantial evidence.[12] Would Judge Frankel hold that to make the instrumentally true seem false, in order to prevent the ultimate untruth (arguments on the unreliability of the circumstantial evidence are not always persuasive) constitutes a service or disservice to the interests of truth?

Inescapably, the supremacy of truth is easier to assert than to define. Consider the matter of justice in the result. The "search-for-the-truth" view of a criminal trial is usually employed to mean maximum correspondence between the judgment of guilt and the defendant's prior performance of the culpable conduct alleged. Yet we have developed a process which is designed, over the long haul, to preclude conviction of an innocent person at the social expense of acquitting some guilty defendants. I am sure Judge Frankel has no quarrel with the design of such a process. There is, then, an interest in the preservation of the process in every case, though the result in a given case does not correspond to the extra-legal truth. Does Judge Frankel suggest that a lawyer, who believes his client to be clearly guilty, perverts truth by holding the prosecution strictly to the burden of due process: to prove the charge beyond a reasonable doubt by admissible evidence?

When the famed Judge Sirica opened the Watergate trial by announcing that rules of evidence might be relaxed, in the interests of finding the "truth"[13] did his New York brother feel no qualm that important safeguards of general application might be sacrificed to a result the court deemed correct?

In short, while the truth (at least as to facts) may seem simple— admitting of no "legalistic" quibbles, no shadings or interpretations—law cases are tried only on evidence of the truth. And evidence is rarely unflawed and unambiguous. Since fact finders must rely largely on human observation, recall, veracity, and interpretation and implication, the truth is often uncertain and unclear. Indeed, the process, designed primarily to discover truth, may at times obscure it. It is no fault of lawyers (or of the process) that the evidentiary manifestations of truth do not invariably lead to it.

Less Drastic Remedies for More Frightful Ills

In conclusion, I must voice my guess at the latent object of Judge Frankel's endeavor. He is at least as subtle and perceptive as I am in regard to the difficulties to which I have alluded. He knows far better than I the various manifestations of truth, and the uncertainties of evidence. He cannot assume blithely that truth shines like a compass-star, by which the lawyer may navigate his case. He understands that, to the advocate in litigation, "facts" are usually a bewildering collection of shifting and contradictory fragments of professed human recollection, unverifiable hunches concerning veracity, and bits of data of uncertain import. Surely, Judge Frankel admits, as we all do, that the lawyer is gifted with no special clairvoyance to appraise the accuracy of the stories his clients or others tell him. He certainly appreciates that, whatever the pleas of the lawyer for truth, a defendant tries to supply a winning tale. And no reformation of any cannon can alter this basic fact in the human interaction we call the lawyer-client relationship.

What, then, has set the judge to worrying over our adversary model and its product? By respectful and altogether friendly intuition, I suspect it is the grievous case of blatant disregard for truth by counsel that sends the judge's hackles into the air. He is outraged by the lawyer's feigned tone of disbelief on hearing adverse testimony, his irate argument to the jury that his client was "framed" when he or his client has openly conceded culpability in another proceeding. When a lawyer during plea negotiations acknowledges his client's factual guilt, when he hears his client admit culpable facts under oath during a pretrial hearing, and thereafter challenges, as fabricated, trial evidence of those same facts—under these circumstances, Judge Frankel concludes that the adversarial system has overstepped the bounds of fair truth detection. If a lawyer puts a witness on the stand, rehearsed to testify to partial truths in order to mislead the fact finder as to the whole truth, the judge's wrath boils. In these (hopefully) rare cases, perhaps we can, along with Judge Frankel, postulate a known or knowable truth; we can, along with Judge Frankel, perceive the advocate's unethical devices of distortion outside of the legitimate employment of procedural or constitutional safeguards.

To purge abuses of this nature, perhaps a more limited physic than Judge Frankel's might suffice. For example, if DR 1-102 (A)4 and (5)[14] are too vague, and DR 7-101 and 102[15] are not much better, how about a formulation such as this:

> It is unprofessional conduct for a lawyer, during the trial of a matter in which he represents a party, to express, convey, or indicate to the fact finder by word, gesture, or in any manner whatever his personal opinion or belief concerning any of the facts in issue or the veracity of any testimony or other evidence.

And to the wily half-truth artist, a few words might be addressed in this vein:

> It is unprofessional conduct for a lawyer to counsel or countenance testimony by a witness in his favor which, although true in the part stated, omits matters which if stated might reasonably alter the meaning or significance of the testimony.

I recognize some overlap between my formulation and that proposed by Judge Frankel. But, I advance my alternative in the spirit of the adversary system as we know it. I have no purpose to reduce acknowledged faults of our adversary mechanism by altering dramatically the obligations or fealty of attorneys. Rather, I submit ethical commands—sharing Judge Frankel's faith that they are in some measure efficacious—which address specific evils within the adversary framework.

For in my opinion, it is not the adversary model itself which is to blame for the excesses which so trouble Judge Frankel, although it certainly provides the means for their employment. Victory will always be a potent lure for unscrupulous advocacy. And criminal litigation, at least, has always tempted the participants to zeal. The occasional compromise of factual truth in the process, or in the outcome, is only one of the several sorts of anguish inherent in any system of penal response. And such errors must be borne as the price of a system of controlled contention which—like ours—gropes unsurely toward some form of justice.

Notes

1. I think Judge Frankel speaks throughout (as I do) of the judge's role in a jury trial. To me, a bench trial is an altogether different event. To allow counsel to manage the production of proof before a judicial fact finder, as though he were a naive, lay, mute jury, may be a blind and wasteful devotion to an inappropriate trial format. Perhaps, after a full and proper introduction to the issues, and with continuing guidance, counsel should allow the case to be developed by the judge. In bench trials, then, a major role in the interrogation of witnesses should be taken by the judge, who should explore the issues of importance to him to the extent he deems necessary for his own illumination. Choosing to waive a jury, the parties might be deemed to have endowed the court with greater initiative and freedom in the factual inquiry, and neither the inquisitorial specter, nor the prospect of a judicial stumble or two, should be allowed to frighten us from an otherwise sensible procedure. But all this is outside the scope of our present concern, I believe, and might be left to some future piece.
2. *See* Uviller, *The Virtuous Prosecutor in Quest of an Ethical Standard,* 71 Mich. L. Rev. 1145 (1973). *See also* ABA Code of Professional Responsibility, DR 7-103, EC 7-13.
3. ABA Code of Professional Responsibility, EC 7-13.
4. Jencks v. United States, 353 U.S. 657 (1957).
5. Brady v. Maryland, 373 U.S. 83 (1963).
6. Napue v. United States, 360 U.S. 264 (1959).
7. ABA Code of Professional Responsibility, DR 7-102.
8. Unless, perhaps, Judge Frankel means to blunt the principal thrust of his argument by the exception provided in the revised canon he sets forth at the end of his piece.
9. I am told, for example, that in the Chinese view, defense counsel serves his client by serving the collective interests in obtaining the reformation of law breakers.
10. A nonpartisan investigating magistrate, who is charged with the development of all the facts in the case. His report is available both to the parties and to the court. *See* Damaska, *Evidentiary Barriers to Conviction and Two Models of Criminal Procedure: A Comparative Study,* 121 U.Pa. L. Rev. 506,556-60 (1973).
11. Freedman, *Professional Responsibility of the Criminal Defense Lawyer,* 64 Mich. L. Rev. 1469 (1966).

12. *Id.,* at 1474-75.
13. *See* Smith, *T*R*U*T*H or Trial?* In N.Y. Times, Nov. 4, 1974, § 1, at 37, col. 2.
14. ABA Code of Professional Responsibility, DR 1-102, Misconduct:

   A. A lawyer shall not:
       (1.-3. omitted)
       4. Engage in conduct involving dishonesty, fraud, deceit, or misrepresentation.
       5. Engage in conduct that is prejudicial to the administration of justice.

15. *Id.,* DR 7-101, 102.

DR 7-101, Representing a Client Zealously.

   A. A lawyer shall not intentionally:
       1. Fail to seek the lawful objectives of his cient through reasonably available means permitted by law and the Disciplinary Rules, except as provided by DR 7-101(B). A lawyer does not violate this Disciplinary Rule, however, by acceding to reasonable requests of opposing counsel which do not prejudice the rights of his client, by being punctual in fulfilling all professional commitments, by avoiding offensive tactics, or by treating with courtesy and consideration all persons involved in the legal process.
       2. Fail to carry out a contract of employment entered into with a client for professional services, but he may withdraw as permitted under DR 2-110, DR 5-102, and DR 5-105.
       3. Prejudice or damage his client during the course of the professional relationship, except as required under DR 7-102(B).

   B. In his representation of a client, a lawyer may:
       1. Where permissible, exercise his professional judgment to waive or fail to assert a right or position of his client.
       2. Refuse to aid or participate in conduct that he believes to be unlawful, even though there is some support for an argument that the conduct is legal.

DR 7-102, Representing a Client Within the Bounds of the Law.

   A. In his representation of a client, a lawyer shall not:
       1. File a suit, assert a position, conduct a defense, delay a trial, or take other action on behalf of his client when he knows or when it is obvious that such action would serve merely to harass or maliciously injure another.
       2. Knowingly advance a claim or defense that is unwarranted under existing law, except that he may advance such claim or defense if it can be supported by good faith argument for an extension, modification, or reversal of existing law.
       3. Conceal or knowingly fail to disclose that which he is required by law to reveal.
       4. Knowingly use perjured testimony or false evidence.
       5. Knowingly make a false statement of law or fact.
       6. Participate in the creation or preservation of evidence when he knows or it is obvious that the evidence is false.
       7. Counsel or assist his client in conduct that the lawyer knows to be illegal or fraudulent.

8. Knowingly engage in other illegal conduct or conduct contrary to a Disciplinary Rule.

B. A lawyer who receives information clearly establishing that:

1. His client has, in the course of the representation, perpetrated a fraud upon a person or tribunal shall promptly call upon his client to rectify the same, and if his client refuses or is unable to do so, he shall reveal the fraud to the affected person or tribunal.

2. A person other than his client has perpetrated a fraud upon a tribunal shall promptly reveal the fraud to the tribunal.

The Attorneys' Duty to Disclose the Commission of Criminal Acts—Two Views on the Lake Pleasant Case

The Impropriety of the Attorney's Actions in the Lake Pleasant Case

Thomas Hobin
David J. Jensen

In the summer of 1974, members of the public were shocked to learn that two lawyers for Robert Garrow, a man on trial for murder, did not disclose that they knew the location of the bodies of the two young women killed by their client. Garrow admitted killing Philip Domblewski, a twenty-two-year-old Harvard student; Susan Petz, a twenty-one-year-old journalism student at Boston University; and Alicia Haucks, a sixteen-year-old Syracuse High School student. Only the body of Domblewski had been found. Garrow gave the attorneys, Armani and Belge, details of the other crimes and a rough map of the area where he had left one of the bodies. The attorneys searched the area thoroughly. On their fifth attempt they found the body of Susan Petz in a hole in the ground. Mr. Armani lowered Mr. Belge by his feet into the hole, and Mr. Belge took pictures of the girl's body. They also found the body of Alicia Haucks without the aid of a diagram. Both bodies were badly decomposed when the attorneys found them. Animals had removed the head of the corpse of Alicia Haucks and dragged it some distance away. Attorney Belge took the skull and placed it back with the remains.

The attorneys decided not to disclose the location of the bodies; they believed it was privileged information, and could only be disclosed if their client consented. The attorneys resisted direct inquiries from the parents of the girls and other interested parties. They did not disclose the location until Garrow admitted to specific details of the crimes on the witness stand in another case. The attorneys reasoned that the confidences of their client outweighed the interests that would be served by disclosure of this information.

145

The Attorney-Client Privilege is Not Absolute and Immutable.

At the root of these attorneys' dilemma of whether or not to remain silent about the location of the corpses was a question regarding the conflicting nature of their obligation. Did they have a duty to protect their client's right to remain silent, a duty which was buffered from sanction by the attorney-client privilege, or did they owe a greater duty to society? The Appellate Division of the Supreme Court of New York stated the dilemma as follows:

> Attorney-client privilege is not all-encompassing; an attorney must protect his client's interests, but also must observe basic human standards of decency, having due regard to the need that the legal system accord justice to the interests of the society and its individual members.[1]

Faced with a perplexing situation, Armani and Belge decided that their client's Fifth Amendment right against self-incrimination had been entrusted to them through an absolute attorney-client privilege, or at least that the privilege outweighed any other consideration. Mr. Armani justified their actions by saying "I want to emphasize that my associate, Mr. Belge, and I took [the lawyer's oath] and that to us an oath is a very sacred thing."[2] As honorable as their intentions might have been, they were, sadly, not consistent with the law. The attorney-client privilege is not an absolute, immutable proposition, but a limited privilege that should be strictly construed.

Any claim of attorney-client privilege should be subject to strict scrutiny.[3] California courts, among others, have recognized the need for examining claims of privilege in the light of all pertinent facts.[4] The courts have held that "since attorney-client privilege suppresses relevant facts, the privilege is to be strictly construed."[5] Particularly on the issue of evidentiary privilege, there have been some major steps forward in loosening the hold of attorney-client privilege in recent years. In regard to future crimes, the ABA has suggested that an attorney has a duty to reveal information necessary to the prevention of a crime.[6] ABA Opinion 314 (1965) states that an attorney must disclose confidences "if the facts in the attorney's possession indicate beyond reasonable doubt that a crime will be committed."[7] In the case of danger to the life of others—if, for instance, Garrow's lawyers had discovered that the bodies were diseased, and that the disease would spread if they were not interred—there would be little argument that the disclosure should not be made.[8] To hypothesize further, what if another individual were charged with the girls' murders? Professor Edwards discusses the hypothetical in his article in the Criminal Law Bulletin.[9] In his answer to this article, Dean Monroe Freedman argues that disclosure would only be necessary if the individual were sentenced to death.[10] Dean Freedman is unable to bring himself far enough away from the absolute privilege to come to the aid of the person falsely imprisoned for life.

Absolute privilege has been limited in other instances. ABA Formal Opinion 314 (1965) states that "in practice before the IRS . . . the lawyer is under a duty not to mislead the Service, either by misstatement, *silence* or through his client, but is under no duty to disclose the weakness of his client's case. He must be candid and fair, and his defense of his client must be exercised within the bounds of the law and without resort to any manner of fraud or chicane."[11]

The trend in judicial decisions has been away from the absolute privilege of attorney-client relations to a narrower, more strictly construed theory of the privilege. The Supreme Court of the United States has held that "a tax-payer's Fifth Amendment privilege was not violated by enforcement of documentary summonses directed toward their attorneys for production of accountants' documents which had been transferred to the attorney in connection with an Internal Revenue Service investigation."[12] More generally, in another case concerned with organizational records, the Supreme Court said "an individual can not raise a Fifth Amendment claim to avoid production of records of an organization held by him in a representative capacity as custodian for the group."[13] In the field of securities transactions, the case of *United States* v. *Mackey*—405 F. Supp. 854 (1975)—held that if the lawyer in the case had not disclosed the information concerning a secret transfer of stock, which information his client claimed to be privileged, he would have been aiding in the fraud. This was not permissive disclosure; rather, it was mandatory disclosure.[14] Moreover, the attorney-client privilege generally does not extend to confidences concerning present and future criminal activity[15] (*See Grieco* v.*Meachum*, 533 F.2d 713 (1976)). This includes such crimes as bribery, perjury and mail fraud,[16] and borders on the separate area of continuing crimes which will be discussed below.

The courts have also limited the attorney-client privilege in cases like *In re Michaelson*—511 F.2d 882 (9th Circ. 1975)—where the Court of Appeals ruled that "a grant of use immunity precludes any Fifth Amendment claim of privilege."[17] The court stated that

> in striking the delicate balance between the informational needs of the court and administering justice and a party or witnesses' right to privacy, it is sufficient that testimony elicited from a person not be used against him without a valid waiver of his Fifth Amendment privilege or the granting of immunity.[18]

The courts have also recognized the need for lawyers to protect themselves in post-judgment cases when clients level charges of incompetence. If a lawyer was not able to counter these charges by using normally privileged information, he would be virtually helpless before such attacks.[19] In *Pruitt* v.*Peyton*—243 F.Supp. 907 (D.C. Va. 1965)—the court pointed out that "increasing problems confronting court appointed attorneys in criminal and post-conviction cases compel some relaxation of the attorney-client privilege rule."[20]

This relaxation can be seen most readily in regard to the evidentiary privilege that is part of the attorney-client privilege. In the celebrated case of *State ex rel. Sowers* v. *Olwell*—64 Wash. 2d 828, 394 P.2d 681, 16 A.L.R. -3d 1021 (1964)—the Washington Supreme Court stated:

> Although the attorney-client privilege is applicable to criminal evidence, such as a knife or other weapons, given to the attorney by his client during legal consultation for information purposes and used in preparing the client's defense, and although such evidence may be withheld for a reasonable period of time, nevertheless the attorney, after a reasonable period, should, as an officer of the court on his own motion turn the same over to the prosecution, and the privilege does not warrant the attorney in withholding such evidence after being properly requested to produce it.[21]

Under the authority of *Sowers*, Armani and Belge could have turned over the information that had been disclosed to them and "as officers of the court" aided the court in its truth-seeking function. Using the balancing test that we believe should govern privilege situations, we find that the slight chance of harm to Garrow's case does not outweigh the societal benefit that would have been afforded by the disclosure of the girls' deaths to their parents. Attorney-client privilege and facilitation of full disclosure by the client would be protected under *Sowers*, because the state would have to take extreme precautions to see that the source is not disclosed.[22]

Garrow was a client who was engaged in a continuing crime—in that he was violating a New York Public Health Law,[23] as well as New York Penal Law § 55.10 (2)(B): "a willful and intentional act of secreting, or of permitting bodies to remain concealed, involves a direct and continuing interference with the rights of interment, such interference is a Class A misdemeanor."[24] In the area of continuing crime, the ABA's Committee on Professional Ethics has attempted to narrow the scope of the attorney-client privilege. ABA Formal Opinion 155 (May 4, 1976) attempts to deal with the privileged information concerning a client who has jumped bail:

> An attorney, whose client has fled the jurisdiction of the court while out on bail, must reveal the whereabouts of his client even if received in confidence from the client. If the client refuses to surrender to the authorities upon the attorney's advice the attorney should withdraw from the case.[25]

Obviously, this is one instance when the attorney's duty to the legal system and to society outweighs his duty to the client. In another opinion released the same day, the ABA said, "Information that a client has violated the terms of his parole is not privileged. Thus, when such information comes to the attention of the attorney, he must advise his client of the consequences of his act and if the client persists, the attorney must advise the proper authorities."[26] And, more generally, ". . . a continuing wrong is not privileged from disclosure. Public policy forbids that the relation of attorney and client should be used to conceal wrongdoing on the part of the client."[27]

The attorney's duty to society has been relegated to a position of little importance in recent years. The attitude that seems to have prevailed is the negative one of "How far can I go?"—instead of the more positive "What should I do?" The Canons of Professional Ethics were originally an attempt to outline the workings of a profession at its best. Underlying the canons is the philosophy that the guidelines therein provided will aid the profession to live up to the public demand for a just legal system.

Canon 9 recognized this need by requiring lawyers to avoid even the appearance of impropriety: "When explicit ethical guidance does not exist, a lawyer should determine his conduct by acting in a manner that promotes public confidence in the integrity and efficiency of the legal system and the legal profession."[28] Canon 15 points out that

> nothing operates more certainly to create or foster popular prejudice against lawyers as a class and to deprive the profession of that full measure of public esteem and confidence which belongs to the proper discharge of its duties than does the false claim . . . that it is the duty of the lawyer to do whatever may enable him to succeed in winning his client's cause . . . He must obey his own conscience and not that of his client.[29]

The question then becomes not what I may do, but what humanity, reason, and justice tells me I ought to do.[30]

The early English case which established the lawyer-client privilege contains several justifications for the rule:

1. A "gentleman of character" does not disclose his client's secrets.
2. An attorney identifies himself with his client, and it would be "contrary to the rules of natural justice and equity" for an individual to betray himself.
3. Attorneys are necessary for the conduct of business, and business would be destroyed if attorneys were to disclose the confidences of their clients.[31]

These justifications do not hold much weight today. In light of the growth of our legal system to its present status—a system which attempts to be consistent and still flexible enough to conform to the changing standards of our time—one could hardly argue for a legally recognized immunity from disclosure of a friend's secrets. Nor is it plausible to accept the privilege on the basis of a betrayal of one's self through disclosure. Finally, the rationale that attorneys are essential to the conduct of business, and should therefore be privileged from disclosing confidences falls flat; attorneys should, by this rationale, be accorded no more privileges than bankers or accountants.

This is not to say that the privilege serves no purpose in the legal process, but only that it is time for a re-evaluation of the privilege and its application. The privilege of confidentiality between a lawyer and his client has in many respects become a bar to the search for truth, and the attainment of justice.[34]

The "fullest disclosure of facts will lead to the truth and ultimately to the triumph of justice."[35] Thus, if we consider the function of the advocate to be to assist in the formulation of wise and informed decisions, we must limit the confidentiality of communications between client and counsel. The partisanship involved in keeping a communication confidential must be restricted when it leads to conduct which destroys the truth.[36]

Former Associate Justice Arthur Goldberg said that the most crucial challenge confronting lawyers is the "need to make our declared legal principles and our constitutional protections into a working reality."[37] He noted that the Warren Court recognized the need to bring legal rules into consonance with the human reality to which they purport to respond.[38] If one purpose of the adversary system is to be to promote a wise and informed decision of cases,[39] adherence to rules which would deny this goal is ludicrous. We must realize that the law is a dynamic (not a static) force in society.[40] Rigid rules of confidentiality will serve only as a barrier to justice.

The situation that Robert Garrow's lawyers found themselves in is illustrative of the dilemmas created by overly rigid rules. The attorneys felt that they were prohibited from disclosure, even though public policy would seem to have called for it. "It is undoubtedly true that our respect for the dignity of the individual provided the foundation for our adversary system, as well as the accompanying procedural rights. Yet, none of these rights are absolute: not the right to counsel,[41] trial by jury,[42] or even the privilege against self-incrimination.[43] And of course, the bounds of due process are invariably determined by balancing risks, values, and responsibilities."[44]

> Thus, it appears that neither confidentiality nor the adversary system is absolute; each is justified pragmatically by its ability to serve certain social needs . . . Absolute confidentiality is inimical to a system which has at its end rational decision making.[45]

What is required is a consideration of competing considerations. "The privilege remains an exception to the general duty to disclose. The benefits are indirect and speculative, its obstruction is plain and concrete."[46] As recognized in the Garrow case itself, a balancing of social interests is always difficult, and there can be no hard and fast rules to cover all circumstances. *See Garrow* 219. The rule is worth preserving for the sake of general policy, but it is nonetheless an obstacle to the investigation of truth. "It ought to be strictly construed within the narrowest possible limits consistent with the logic of its principle."[47] Only when so construed will the rules allow the lawyer to effectively fulfill his three primary obligations: loyalty to the client, candor to the court, and fairness to the opposition.[48] The lawyer cannot, as has been suggested by Dean Freedman,[49] subordinate all other professional obligations he may have in favor of the preservation of a confidence.

Justice Blackman questioned the nature of the relationship between law and moral principles: "Are we too much concerned always with rights—the rights of the client, our rights as persons and lawyers—and never enough concerned with duties and responsibilities to what is just, and to what is moral as well as barely legal?"[50] He went on to note that "rights imply power and with that power inevitably comes the obligation to exercise it responsibly."[51] Lawyers have a duty to remain within certain moral, as well as legal bounds. "Once we step beyond the boundary of responsible exercise of power, even though in the client's behalf, we encounter professional inconsistency, difficulty, and possible chaos."[52] Furthermore, "if law is to be believed in, we have no choice but to labor to build and maintain its moral integrity and its sense of the ethical, in appearance and in dispensation."[53] Those in the legal profession must be dedicated to the effort to retain high standards of ethics. This may not always be the simplest of tasks, but lawyers must assume it if they are to maintain the integrity of the profession. "In fulfilling his professional responsibility, a lawyer necessarily assumes various roles that require the performance of many difficult taks."[54]

It has been many years since Jeremy Bentham advocated total abolishment of the privilege.[55] Few would deny that it has its place in the profession today. The mere fact that the privilege is recognized, however, does not mean that it is without its conditions or exceptions.[56] Social policy will often dictate that there must be exceptions to a particular rule. "The social policy that will prevail in many instances will run afoul in others of a different social policy, competing for supremacy."[57] Perhaps the fourth principle governing privileged communications in Wigmore's *Handbook on Evidence* is most illustrative. It states that "the *injury* that would inure to the relation by the disclosure of the communications must be *greater than the benefit* thereby gained by the correct disposal of litigation."[58] Only if this condition is met, along with several others, should there be recognition of the privilege.

The duty to the client of secrecy would still be recognized and protected in the ordinary course, but the lawyer's duty as an officer of the court to lend his aid in the last resort to prevent a miscarriage of justice would be given the primacy which a true balancing of the two interests would seem to demand.[59]

At the present time, there are four theories to which a lawyer can refer in deciding how to resolve a problem similar to that faced by attorneys Armani and Belge:

A. the theory contained in the ABA Code of Professional Responsibility;
B. the theory of absolute confidentiality;
C. the theory of truth as a paramount value; or
D. the theory of personal conscience.[60]

The exceptions found in the Code of Professional Responsibility do not offer the attorney adequate guidelines for resolution of the problem at the present time. The theory of absolute confidentiality would guide the lawyer, but it would also serve to create injustice in many cases. The theory of truth as a paramount objective avoids the ambiguities of the code, but would infringe upon the client's Fifth Amendment protection against self-incrimination, and Sixth Amendment right to effective assistance of counsel. The fourth alternative, the conscience theory, would still subject the lawyer to a choice between betrayal of his client's trust and a possible miscarriage of justice.

An alternative approach to confidentiality has recently been suggested.[61] Legislatures are free to make two procedures available which would reconcile the conflicting values: in camera review and use immunity. Statutory enactments could make it mandatory for lawyers to disclose to a court, in camera, information which an attorney felt would be necessary to avoid a miscarriage of justice. The court would then review the information and decide whether an injustice had or would be done (such as that suffered here). If such an injustice had been done, the court would forward the information to the appropriate prosecutor. This would, of course, be contingent on a grant of use immunity to the client. The innocent victim would have the benefit of disclosure, and the client would be in substantially the same position as if the lawyer had not gone to the court with the information.

The Supreme Court, in *Kastigar* v. *United States*,[62] considered the constitutionality of immunity statutes where two grand jury witnesses asserted their Fifth Amendment privilege against self-incrimination. The court held that the statute "leaves the witness and the prosecutorial authorities in substantially the same position as if the witness had claimed the Fifth Amendment privilege."[63] Such an application indicates an equitable balance of competing interests.

The Ninth Circuit has held that where attorney and client had been granted use immunity prior to the attorney being ordered to testify before a grand jury, the attorney could not refuse on the basis of confidentiality stemming from the attorney-client relationship.[64] The court held that a "witness's residual right of privacy; that is, the discomfort any witness has in testifying against his wishes about matters within his knowledge, cannot outweigh the court's interests in getting the facts necessary to make a reasoned and informed decision."[65] The grant of immunity would protect the attorney and client from any civil or criminal liability, and a protective order would insure the protection of the client's expectations of privacy.

If attorneys Belge and Armani had followed this procedure, it is probable that the considerations of simple decency would have led to an accommodation of public interest. "In camera disclosure shifts the locus of this conflict from the individual attorney to the courts. The interests of the client are no longer a part of the conflict; they are protected whether the court discloses the information to the prosecution—thus requiring the grant of immunity—or decides to retain the information in camera without disclosure."[66] The interests of the client, and of justice could have been well served.

Notes

1. People v. Belge, 50 A.2d 1088, 376 N.Y.S.2d 771 (1975).
2. Chamberlain, *Legal Ethics: Confidentiality and the Case of Robert Garrow's Lawyers,* 25 Buff. L. Rev. 211 (1975).
3. Greyhound Corp. v. Superior Court in and for Merced County, 15 Cal. Rptr. 90, 364 P.2d 266 (1961); Brown v. Superior Court in and for Butte County, 218 A.2d 430, 32 Cal. Rptr. 527 (1963); City of Philadelphia v. Westinghouse Electrical Corp., 205 F.Supp. 830 (E.D.Pa. 1962).
4. Brown v. Superior Court in and for Butte County, 218 A.2d 430, 32 Cal. Rptr. 527 (1963).
5. Greyhound Corp. v. Superior Court in and for Merced County, 15 Cal. Rptr. 90, 364 P.2d 266 (1961).
6. ABA Opinion 314 (1965); ABA Opinion 155 (1936); ABA Opinion 156 (1936).
7. ABA Opinion 314 (1965).
8. Edwards, *Hard Answers for Hard Questions: Dissenting in Part from Dean Freedman's Views on the Attorney-Client Privilege,* 11 Crim. L. Bull. 478 (1975).
9. Ibid., at P.6.4.
10. Freedman, *In Rebuttal to Professor Edwards,* 11 Crim. L. Bull. 478 (1975).
11. ABA Opinion 314 (1965).
12. Fisher v. United States; United States v. Kasmir, 425 U.S. 391, 96 S.Ct. 1569, 48 L.Ed.2d 2039 (1976).
13. Matter of Berry, 521 F.2d 179 (1975).

14. United States v. Mackey, 405 F.Supp. 854 (1975).
15. Grieco v. Meachum, 533 F.2d 713 (1976), *cert. denied.*
16. In re Sawyer's Petition, 229 F.2d 805 (7th Circ. 1956); United States v. Aldrich, 484 F.2d 655 (7th Circ. 1973).
17. In re Michaelson, 511 F.2d 882 (9th Circ. 1975), *cert. denied* 421 U.S. 978 (1975).
18. Ibid, at P.6.891.
19. Pruitt v. Peyton, 249 F.Supp. 907 (D.C.V. 1965); Jacobs v. State of Arkansas, 253 Ark. 37, 484 S.W.2d 345; State of Missouri v. Brizendine, 433 S.W.2d 321; Meyerhofer v. Empire Fire And Marine Ins. Co., 497 F.2d 1190 (2d Cir. 1974), *cert. denied,* 419 U.S. 998 (1974).
20. Pruitt v. Peyton, 249 F.Supp. 907 (D.C.V. 1965).
21. State Ex Rel. Sowers v. Olwell, 64 Wash.2d 828, 394 P.2d 681, 16 A.L.R.3d 1021 (1964).
22. Ibid.
23. N.Y. Public Health Law § 4200 (McKinney 1971); N.Y. Public Health Law § 12-B(2) (McKinney 1971).
24. N.Y. Penal Law § 55.10(2)(B) (McKinney 1975).
25. ABA Formal Opinion 155 (May 4, 1936).
26. ABA Formal Opinion 156 (May 4, 1936).
27. Ibid.
28. ABA Code of Professional Responsibility, EC9-2.
29. ABA Canons of Professional Ethics, Canon 15.
30. Weinstein, *Educating Ethical Lawyers,* 47 N.Y. St. Bar J. P.6.260 (June 1975).
31. Noonan, *The Purposes of Advocacy and the Limits of Confidentiality,* 64 Mich. L. Rev. 1485 (1966).
32. *See* Edwards, *supra* note 8, at 483.
33. Noonan, *supra* note 31, at 1485.
34. Blackman, *Thoughts about Ethics,* 24 Emory L.J.3, 12-13 (1975).
35. 16 A.L.R.3d 1050.
36. Noonan, *supra* note 31, at 1488.
37. Goldberg, *The Search For Relevant Justice,* 8 Conn. L. Rev. 603 (1976).
38. *Id.,* at 603.
39. Noonan, *supra* note 31, at 1487.
40. Goldberg, *supra* note 37, at 605.
41. Arpersinger v. Hamlin, 407 U.S. 25 (1972).
42. Cheff v. Schrackenberg, 384 U.S. 373 (1966).
43. *See* Harris v. New York, 401 U.S. 222 (1971).
44. Edwards, *supra* note 32, at 480.
45. Noonan, *supra* note 31, at 1489.
46. 8 WIGMORE, EVIDENCE § 2291 (3d ed.).
47. *Id.*
48. Blackman, *supra* note 34, at 12.
49. Meagher, *A Critique of Lawyers' Ethics in an Adversary System,* 4 Fordham Urban J. 289,290 (1976).
50. Blackman, *supra* note 34, at 13.
51. *Id.*
52. Ibid.
53. *Id.,* at 14.

54. ABA Code of Professional Responsibility, Preamble.
55. BENTHAM, Rationale of Judicial Evidence, 7 THE WORKS OF JEREMY BENTHAM (Bowring Ed.1842).
56. Clark v. United States, 289 U.S. 1,13 (1932).
57. *Id.*
58. 8 WIGMORE. EVIDENCE § 2285-96 (3d ed.).
59. MCCORMACK, HANDBOOK ON THE LAW OF EVIDENCE 177 (2d ed.)(McCleary Ed.1972).
60. Heather, *Attorney-Client Confidentiality: A New Approach,* 4 Hofstra L. Rev. 685,686 (1976).
61. *Id.,* at 691.
62. Kastigar v. United States, 406 U.S. 441 (1972).
63. *Id.,* at 462.
64. *In re* Michaelson, 551 F.2d 882 (9th Cir.), *cert. denied* 421 U.S. 978 (1975).
65. *Id.,* at 891.
66. Heather, *supra* note 60, at 699.

The Propriety of the Attorneys' Actions in the Lake Pleasant Case

Michael S. Callahan
Hal C. Pitkow

Statement of Facts

In the summer of 1973, Robert Garrow, Jr. stood charged in Hamilton County, New York for the murder of Philip Domblewski. Two attorneys, Armani and Belge, were assigned by the court to defend the indigent Mr. Garrow. A defense of insanity was interposed by counsel for Mr. Garrow. During the preparation for the trial, Garrow admitted to counsel that he had murdered three other people. Mr. Armani and Mr. Belge, acting on their own, searched for and eventually located the bodies. The body of Susan Petz was found in a mine shaft. The body of Alicia Haucks was discovered in a Syracuse cemetery.[1]

This was not disclosed to the authorities. Their knowledge became evident only in their efforts to plea bargain, when the two attorneys offered to help solve the mystery of Alicia Haucks and Susan Petz, in exchange for their client's committal. Neither Mr. Armani nor Mr. Belge was ever requested to reveal their information to any judicial, administrative, or legislative tribunal. Mr. Armani was asked as to the whereabouts of the missing women by the district attorney of Onondaga County, and by the New York State Police on several occasions. The father of Ms. Haucks also requested information. To all of these requests the attorneys claimed they had nothing to tell.

In June of 1974, during the trial of Mr. Garrow, in order to affirmatively establish the defense of insanity, these three other murders were raised by the defense—through the testimony of Mr. Garrow. At this point, the attorneys felt that their client had waived his right to confidentiality by implicating himself in the other slayings; therefore, they informed the authorities as to the locations of the bodies.[2]

A great outcry followed the attorneys' revelations. "Members of the public were shocked at the apparent callousness of these lawyers, whose conduct was seen as typifying the unhealthy lack of concern of most lawyers with the public interest and with simple decency."[3] Public indignation reached a fever pitch that summer. The district attorney caused the Grand Jury of Onondaga County, then sitting, to conduct a thorough investigation. As a result of this investigation, an indictment was brought against Mr. Belge for having violated § 4200(1) of the Public Health Law, which requires that a decent burial be accorded the dead; and § 4143 of the Public Health Law, which requires anyone knowing of the death of a person without medical attendance to report the same to the authorities.[4]

However, not all reaction was adverse. Monroe Freedman, dean of Hofstra Law School, stated that "the conduct of the attorneys is absolutely correct. If they had acted otherwise it would have been a serious violation of their professional responsibility."[5] The president of the Albany County Bar Association stated that there was neither an ethical nor a legal way the attorneys could have revealed this confidential information, heinous as it may have been."[6] The attorney-client privilege and the ethical canons absolutely forbid an attorney to do so. If this is so, then why the public outcry?

Introduction

The problems faced by the attorneys in their defense of Robert Garrow brought to the forefront the public's lack of understanding of the fundamentals of justice in a democratic society under the adversary system. Most people can certainly understand the moral compulsion to aid the parents, in order to end their anguish and endless waiting, to accord the victims a proper burial, and to allow the parents to start living their lives again. Therefore, it must follow that, since the two attorneys knew where the bodies were and did not disclose the information until months later, they should not only be guilty of violating the health ordinance, but also of breaching some moral duty. This interpretation is, however, improper. The attorneys were compelled by a higher duty; the obligation of lawyers to their clients, and to the system of administering justice as guaranteed in the Constitution, Common Law, and Statute.

This system demanded that the attorneys not disclose where the bodies were buried. As defense counsels they were prevented from disclosing what they had learned in confidence from their client.[7] They may have personally believed that certain rules of law which benefited their client were wrong and in need of change. However, it was their obligation, in the course of representation, to invoke these rules on their client's behalf.[8]

Argument

Few subjects in the administration of criminal justice are more in need of clarification than the role of defense counsel in a criminal prosecution. Both the public and the legal profession sometimes exhibit grave misconceptions as to defense counsel's function and the limits of proper conduct in his relationship with his client.[9] Examples of this were visible in newspapers across the country following the disclosures of Attorneys Armani and Belge,[10] and during James St. Clair's performance in the Watergate scandal.[11]

To understand the role of the defense attorney in the United States it is useful to contrast it with that of a totalitarian country. In the People's Republic of China, for instance, "there is no legal representation for criminals."[12] The "judge" represents the interests of the accused. Sentencing in China is set according to community passions. This indignation is registered by a "street committee," which oversees neighborhoods of as many as 65,000 people. Assisting the "street committee" is a smaller residential committee which manages the affairs of smaller sections of each neighborhood. "When a serious crime is committed, these committees prepare a report on the offender, the victim, and the community reaction to the crime. If the reaction is high, so is the sentence. The court only infrequently disregards the community report."[13]

The role of the criminal defense attorney in Cuba is also quite different from that of his counterpart in the United States. "The first job of a revolutionary lawyer is not to argue that his client is innocent, but rather to determine if his client is guilty and if so, to seek the sanction which will best rehabilitate him."[14]

In Bulgaria, again we see that the defense attorney is but an arm of the state. In the trial of Traicho Kostov, former vice premier of Bulgaria, for treason and espionage, his attorney began by distinguishing the roles of defense counsel in a socialist state. He said a lawyer could not defend a criminal he knew was guilty "merely by scoring technical points" against the prosecution. "In a socialist state there is no division of duty between the judge, prosecution and defense counsel . . . the defense must assist the prosecution to find the objective truth in the case." During the trial, defense counsel ridiculed his client's defense. Kostov was convicted and executed.[15] Unfortunately for the defendant, those conducting the trial did miss "the objective truth." This seems rather odd, since both the prosecution and defense were searching for it. Six years later, a re-examination of the trial cleared Kostov's name, and he was "rehabilitated."[16]

The emphasis in a free society is, of course, sharply different. The attorney functions in an adversary system based upon the supposition that justice is best achieved by presenting both sides of a controversy to an impartial judge or jury. Under this system, the needs or interests of the state are neither absolute nor paramount. Under our criminal justice system, it is the dignity of the individual, the accused, that is and should be absolutely protected. "The dignity of the individual is respected to the point that even when the citizen is known by the state to have committed a heinous offense, the individual is nevertheless accorded such rights as counsel, trial by jury, due process, and the privilege against self-incrimination."[17] The individual is also presumed to be innocent until proven guilty, and the state has the burden of proving guilt beyond a reasonable doubt.[18]

To the casual observer, it would seem that the defendant in a criminal prosecution is in a fairly secure position, fully protected by the cloak of due process, surrounded by a legion of constitutional amendments, and guided by his lawyer. But, upon closer observation, the converse is probably true. It is a fact that most people who are arrested and charged with a crime are indeed guilty. It is also true that, in most cases, the prosecution has sufficient evidence to convict the defendant, and that most defendants who plead guilty usually are found guilty.[19]

This follows naturally, if the prosecution, grand jury, magistrate, and police are performing their jobs properly.[20] Moreover, by the time the defense counsel is obtained he is already at a disadvantage. He must sift through state evidence and contend with any statements which his client may have given the police.

Therefore, it can be seen that, in spite of the defendant's guarantees of due process, his attorney undertakes the defense after a series of events has placed his client under a very real cloud, notwithstanding the presumption of innocence.[21] In truth, the defendant in a criminal prosecution and his counsel are faced with a host of governmental agencies and officials, with endless time and money, moving toward conviction.

Innocent persons do, however, get arrested and tried. Some have even been convicted. This should be sufficient to remind us of the underlying purposes of the constitutional safeguards in the Bill of Rights—to protect the innocence and dignity of the individual. For this reason, we must remain vigilant to insure that our criminal, procedural safeguards are strong and constantly applied. The defense counsel performs this function on behalf of an accused and for the benefit of society, by challenging the government's evidence and seeing that the accused's rights are protected.[22]

The indictment of Attorney Belge for not disclosing his client's confidences represents not only an attack by the government on the traditional attorney-client privilege, but also an attempt to undermine the effectiveness of the Fifth and Sixth Amendments. The government attempts to circumscribe these constitutional rights by claiming that a New York health law may vitiate the effectiveness of two constitutional amendments. Plainly this interpretation is incorrect.

To say that a criminal trial is a search for the truth, and that getting the truth is the most important function of the trial is surely incorrect. Our system of law has developed procedural safeguards which could be characterized as impeding the disclosure of truth. Perhaps the greatest of these procedural safeguards—or impediments—is the Constitution of the United States. "The illustrious men who framed that instrument were guarding the foundations of civil liberty against the abuses of unlimited power."[23] Some argue, however, that because of these individual rights "[i]t becomes evident that the search for truth fails too much of the time. The rules and devices accounting for the failures come to seem less agreeable and less clearly worthy than they once did."[24] To interpret the Constitution in this light is simply improper. For the Supreme Court has stated: "The Constitution of the United States is not intended as a facility for crime, it is intended to prevent oppression."[25] "Before we will permit the state to deprive any person of life, liberty or property we require that certain processes be duly followed which ensure regard for the dignity of the individual, irrespective of the impact of those processes upon the determination of the truth."[26]

The right of a criminal defendant to have the assistance of counsel, as secured by the Sixth Amendment of the Constitution, has been declared by the Supreme Court as ". . . one of the safeguards deemed necessary to insure fundamental human rights of life and liberty."[27]

In *Powell* v. *Alabama*, the Supreme Court stated that "the right to be heard would be, in many cases, of little avail if it did not comprehend the right to be heard by counsel."[28] This philosophy was imposed upon the states in *Gideon* v. *Wainwright,* which incorporated the Sixth Amendment into the Fourteenth Amendment.[29] State courts were now constitutionally required to appoint counsel for all indigents defending against felony charges.[30] The high court declared criminal defense attorneys to be "necessities not luxuries,"[31] since "any person hauled into court, who is too poor to hire a lawyer cannot be assured a fair trial unless counsel is provided for him."[32] This right of counsel was recently extended to indigents defending against misdemeanors punishable by imprisonment in state courts.[33] This absolute need for defense counsel has been expanded to include almost all phases of criminal prosecution. The individual has the right to counsel: as soon as the investigation has "begun to focus on a particular suspect,"[34] at custodial interrogations,[35] lineups,[36] arraignments,[37] preliminary hearings,[38] and post-conviction appeals.[39]

"To fulfill the role of the truly professional advocate, the lawyer must be free to bring to bear in the preparation of defense the skills, experience and judgment he possesses. He can do this only if he knows all that his client knows concerning the facts. The client is not competent to evaluate the relevance of significant facts; hence the lawyer must insist on complete and candid disclosure." Secondly, he must be able to conduct the case free from interference.[40]

Although our law recognizes the right of a defendant to defend himself without assistance of counsel if he so chooses, judges, prosecutors, and defense counsel are unanimously of the opinion that justice is undermined when a party proceeds without a professional advocate. The accused lacks the knowledge which would permit him to take full advantage of his legal rights, and demonstrate his position if he elects a trial.[41]

Why has the Supreme Court, the highest court of our land, stated that defense counsels are "necessities" in criminal prosecutions?[42] The reason is that defense counsel will protect the constitutional rights of the accused. In *Miranda* v. *Arizona,* the Supreme Court stated that "the presence of counsel . . . would be the adequate protective device necessary to make the process of police interrogation conform to the dictates of the privilege"[43] of the Fifth Amendment. Defense counsel will also challenge the evidence of the government, every step of the way. "It is the lesson of human experience that even in the case of the most well intentioned prosecutor the absence of such a challenge can result in carelessness and failure to review the evidence and properly prepare the case which makes it easier to convict the innocent."[44] By using the Sixth Amendment guarantee to counsel, and interposing the skills, knowledge, and experience of an effective defense attorney between the defendant and the state, life is given to the individual's constitutional rights. This is in perfect harmony with the concept of justice seen by the framers of the Constitution. They were ". . . deeply committed to perpetuating a system that minimized the possibilities of convicting the innocent; they were not less concerned about the humanity that the fundamental law should show even the offender . . . [I]n a free society based upon respect for the individual, the determination of guilt or innocence by just procedures . . . was more important than punishing the guilty."[45]

It would seem that since defense counsel is absolutely necessary to protect the rights of an individual in a criminal prosecution, something must be said about how he accomplishes this. For, as in most cases, not everyone is in agreement. To begin, an advocate must give his "undivided loyalty" to his client.[46] Some critics feel that he appears to be an even greater obstacle to the efforts of law enforcement agencies to protect society from the criminal.[47] Judge Walter Schaefer states:

> What's bothersome is that almost never do we have a genuine issue of guilt or innocence today. The system has so changed that what we are doing in the courtroom is trying the conduct of the police and that of the prosecution all along the line. Has there been a misstep at this point? At that point? You know very well that the man is guilty; there is no doubt about the proof. But you must ask for example: Was there something technically wrong with the arrest? You're always trying something irrelevant.[48]

These rights may seem irrelevant to Judge Schaefer, but they are certainly not to a defendant—especially an innocent one. The Supreme Court has stated that these are "the restraints society must observe consistent with the federal Constitution in prosecuting individuals for crime."[49] Defense counsel is professionally obligated to prevent the introduction of evidence that may be wholly reliable (such as a murder weapon), seized in violation of the Fourth Amendment, or a truthful but involuntary confession. He may also advise a client to withhold the truth. As Justice Jackson noted, "Any lawyer worth his salt will tell the suspect in no uncertain terms to make no statement to police under any circumstances."[50]

> Such conduct by defense counsel does not constitute obstruction of justice. On the contrary, it is part of the duty imposed on the most honorable defense counsel, from whom "we countenance or require conduct which in many instances has little, if any, relation to the search for truth." The same observation has been made by Justice Harlan, who noted that "necessity may become an obstacle for truth finding." Chief Justice Warren has also recognized that when the criminal defense attorney successfully obstructs efforts by the government to elicit truthful evidence in ways that violate constitutional rights, the attorney is "merely exercising . . . good professional judgment" and "carrying out what he is sworn to do under his oath—to protect to the extent of his ability the rights of his client." Chief Justice Warren concluded: "In fulfilling this responsibility the attorney plays a vital role in the administration of criminal justice under our Constitution."[51]

Are communications disclosed to an attorney in confidence protected from disclosure by the client's Fifth Amendment privilege against self-incrimination?

During the course of representation in a criminal prosecution, the client may make many incriminating statements. The Fifth Amendment states that ". . . no person shall be compelled in any criminal case to be a witness against himself."[52] From the beginning, the view has been adopted that this provision must have a broad construction. The cases hold that the privilege is not limited to the literal language.[53] There are several policies underlying the privilege against self-incrimination. It serves to assure that even guilty individuals are treated in a manner consistent with basic respect for human dignity. "[W]e do not make even the most hardened criminal sign his own death warrant, or dig his grave, or pull the lever that springs the trap on which he stands. We have through the course of history developed considerable feeling for the dignity and intrinsic importance of the individual man. Even the evil man is a human being."[54] It also includes "an unwillingness to subject those suspected of a crime to the cruel trilemma of self-accusation, perjury, or contempt, a preference for an accusatorial rather than an inquisitional system of criminal justice, [and] a fear that self-incriminating statements will be elicited by inhumane treatment and abuse . . ."[55]

The foregoing constitutional principles are well settled and defined. Their application would not be difficult if the government and criminal defendant were the sole participants in the prosecution. But, because of the defendant's constitutional right to counsel, this question must be asked: does the attorney have standing to assert his client's Fifth Amendment privilege?[56]

If this question is answered affirmatively, counsel becomes a conduit for incriminating evidence. This evidence would be used by the prosecution to convict the defendant. This procedure would have a devastating effect on the attorney-client privilege. It would hurt the defendant's trial preparation, for he would not know what he could disclose in safety to his attorney. "For example, one client was reluctant to tell her lawyer that her husband had attacked her with a knife, because it tended to confirm that she had in fact shot him (contrary to what she had at first maintained). Having been persuaded by her attorney's insistence upon complete and candid disclosure, she finally 'confessed all',—which permitted the lawyer to defend her properly and successfully on the grounds of self-defense."[57]

It would also affect the prosecution's investigation. The need to investigate thoroughly would be diminished, since highly inculpatory evidence disclosed to defense counsel by the defendant could be demanded by the prosecution. Furthermore, this lack of investigation may deprive the defendant of exculpatory matter which may have been uncovered by the state. More importantly, if allowed, this procedure would greatly diminish the defendant's Fifth and Sixth Amendment rights. This proposal is completely unconstitutional, yet this is exactly what the prosecution in *People v. Belge* is advocating. Fortunately, the Supreme Court in *Couch v. United States*[58] offered a two-part test for determining when the privilege against self-incrimination can be asserted as evidence in the hands of third persons. First, the element of personal compulsion must be directed against the accused.[59] Second, the claimant of the privilege must have a legitimate "expectation of protected privacy or confidentiality" in the incriminating evidence possessed by the third person. How would this test apply to the facts in the Lake Pleasant incident? If Robert Garrow possessed the only knowledge of where the bodies of his victims were buried, the state would have no opportunity of reaching that knowledge without giving him immunity that would be coextensive with his Fifth Amendment privilege; for surely, that information would tend to incriminate him.[60] If Garrow possessed photographs of the victims' bodies, I feel that he would still be able to assert his Fifth Amendment privilege against compelled disclosure,[61] for the pictures would tend to incriminate him—for violating the health ordinance, if nothing else.

The recent case of *United States* v. *Kasmir* held, *inter alia,* that the individual attorney may assert the client's privilege against self-incrimination if the client himself could have successfully asserted it.[62] I feel that Robert Garrow could have asserted the privilege. Therefore, it follows that if his attorneys had been ordered by the state to produce the pictures, disclose the location of the bodies, or testify to any of the conversations they had with Mr. Garrow concerning this, they could have asserted Mr. Garrow's Fifth Amendment privilege successfully (the attorneys could have asserted their own Fifth Amendment privilege because they were in violation of Public Health Law § 4200(1) and § 4143).

A declaration by a court that a defense attorney must disclose incriminating evidence made available to him by his client in confidence during the attorney-client relationship, would not only interfere with the client's exercise of his Fifth Amendment privilege, but would vitiate it, as well. The attorney would become a spy for the state or face contempt charges. In *Bursey* v. *Weatherford,* the Fourth Circuit held that any deliberate intrusion by the prosecution into the confidential relationship between the defendant and his counsel constitutes a violation of the Sixth Amendment guarantee.[63] But the facts in the Lake Pleasant case can be distinguished from those in the above mentioned case. There, the informant or agent of the state law enforcement division was a co-defendant; here, the government attempts to force the defense attorney to become the informant or a defendant for violation of a public health ordinance.

The defense attorneys in *People* v. *Garrow* were able to give the accused a proper defense, for the defendant could freely disclose not only everything about his particular crime, but also everything about other crimes. Thus, it was because of the privilege that the attorneys were able to learn about Mr. Garrow's other victims; and, in the exercise of their professional responsibility, they were able to ethically and legally provide for its disclosure without violating the defendant's individual rights.

What is the relation between the attorney-client privilege and the adversary system of justice?

Our adversary system assumes that the most effective method for ascertaining the truth is through the presentation of legal issues with maximum zeal.[64] The parties and their attorneys represent opposing viewpoints, and present evidence to support their position or to attack their opponent's. The attorneys are the critical figures in the adversary system. They are the nexus between the complicated legal workings of the judicial system and the usually uninformed and wary client. As an officer of the court,[65] the attorney must see that justice is done. He may not "suppress evidence that he or his client has a legal obligation to reveal"[66] In all his actions, he must act in good faith and within the framework of the law.[67] But at the same time, the lawyer must serve as an advocate for the client. He must represent his client's interests "zealously"[68] and with "undivided loyalty."[69] He must do nothing to prejudice or damage the client during the course of their professional relationship.[70] The attorney must be sure to safeguard the interests of the client[71] and to preserve his "confidences and secrets."[72]

One essential ingredient to the proper functioning of our adversary system is the attorney-client privilege. The privilege, as construed with its exceptions, is an accommodation of competing public interests.[73] The testimonial duty, and the obligation to provide all relevant evidence in the interest of truth and justice is balanced against the constitutional underpinnings of both the Fifth Amendment privilege against self-incrimination, and the Sixth Amendment right to effective counsel.[74] The lawyer can serve effectively as a constitutionally mandated advocate and protector of his client's rights only if he knows all that his client knows concerning the facts of the case.[75] If the lawyer cannot get all the facts about the case, he may be surprised at trial, and will only give the client "half of a defense."[76] "[T]he client is not competent to evaluate the relevance or significance of particular facts. What may seem incriminating to the client, may actually be exculpatory."[77] For example, an innocent client who maintains he acted in self-defense is on trial for the stabbing death of man, and is reluctant to tell you he carries his penknife with him every day, for fear that this could be used against him. Assuming the charge to be first-degree murder, the client does not realize that his routine carrying of the knife would negate the element of premeditation, which the prosecutor would have to prove beyond a reasonable doubt.[78] To avoid this type of problem, the client must feel free to tell his attorney everything.[79] It should be obvious why the basic rationale of the attorney-client privilege is to encourage the complete disclosure of information between an attorney and his client, without apprehension of subsequent compelled disclosure.[80] If disclosure responsibilities were placed upon attorneys, clients would not confide in their attorneys, and attorneys would caution their clients against disclosure.[81] This would destroy the lawyer's role as an effective advocate for his client, and the proper functioning of our adversary system would be severely undermined.[82]

It is argued, however, that the privilege is not needed by an innocent party, and the guilty should not be given its aid.[83] In response, Professor Wigmore points out that in lawsuits "all is not black and white." A client's case may be one where there is no clear preponderance of morals and justice on either side, and he may mistakenly think a fact fatal to his case when it is not and thus be compelled, if there were no privilege, to forego resort to counsel in a fair claim.[84]

Opponents of the privilege also suggest that rightful punishment or liability could be avoided solely because of nondisclosure of confidential information.[85] The rules against disclosure of confidential communications, however, represent deliberate tolerance of the suppression of some pertinent information on the grounds that the protection of confidentiality is vital to the accusatorial process.[86]

[Despite the many criticisms, the privilege does accomplish the purpose of fostering free communication between client and attorney. This results in each side learning the truth, and presenting its case in the best light possible, before a neutral judge and jury who apply the law to the facts and then ". . . render impartial judgments."[87]

Is the attorney-client privilege applicable to the facts of the Lake Pleasant case?

The most common formulation of the privilege is that summarized by Professor Wigmore from common law. The substantive elements of the privilege are:

1. Where legal advice of any kind is sought;
2. from a professional legal advisor in his capacity as such;
3. the communications relating to the purpose;
4. made in confidence;
5. by the client;
6. are at his insistence permanently protected;
7. from disclosure by himself or by the legal advisor;
8. except if the protection be waived.[88]

When the facts of the Lake Pleasant case are applied to the prima facie elements, they establish the existence of the privilege.

(1)—"Where legal advice of any kind is sought"—Attorneys Armani and Belge were appointed as counsel for Mr. Garrow when the disclosure was made for the express purpose of providing him with the legal advice he sought and accepted.

(2)—"from a professional legal advisor in his capacity as such"—Both Mr. Armani and Mr. Belge are licensed by the New York State Bar Association to practice law and thus, are professional legal advisors. The advice they offered was in their capacity as professional legal advisors. Indeed, if they had not been court appointed counsel, Mr. Garrow would never have become associated with attorneys Armani and Belge, and would not have been the recipient of their legal advice.

(3)—"the communications relating to that purpose"—There is no question that the communication at issue was the cornerstone of the insanity defense and, as such, was intimately related to the legal advice Mr. Garrow received.

(4)—"made in confidence"—The client must have intended the communication to remain confidential[89] and been warranted in having this expectation to sustain a finding that the communication was made in confidence. Mr. Garrow did not divulge the information in issue to his attorneys during their first meeting. Only after repeated assurances that information disclosed to them was confidential and could not be introduced at trial, did Mr. Garrow reveal the location of the bodies.[90] The information was neither disclosed in the presence of third persons, nor did Mr. Garrow necessarily contemplate the disclosure of this information to third parties. Furthermore, this information was not disclosed for the purpose of public disclosure. If Mr. Garrow had revealed the information to his attorneys under such conditions, he could not have intended, or would not have been warranted in believing that the communication was confidential.[91] A critic of this subjective-objective test for determining confidentiality asserts that whether a client knows it or not, whenever he speaks he assumes the risk that the attorney will be required to disclose the information[92] and therefore, is never warranted in believing that the information will remain confidential. This statement seems very shortsighted when considered in light of the Sixth Amendment right to effective counsel, which necessarily implies the free disclosure of information between client and attorney without fear of subsequent disclosure,[93] and the Fifth Amendment privilege against self-incrimination which allows the attorney to assert the right on behalf of the client, if the client could assert the right on his own behalf.[94]

(5)—"by the client"—The only evidence on record as to how the location of the bodies came to the attention of the attorneys was presented by the attorneys, who claim it was disclosed to them by their client. The courts realize this will usually be the case, and have fashioned their decisions to accommodate the realities of this situation. For instance, where there was no evidence as to how a murder weapon came into an attorney's possession, it was assumed to have been obtained through the confidential relationship;[95] and an attorney's handwritten notes were found to be protected by the attorney-client privilege—because the information contained in the notes could only have been obtained from the client.[96] This rationale seems applicable to the information possessed by the attorneys in the Lake Pleasant case. Since there is no contrary evidence, the information must have been obtained through the attorney-client relationship. Assuming the information regarding the location of the bodies was relayed to the attorneys by a third party (although there is no evidence to this effect), there is now case law in addition to the comment that the Sixth Amendment would protect this information because of the chilling affect which disclosure or questioning an attorney would have on the free exercise of an accused's right to counsel.[97]

(6)—"are at his insistence permanently protected"—Mr. Garrow asserted the privilege, as evidenced by the subsequent appeal of his conviction on the grounds that Armani and Belge violated the confidentiality of the attorney-client privilege. The court held that the privilege existed until Mr. Garrow disclosed the nature of his communications with his attorneys in court. Until that time, the communications were protected.

(7)—"from disclosure by himself or by the legal advisor"—The confidential communication was known only by Mr. Garrow and his attorneys, Mr. Armani and Mr. Belge. The lawyers did not seek to prevent any third party with knowledge of the past crimes from going forward with such information to the authorities. They merely held themselves to the oath they were required by law to uphold.[98]

(8)—"except if the protection be waived"—The privilege may be waived by either the client[99] or the attorney, if he has been so instructed by the client.[100] Waiver includes not only words, but also conduct expressing an intention to relinquish the privilege (such as partial disclosure, or failure to claim the privilege when a witness takes the stand to testify about the confidential communication).[101] Any testimony, given on direct or cross-examination, relating to the privileged communication usually constitutes waiver, also.[102] The facts of the Lake Pleasant case make it clear that Mr. Garrow did not waive the privilege through any of these conventional techniques.

The argument has been raised, however, that Mr. Garrow implicitly authorized Armani and Belge to disclose confidential information to the prosecutor, in so far as it might further his position during plea bargaining, and thus waived the general right to the confidentiality of such information. This reasoning fails for two reasons. First, the information relating to the confidential communications was not disclosed to the prosecutor. Armani and Belge merely offered to help solve the mystery of the missing bodies, if the prosecutor would agree to commit Mr. Garrow. This offer was refused and the negotiations went no further. Second, even if the promise to help solve the mystery of the missing bodies can be considered information which was part of the confidential communication, the interests of justice dictate this should not constitute a waiver of the attorney-client privilege. The plea negotiation process has become a recognized part of the criminal proces.[103] Unless most of the cases are disposed of by pleas, the courts will be crippled with a mass of cases, resulting in long delays, an increased number of crimes committed by defendants awaiting trial, and a general breakdown in the machinery of justice.[104] Indeed, by simply requesting their constitutional right to a trial by jury, defendants who are awaiting trial can cripple the entire criminal justice system. This would most certainly occur if defendants knew that disclosures which they authorized their attorneys to make during plea bargaining would subsequently become evidence in their prosecution. To avoid this, the courts must consider disclosures made during plea negotiation to be confidential, and within the attorney-client privilege.

Did the disclosure by Mr. Garrow to his attorneys fall within an exception to the attorney-client privilege as enumerated by New York law or the Code of Professional Responsibility?

The attorney-client privilege, as codified in New York, does not protect communications between an attorney and a client where the client's purpose is "to commit a crime" or to seek aid in the "accomplishment of an unlawful purpose."[105] However, "advice secured in aid of legitimate defense by a client against a charge of past crimes or past misconduct, even though he is guilty, stands on a different footing and such consultations are privileged."[106] "The privileged communications may be a shield of defense as to crimes already committed, but it cannot be used as a sword or weapon of offense to enable persons to carry out contemplated crimes against society."[107] This represents the legislature's recognition that the value of the attorney-client privilege outweighs the need for disclosure of all relevant evidence. But, when disclosure of the confidential information would prevent injury to life or property, the legislature has found the scales tipped against the privilege. Thus, if the lawyers in Lake Pleasant were told that the missing girls were still alive, or if their investigation had revealed that the bodies were infected with a deadly disease,[108] they should not have hesitated to call the authorities to prevent further injury, even though to do so would be a violation of their client's confidence and their oaths as attorneys.[109] The obligation to disclose information received in the furtherance of a crime[110] and to permissively reveal "the information necessary to prevent the crime"[111] does not mean the attorney-client privilege is afforded a secondary role in relation to the truth-seeking function. The duty to maintain the confidentiality of the privilege is paramount, except when the lawyer's advice is sought to aid in the furtherance of a crime.[112] The confidential information received by the attorneys in the Lake Pleasant case was not to aid in the furthering of a crime. Mr. Garrow did not reveal the location of his victims to attorneys Armani and Belge in order to perpetrate a future crime. He did so to aid a legitimate defense of a crime which had been completed prior to the disclosures. Indeed, the main purpose for the creation of the attorney-client privilege is to allow just such communications to be made in the interest of establishing a legal defense.[113] To reveal information obtained under these circumstances would reduce the attorney's role to that of a conductor of evidence for the benefit of the state. In the United States, the interests of the government are indeed very important. But when they clash with the rights of the individual citizen, the very essence and continued existence of our democratic system requires that governmental interests occupy a subservient position to our rights as citizens.

The Code of Professional Responsibility imposes an ethical obligation upon the lawyer "to guard the confidences and secrets of his client" which is broader than the attorney-client privilege.[114] Accordingly, the Code of Professional Responsibility neither requires nor recommends, but simply allows the lawyer to reveal:

1. Confidences or secrets with the consent of the client or clients affected, but only after a full disclosure to them.
2. Confidences or secrets when permitted under Disciplinary Rules or required by law or court order.
3. The intention of his client to commit a crime and the information necessary to prevent the crime.
4. Confidences or secrets necessary to establish or collect his fee or to defend himself or his employees or associates against an accusation of wrongful conduct.[115]

Canon 4 also states that "[a] lawyer should not use information acquired in the course of the representation of a client to the disadvantage of the client. . ."[116] and "[t]he obligation of a lawyer to preserve the confidences and secrets of his client continues after the termination of his employment."[117] Furthermore, "this ethical precept, unlike the evidentiary privilege, exists without regard to the nature or source of information or the fact that others share the knowledge."[118]

Only one exception to the ethical obligation of confidentiality seems applicable. DR 4-101(C)(1) does not apply, since Mr. Garrow did not consent to disclosure. DR 4-101(C)(3) does not apply because Mr. Garrow had no intention to commit further crimes. DR 4-101(C)(4) does not apply because disclosure as construed in that section pertains to actions where the attorney has to defend himself against an accusation of wrongful conduct by the client.[119] DR 4-101(C)(2), at first glance, appears to pose a legitimate possibility of disclosure upon the two attorneys. After a reasoned analysis, it would be most hypocritical to have such an exception and to suppose the attorney-client privilege served any purpose at all. DR 4-101(C)(2) says that "a lawyer may reveal. . . [c]onfidences or secrets when permitted under Disciplinary Rules or required by law or court order." The only Disciplinary Rule which could permit disclosure under DR 4-101(C)(2) is DR 7-102(B)(1). This rule requires "[a] lawyer who receives information clearly establishing. . . [h]is client has. . . perpetrated a fraud upon a. . . tribunal [to] promptly call upon his client to rectify the same, and if his client refuses. . . he shall reveal the fraud to the. . . tribunal, except when the information is protected as a privileged communication."

This language clearly indicates the rule only applies to fraudulent acts which have been committed in the past. "Virtually every ethics opinion which has addressed this issue has held that an attorney has no ethical duty to reveal a client's past crimes. [120] Indeed, any rule of ethics which required an attorney to disclose information concerning his client's past crimes would interfere with the client's exercise of his Fifth Amendment privilege against self-incrimination and seriously undermine the proper functioning of the criminal justice system."[121] Thus, where an attorney learns from his client that the client has committed a past fraud which also constitutes a crime, the duty imposed by DR 7-102(B)(1) does not apply and the lawyer need not make a disclosure. This view is supported by the language in the Disciplinary Rule which requires disclosure, "except when the information is protected as a privileged communication."[122] Communications made after the fact of the commission of the crime (such as those made in the Lake Pleasant case) are protected by the attorney-client privilege.[123]

DR 4-101(C)(2) also allows disclosure when ". . . required by law or court order." To construe laws requiring the reporting of felonies to the authorities, or a court order in the form of a subpoena *duces tecum* as requiring disclosure of information received in the course of the attorney-client relationship is total nonsense. To maintain this position would mean the privilege applies only when the court does not request disclosure. This cannot be so, for it is exactly this sort of protection that is the essence of the evidentiary protection for confidential communications. The attorney must be able to refuse disclosure of information which he, in good faith and without disrespect, believes is protected by the attorney-client privilege, or there would be no such thing as a lawyer-client privilege.

The above analysis either subverts the rule to a position totally inconsistent with the attorney-client privilege (if it requires disclosure when the privilege dictates otherwise) or interprets it to be totally meaningless (if the privilege can always be asserted despite the court order). There is one possible interpretation which avoids this dilemma. This construction limits the application of the Disciplinary Rule to situations in which a pre-existing court order or legal obligation mandates disclosure.[124]

For example, when a defendant is admitted to bail, both the defendant and his lawyer are promising that the defendant will appear at trial. If the client jumps bail and informs his attorney of his whereabouts, the attorney is bound by a "specifically directed legal requirement to assure the presence of his client at trial."[125] "Failure to disclose the client's whereabouts under these circumstances would aid the client in escaping a trial for the crime for which he was indicted, [and] would likewise aid him in evading prosecution for the additional offense of bail jumping."[126] This rationale can be extended to situations where the attorney has applied for probation or suspension of sentence on his client's behalf, and he represents to the court, at least by implication, that his client will abide by the terms and conditions of the court's order. Furthermore, by reason of his appearance and application before the court, the attorney is under an affirmative duty to assist his client to obey the court's order, which includes disclosure of information ordinarily within the attorney-client privilege.[127] Mr. Garrow's attorneys, however, were not under the auspices of a specifically directed, pre-existing court order which required disclosure.

Would an anonymous disclosure of evidence by an attorney (received in confidence) accommodate the public interest without violating the attorney-client privilege?

Despite the preceding analysis, which clearly illustrates the existence of the attorney-client privilege as applied to the circumstances of the Lake Pleasant case, there are those who believe other interests are more important than the preservation of the attorney-client privilege. Various concepts have been formulated, which they believe circumvent the privilege without forcing the lawyer to break his oath of confidentiality. One suggestion is that the lawyers should have anonymously disclosed the location of the bodies. This course of action, they claim, would serve the public interest by allowing the prosecution to discover the location of the bodies. The client's privilege would be preserved because the source of the evidence would remain unknown. This reasoning fails for several reasons. First, it assumes the prosecution will neither discover who made the anonymous disclosure, nor obtain evidence which will later implicate the defendant. If either of these contingencies occurs, the lawyer has assisted in the conviction of his client. At the very least, the attorney has violated his oath of confidentiality,[128] disclosed evidence which could result in the conviction of his client,[129] and has not avoided the appearance of impropriety.[130] Furthermore, one must question the value of a system of justice (and the integrity of the profession that serves this system) if they condone deception and trickery as techniques for learning the truth.

Does granting a lawyer immunity relieve the lawyer of his obligation under the attorney-client privilege?

Supporters of this position correctly maintain that the court has the power to compel testimony.[131] This power is not absolute and is subject to a number of exceptions, the most important of which is perhaps, the privilege against self-incrimination.[132] Immunity statutes seek a rational compromise between these two competing interests.[133] A recent case raised the issue of whether the granting of immunity to an attorney was coextensive with the liability incurred by requiring disclosure in violation of the attorney-client privilege.[134] The court decided that the attorney was under obligation to disclose the information conveyed to him in the course of the attorney-client relationship, without deciding whether the immunity granted to him also protected the client from prosecution as a result of the testimony.[135] Here lies the crucial decision. The attorney placed in this situation will avoid disclosure for two reasons: first, to avoid liability for violating the attorney-client privilege; and second, to preserve his oath of confidentiality and the viability of the attorney-client privilege. If the immunity only extends as far as releasing the attorney from liability, the purpose behind the attorney-client privilege will be disregarded, and the functioning of the lawyer in the legal system will be undermined. In addition, the client has now seen his "champion against a hostile world"[136] turn against him; what was his only defense has now become another weapon in the prosecutor's arsenal. Under such circumstances, the attorney who might be a witness against his client is compelled by ethical and practical considerations to decline to represent the client.[137] Thus, the prosecution would be given the power to decide who could represent a prospective defendant.[138] It should be obvious that to preserve the effectiveness of the attorney-client privilege, the grant of immunity must protect both the attorney and client from subsequent use of the confidential communication by the prosecutor.

Is an attorney who in good faith maintains his oath of confidentiality subject to prosecution for violation of criminal or health laws?

Implicit in the role of the lawyer in an adversary system is the fact that he will frequently be a depository of highly incriminating evidence, and may even (as in the Lake Pleasant case) learn that his client has caused the death of another human being. If the attorney was required to divulge such information, there would not have been any reason to adopt an attorney-client privilege. The lawyer's role would not be that of a partisan advocate representing his client with maximum zeal.[139] Even so, it is suggested that a lawyer who does not divulge a client's self-incriminatory information would be guilty of such crimes as obstruction of justice, misprision of a felony, or health violations. The duty to insure a decent burial, and the duty to report a death occurring without medical attendance were brought against the attorneys in the Lake Pleasant case. Statutes such as these should not apply to lawyers for a number of reasons. First, while serving as advocates, lawyers should resolve doubts as to the bounds of the law in favor of their clients.[140] Therefore, any doubt as to whether a duty to disclose exists that is resolved against disclosure should not be punished. Second, "... criminal statutes should be interpreted to avoid raising constitutional issues unnecessarily particularly when there is a likelihood that the statute would have to be ruled constitutionally invalid."[141] Any attempt to apply these statutes against lawyers would certainly be met by raising the Fifth and Sixth Amendments as a defense. Third, ". . . criminal statutes should be narrowly confined to avoid applying them more broadly than the legislature intended or to those who may have been ignorant of the laws' application to them.[142] Finally, to construe a criminal law in a way that would subvert the attorney-client privilege would also undermine the adversary system, and violate the constitutional rights to counsel, due process of law, and the privilege against self-incrimination.[143]

The criminal statutes that cannot be applied to attorneys who do not reveal their client's confidences, may apply to attorneys who actively participate in the concealment of evidence or the obstruction of justice. For example, in the *Ryder* case, an attorney removed the weapon used in the commission of the crime (and the monetary proceeds of the crime) from his client's safe deposit box, and put them in his own safe deposit box.[144] The important difference between the *Ryder* case and the Lake Pleasant case lies in the role performed by the attorneys. In *Ryder,* the attorney actively concealed evidence, while in Lake Pleasant, the attorneys merely maintained the confidentiality of the information received from their client. Indeed, when a lawyer who faced the same dilemma which confronted attorneys Armani and Belge decided on the course of disclosure, his client's subsequent conviction was reversed on a finding of prejudicial error—which resulted from violation of the attorney-client privilege.[145] The court made it quite clear that the client's disclosure to her defense counsel of the location of her husband's remains was a confidential communication which was protected by the attorney-client privilege.[146]

It has been brought out, however, that one of the attorneys in the Lake Pleasant case discovered the head of one of the victims severed from the body and placed it next to the body. While it is clear the attorney touched the body, this action did not result in the concealment of evidence. The contrary conclusion seems to be warranted. By keeping the human bones together, the attorney assisted in preserving the corpse for future identification.

Does the undertaking of an investigation by a lawyer to corroborate his client's story relieve him of his obligation to his client under the attorney-client privilege?

Another possible solution suggested is ". . . that the attorneys in the Lake Pleasant case were not bound by their oath of confidentiality once they had undertaken to corroborate their client's information through their own investigation."[147] This suggestion fails for two reasons. First, information which an attorney obtains as a result of information disclosed to him in the course of a confidential communication is also privileged.[148] Applying this to the facts, any evidence which was uncovered by Armani and Belge during their investigation would not have been discovered if their client had not confided in them. Accordingly, this information is also privileged. Second, this argument does not recognize that a defense counsel in a criminal case is under an affirmative duty to investigate the facts of the matter,[149] "regardless of the accused's admissions or statements of facts constituting guilt."[150] The accused has a right to expect that his court-appointed counsel will make "such investigation of the facts as the circumstances require."[151] If any attorney does not fulfill this duty to investigate, he may be cited for providing ineffective assistance.[152] Furthermore, if an attorney does not make a sufficient investigation, he may render the quality of the defendant's representation constitutionally inadequate; a conviction may have to be reversed.[153] Although the investigation by the attorneys did not result in the discovery of new evidence, it might have revealed that their client's belief that he had killed three other people was false. This would have had an important bearing on the insanity defense. The attorneys in this case were performing a duty which Mr. Garrow's constitutional right to counsel required. Any suggestion that this course of action excuses an attorney from his obligation under the client's privilege disregards our constitutional principles.

Were the pictures taken by Armani and Belge subject to discovery by the prosecution?

Critics of Armani and Belge have also suggested that the pictures they took were evidence subject to the rules of discovery pertaining to criminal actions. This suggestion also fails for two reasons. First, as previously mentioned, evidence which owes its existence to information disclosed in the course of the attorney-client privilege is also privileged.[154] The pictures would never have been taken if Mr. Garrow had not told his attorneys where the bodies were buried, and, accordingly they are privileged information. Second, the pictures are not discoverable evidence as defined by the Federal Rules of Criminal Procedure. The pictures are exempted from discovery by Rule 16(b), since they will not be introduced as evidence in chief at trial,[155] and also because they are ". . . internal defense documents made by the defendant, or his attorneys, or agents in connection with the investigation or defense of the case. . ."[156] It is the prosecutor who would be violating the law in this case by requesting discovery of material which is not subject to discovery. The prosecutor's primary duty to the state is not to convict, but to see that justice is done.[157]

Conclusion

In *Gideon* v. *Wainwright,* the Supreme Court declared criminal defense attorneys to be "necessities not luxuries." Anyone subjected to the harshness of our criminal justice system would most certainly agree. Without a lawyer to protect his rights, the defendant would be easy prey for a district attorney, particularly one hungry for headlines. To protect people in this position even if we believe them to be guilty, our constitutional system has developed procedural safeguards which assure that anyone accused of a crime will be convicted in a manner becoming to civilized men and women. The lawyer's role is to insure that these rights are not violated. By doing so he preserves the integrity of our criminal justice system—a reflection of our ethics, morals, and integrity.

The constitutional representation of indigent defendants (such as Mr. Garrow) requires the attorney to provide effective assistance to his client. The attorney's first, and perhaps most important step in performing his constitutionally mandated role is to learn everything from his client which may serve as an aid in a legitimate defense. To assure this free flow of information, the federal government and each of the states have developed an attorney-client privilege. This privilege encourages clients to confide in their attorneys and tell them everything, by suppressing information related in the course of this relationship from disclosure or use at trial. The privilege also encourages men and women of high character to enter the legal profession who might not, if they had to turn around and disclose information which they received from their clients in the strictest confidence. Furthermore, the mere existence of this privilege is a recognition that there are societal interests more important than discerning the truth. This view is totally consistent with the Bill of Rights—an express declaration of individual rights which was crucial to the ratification of the Constitution. The construction given to the attorney-client privilege allows the defendant to freely disclose all information, without placing upon him the onus of determining whether the evidence is relevant or irrelevant, incriminating or exculpatory. Thus, the attorney-client privilege is both fair and practical. Through it, the court recognizes that most people are ill equipped to take on a lawyer's responsibility, and that a blunder or misstep could result in the conviction of an innocent person—which is an affront to justice.

The function of defense counsel in our adversary system is to represent the client zealously. His duty to both the court and the client are the same—to assure that innocent persons are not convicted. The attorney-client privilege protects the individual and society. This can be readily seen in the Lake Pleasant case. Robert Garrow was induced to disclose the fact that he had murdered three other people. Attorneys Armani and Belge were able to take this information and interpose a plea of insanity for the defendant. During the trial, the attorneys allowed this fact to come out via the testimony of the defendant, Mr. Garrow. Under the protection afforded by the attorney-client privilege, information which might never have been disclosed by a defendant came to the fore.

Notes

1. Chamberlain, *Legal Ethics: Confidentiality and the Case of Robert Garrow's Lawyers,* 25 Buffalo L. Rev. 211, 211(1975) [hereinafter cited as *Legal Ethics*].
2. People v. Belge, 272 N.Y.S.2d 798 (1975).
3. Freedman, *Where the Bodies are Buried: The Adversary System and the Obligation of Confidentiality,* 10 Crim. L. Bull. 979, (1974) [hereinafter cited as Freedman].
4. People v. Belge, at 799.
5. *Legal Ethics, supra* note 1, at 222 n.64.
6. *Id..*
7. ABA Code of Professional Responsibility *and* Canons of Judicial Ethics, Ethical Consideration 4-1 (1975) [hereinafter cited as ABA Code]. [Ethical Considerations will be hereinafter referred to as EC in both text and notes].
8. ABA Project on Standards for Criminal Justice, Standards Relating to the Prosecution and Defense Function, at 148 (1971) [hereinafter cited as ABA Project
9.].*Id.,* at 141.
10. *Legal Ethics, supra* note 1, at 221.
11. FREEDMAN. LAWYERS ETHICS IN ADVERSARY SYSTEM, ZEALOUS ADVOCACY AND THE PUBLIC INTEREST 11 (1975) [hereinafter cited as LAWYERS ETHICS].
12. Douglas, Trial, Feb. 1977, at 46, col. 1.
13. *Id.,* col. 3.
14. KAPLAN, CRIMINAL JUSTICE, at 265-66, note 1 (1969).
15. *Id.,* at 266.
16. *Id..*
17. Freedman, *supra* note 3, at 982.
18. Escobedo v. Illinois, 378 U.S. 478 (1964).
19. Dash, *The Emerging Role and Function of the Criminal Defense Lawyer,* 47 N.C. L. Rev. 598,626,N.20 (1966) [hereinafter cited as Dash].
20. ABA Project, *supra* note 8, at 144.
21. *Id..*
22. Dash, *supra* note 19, at 622.
23. Ex parte Milligan, 4 Wall. 2 (1866).
24. Frankel, *The Search for Truth: An Umpireal View,* 123 U.Pa. L. Rev. 1031,1034 (1975) [hereinafter cited as Frankel].
25. Brown v. Elliot, 225 U.S. 392,402 (1911).
26. Freedman, *supra* note 3, at 983.
27. Johnson v. Zerbst, 304 U.S. 452,462 (1938).
28. Powell v. Alabama, 287 U.S. 45,68,69 (1932).

29. Gideon v. Wainwright, 372 U.S. 335 (1963).
30. *Id.,* at 342.
31. *Id.,* at 344.
32. *Id.,* at 346.
33. Argersinger v. Hamlin, 407 U.S. 25,37 (1972).
34. Escobedo v. Illinois, 378 U.S. 478 (1964).
35. Miranda v. Arizona, 384 U.S. 436 (1966).
36. United States v. Wade, 380 U.S. 218 (1967), *after initiation of criminal judicial proceedings.*
37. Hamilton v. Alabama, 368 U.S. 52 (1961).
38. Coleman v. Illinois, 399 U.S. 1 (1970).
39. Douglas v. California, 372 U.S. 353 (1963), *limited to appeals of right in* Ross v. Moffitt, 417 U.S. 600 (1974).
40. ABA Project, *supra* note 8, at 147.
41. *Id.,* at 145.
42. Gideon v. Wainwright, 372 U.S. 335 (1963).
43. Miranda v. Arizona, 384 U.S. 436,466 (1966).
44. Dash, *supra* note 19, at 603.
45. LEVY, ORIGINS OF THE FIFTH AMENDMENT 432 (1968).
46. Grievance Comm. v. Rottner, 152 Conn. 59, 203 A.2d 82 (1964).
47. Dash, *supra* note 19, at 600.
48. Frankel, *supra* note 24, at 1037.
49. Escobedo v. Illinois, 378 U.S. 478,491 (1964).
50. Watts v. Indiana, 338 U.S. 49,59 (1949) (separable opinion).
51. LAWYERS ETHICS, *supra* note 11, at 3.
52. U.S. Const. Amend. V.
53. Counselman v. Hitchcock, 142 U.S. 547 (1892).
54. GRISWOLD, THE FIFTH AMENDMENT TODAY 7 (1955).
55. Callan & David, *Professional Responsibility and the Duty of Confidentiality: Disclosure of Client Misconduct in Our Adversary System,* 29 Rutgers L. Rev. 332,366 (1976) [hereinafter cited as *Disclosure of Client Misconduct*].
56. *Id.,* at 367.
57. LAWYERS ETHICS, *supra* note 11, at 4,5.
58. Couch v. United States, 409 U.S. 322 (1973).
59. *Id.,* at 329.
60. Kastigar v. United States, 406 U.S. 441 (1972).
61. Maness v. Meyers, 419 U.S. 520 (1975).
62. United States v. Kasmir, 425 U.S. 4154 (1976).
63. Bursey v. Weatherford, 45 U.S.L.W. 4154 (1977).
64. ABA Committee on Professional Ethics, Opinion No. 23 (1930) [hereinafter cited as ABA Ethics]; ABA Code, *supra* note 7, EC 7-19.
65. Bowles v. United States, 50 F.2d 848,851 (4th Cir. 1931).
66. ABA Code, *supra* note 7, EC 7-27.
67. *Id.,* Disciplinary Rule 7-102. [Disciplinary Rules will hereinafter be referred to as DR in both text and notes.].
68. *Id.,* DR 7-101.
69. *Id.,* Canon 6.
70. *Id.,* DR 7-101(A)(3).
71. *Id.,* EC 6-1.
72. *Id.,* DR 4-101.

73. State v. Kociolek, 23 N.J. 400, 129 A.2d 417,425 (1957).
74. United States v. Valencia, 541 F.2d 618,622-23 (6th Cir. 1976); State v. Kociolek, 23 N.J. 400, 129 A.2d 417, 425 (1957); Tarlow, *Witness for the Prosecution: A New Role for the Defense Lawyer,* 1 Nat. J. On Crim. Def. 331,336 (1975) [hereinafter cited as Tarlow].
75. ABA Code, *supra* note 7, EC 4-1.
76. Greenough v. Gaskell, 1 Myl. & K. 98, 39 Eng. Rep. 618 (1833) (Lord Chancellor Brougham).
77. Freedman, *supra* note 3, at 485.
78. Freedman, *Professional Responsibility of the Criminal Defense Lawyer: The Three Hardest Questions,* 64 Mich. L. Rev. 1469,1479-80 (1966).
79. Freedman, *supra* note 3, at 485.
80. Handgards v. Johnson & Johnson, 413 F.Supp. 926,929 (N.D. Cal. 1976); Valente v. Pepsico, Inc., 68 F.R.D. 361,367 (D.Del. 1975); Int. Tel. & Tel. v. United Tel. Co. of Florida, 60 F.R.D. 177,185 (D.C.Fla. 1973); ABA Ethics, *supra* note 64, Opinion No. 91 (1933); 8 WIGMORE. EVIDENCE § 2291 (McNaughton rev.) [hereinafter cited as Wigmore].
81. ABA Ethics, *supra* note 64, Opinion No. 250 (1943); Thornton, Attorneys at Law §94 (1914); 2 Meechem Agency § 2297 (2d ed. 1914).
82. ABA Code, *supra* note 7, EC 4-1.
83. BENTHAM. Rationale of Judicial Evidence (1827), 7 THE WORKS OF JEREMY BENTHAM 473-75, 477, 479 (Bowring ed. 1842).
84. Wigmore, *supra* note 80, § 2291.
85. BENTHAM. Rationale of Judicial Evidence (1827), 7 THE WORKS OF JEREMY BENTHAM 473-75, 477, 479 (Bowring ed. 1942).
86. United States v. United Shoe Machinery Corp., 89 F. Supp. 357,358 (D.Mass. 1950); Wigmore, *supra* note 80, § 2291.
87. ABA Code, *supra* note 7, EC 7-19.
88. Wigmore, *supra* note 80, § 2292.
89. United States v. United Shoe Machinery Corp., 89 F.Supp. 357,358 (D.Mass. 1950); *Legal Ethics, supra* note 1, at 344; McCORMICK. EVIDENCE § 91 (2d ed. 1972) [hereinafter cited as McCormick].
90. *Disclosure of Client Misconduct, supra* note 55, at 22-23 n.62.
91. Green v. Fuller, 159 Wash. 691, 294 P.1037,1039 (1930); McCormick, *supra* note 89, § 91.
92. Edwards, *Hard Answers for Hard Questions: Dissenting in Part From Freedman's Views on the Attorney-Client Privilege,* 11 Crim. L. Bull. 478,482 (1975) [hereinafter cited as Edwards].
93. *See supra* note 79.
94. United States v. Couch, 409 U.S. 322 (1973).
95. State v. Olwell, 64 Wash.2d 828, 394 P.2d 681,683 (1964).
96. United States v. Oborn, 409 F.Supp. 406,411 (D.Ore. 1975).
97. Bursey v. Weatherford, 45 U.S.L.W. 4154 (1977); Tarlow, *supra* note 74, at 336.
98. N.Y. Civ. Prac. Law § 4503, note 15 (McKinney 1963).
99. McCormick, *supra* note 89, § 93.
100. *Id..*
101. *Id..*
102. *Id..*
103. United States v. Santobello, 404 U.S. 257,260-61 (1971).
104. Dash, *supra* note 19, at 627.

105. N.Y. Civ. Prac. Law § 4503, note 15 (McKinney 1963).
106. McCormick, *supra* note 89, § 95.
107. Gebhardt v. United Rys. Co., 220 S.W. 677,599 (Mo. 1920); Clark v. State, 261 S.W.2d 339 (Tex.Cr. 1953), *cert. denied* 346 U.S. 855.
108. Edwards, *supra* note 92, at 480-81.
109. N.Y. Civ. Prac. Law § 4503 (McKinney 1963).
110. *Id.,* note 15.
111. ABA Code, *supra* note 7, DR 4-101(C)(3).
112. N.Y. Civ. Prac. Law § 4503, note 15 (McKinney 1963).
113. Duplan Corp. v. Deering Milliken, Inc., 397 F.Supp. 1146,1172 (D.S.C. 1974).
114. ABA Code, *supra* note 7, EC 4-4.
115. *Id.,* DR 4-101(C)(1-4).
116. *Id.,* EC 4-5.
117. *Id.,* EC 4-6; ABA Ethics, *supra* note 64, Opinion No. 154 (1936).
118. *Id.,* EC 4-4.
119. *Id.,* DR 4-101(C)(4), n.19.
120. *Disclosure of Client Misconduct, supra* note 55, at 358, n. 114.
121. *Id.,* at 358, n. 115.
122. ABA Code, *supra* note 7, DR 7-102(B)(1).
123. Duplan Corp. V. Deering Milliken, Inc., 397 F.Supp. 1146,1172 (D.S.C. 1974).
124. *Legal Ethics, supra* note 1, at 230.
125. *Id..*
126. *Id..*
127. ABA Ethics, *supra* note 64, Opinion No. 156 (1936).
128. N.Y. Civ. Prac. Law § 4503 (McKinney 1963).
129. Hoffman v. United States, 341 U.S. 479,486 (1951).
130. ABA Code, *supra* note 7, Canon 9.
131. Murphy v. Waterfront Commission, 378 U.S. 52,93-94 (1964) (White, J. concurring); Kastigar v. United States, 406 U.S. 441,443-444 (1972).
132. Kastigar v. United States, 406 U.S. 441,444 (1972).
133. *Id.,* at 446.
134. *In re* Michaelson, 511 F.2d 882 (9th Cir. 1975).
135. *Id.,* at 893.
136. Freedman, *supra* note 3, at 484, quoting from,
137. ABA Code, *supra* note 7, DR 5-102(B).
138. Tarlow, *supra* note 74, at 363.
139. ABA Code, *supra* note 7, DR 7-101.
140. *Id.,* EC 7-3; ABA Ethics, *supra* note 64, Opinion No. 314 (1965).
141. People v. Terra, 303 N.Y. 332, 102 N.E.2d 576, 577, 111 N.Y.S.2d (1951).
142. Freedman, *supra* note 3, at 486.
143. *Id..*
144. *In re* Ryder, 263 F.Supp. 360 (E.D.Va. 1967).
145. State v. Sullivan, 60 Wash.2d 214, 373 P.2d 474,476 (1962).
146. *Id..*
147. Freedman, *supra* note 3, at 488-489.
148. State v. Sullivan, 60 Wash.2d 214, 373 P.2d 474,476 (1962).
149. Smotherman v. Beto, 276 F.Supp. 579,588 (N.D. Texas 1967).
150. ABA Project, *supra* note 8, § 4.1.

151.   Von Moltke v. Gillres, 332 U.S. 708,721 (1948); Kott v. Green, 303 F.Supp. 821,823 (N.D. Ohio 1968); Abraham v. State, 228 Ind. 171, 91 N.E.2d 358, 360 (1950).
152.   Turner v. Maryland, 303 F.2d 507 (4th Cir. 1962).
153.   Bell v. Alabama, 367 F.2d 243,247 (5th Cir. 1966); Brubaker v. Dickinson, 310 F.2d 30,35,39 (9th Cir. 1962); Jones v. Cunningham, 297 F.2d 851,855 (4th Cir. 1962); Kott v. Green, 303 F.Supp. 821,823 (N.D. Ohio 1968); Abraham v. State, 228 Ind. 171, 91 N.E.2d 358,360 (1950).
154.   State v. Sullivan, 60 Wash.2d 214, 373 P.2d 474,476 (1962).
155.   Fed. R. Crim. P.16 (b)(1)(A).
156.   Fed. R. Crim. P.16 (b)(2).
157.   ABA Ethics, *supra* note 64, Opinion No. 150 (1936).

Attempting to Regulate
Perjurious Testimony:
The Massachusetts Experience

John A. Pino

Canon Seven of the Code of Professional Responsibility states that "a lawyer should represent a client zealously within the bounds of the law." However, neither zealous representation nor the bounds of the law are clearly delineated in the Code of Professional Responsibility. Therefore, determining whether a given course of action is within the limits of permissible adversary conduct often raises perplexing issues. Resolution of these issues often requires consideration of the moral and ethical rules which have been inculcated in us since childhood—the Ten Commandments, the Golden Rule, and a myriad of other standards which society has adopted to separate right from wrong. Thus, it is not surprising that some confusion exists as to the propriety of certain practices in the course of representing a client. This essay is aimed toward clarifying the bounds of zealous representation, and elucidating the role of a zealous advocate in criminal defense cases.

The fundamental touchstone of proper adversary conduct is the attorney's oath which is embodied in various state statutes. In Massachusetts, for example, the oath is found in General Laws, Chapter 221, Section 38, which provides:

> I solemnly swear that I will do no falsehood, nor consent to the doing of any in court; I will not wittingly or unwittingly promote or sue any false or groundless or unlawful suit nor give aid or consent to the same; I will delay no man for lucre or malice; but I will conduct myself in the office of an attorney within the courts according to the best of my knowledge and discretion, and with all good fidelity as well to the courts as my clients, so help me God.

The promise in the oath eschewing falsehoods touches upon an area in which there exists a great divergence of opinion, particularly in a criminal defense setting. Recognizing the need for explicit guidelines in this area, the American Bar Association promulgated Standard 7.7 of the "Defense Function" which provides:

(a) If the defendant has admitted to his lawyer facts which establish guilt and the lawyer's independent investigation establishes that the admissions are true but the defendant insists on his right to trial, the lawyer must advise his client against taking the witness stand to testify falsely.

(b) If, before trial, the defendant insists that he will take the stand to testify falsely, the lawyer must withdraw from the case, if that is feasible, seeking leave of the court if necessary.

(c) If withdrawal from the case is not feasible or is not permitted by the court, or if the situation arises during the trial and the defendant insists upon testifying falsely in his own behalf, it is unprofessional conduct for the lawyer to lend his aid to the perjury or use the perjured testimony. Before the defendant takes the stand in these circumstances, the lawyer should make a record of the fact that the defendant is taking the stand against the advice of counsel in some appropriate manner without revealing the fact to the court. The lawyer must confine his examination to identifying the witness as the defendant and permitting him to make his statement to the trier or the triers of the facts; the lawyer may not engage in direct examination of the defendant as a witness in the conventional manner and may not later argue the defendant's known false version of facts to the jury as worthy of belief and he may not recite or rely upon the false testimony in his closing argument.

If adopted, this standard would eliminate much of the uncertainty surrounding perjured testimony; however, section (c) appears inadvisable as a practical matter. The following hypothetical situation is illustrative:

An attorney is trying a case in which his client is a defendant in a criminal action. During the trial he learns that his client intends to proffer false testimony in an effort to avoid conviction. Accordingly, counsel warns his client about the sanctions associated with perjury but is unable to dissuade him. The attorney then requests the court's permission to withdraw from the case but his request is denied.

Recall that under these circumstances Standard 7.7 (c) enjoins counsel from conducting more than a superficial examination, limiting his questioning to "identifying the witness as the defendant and permitting him to make his statement to the trier[s] of facts." It appears as though such an abbreviated, direct examination of counsel's own witness would be tantamount to an admission that the testimony was perjured. Certainly, the trial judge and opposing counsel would be apprised of this fact, since they would no doubt be aware of the ABA standards in this area. Arguably, the jury's evaluation of the defendant's testimony would not be affected by examination in accordance with Standard 7.7 (c), since they would not know of the rule. However, counsel's limited examination of the defendant would sharply contrast the more detailed examination of other witnesses, and after noting this difference, the jury might well conclude that the testimony was tainted.

It would thus appear that a lawyer's adherence to Standard 7.7 (c) may effectively prejudice his client's right to a fair trial, as guaranteed by the Sixth and Fourteenth Amendments. Because it was felt that the likelihood of obtaining this result was considerable, the Massachusetts and Boston Bar Associations did not include Standard 7.7 (c) in a petition to the Supreme Judicial Court of Massachusetts (which urged the adoption of various standards relating to the prosecution and defense of criminal cases). Their petition did, however, urge the adoption of sections (a) and (b) of Standard 7.7 of the "Defense Function" . . . .

Perjury: Stay In or Pull Out?

Neil Pickett

**ABA BATTLE LOOMS OVER PROPOSED
REVISION OF STANDARD COVERING LAWYER
RESPONSIBILITY WHEN CLIENT LIES**

WASHINGTON, D.C.—A major storm is brewing within the American Bar Association over a lawyer's responsibility to a client who intends to commit perjury. The thunder should start next month when the House of Delegates meets to consider proposed revisions in the association's Standards for Criminal Justice at the ABA mid-year conference.

Several of the changes drafted by the Standing Committee for Association Standards for Criminal Justice will be controversial. But the fiercest debate will probably center on the perjury section, which it left essentially unchanged. Indeed, the perjury suggestion is the only one the powerful ABA committee strongly opposes.

The ABA standards, first published in 1968, are "a general statement of what the law and legal practices should be in a certain area of criminal justice," according to W. Randolph Baker, director of the committee's project to update the standards. The original standards were the first in the criminal law area, and were incorporated in some part in almost every state criminal code. Recent court decisions and policy developments prompted the ABA to begin revising the standards two years ago. Revisions in ten areas of criminal justice have already been completed.

Drafters of the revisions hope to complete the process at the mid-year conference, when changes in standards for the remaining six areas will be presented for approval. But whether several of the standing committee's proposals will be accepted by the House of Delegates remains unclear.

Due Process Threat

The current ABA perjury standard requires and attorney who knows a client intends to commit perjury to withdraw from a case, if the client ignores the attorney's admonitions not to testify falsely. However, two recent court decisions, one on the state and the other on the federal level, made it clear that the ABA standard posed a threat to a defendant's right to due process under the law.

In *Lowery* v. *Cardwell*—575 F.2d 727 (1978)—the Ninth Circuit U.S. Court of Appeals held that counsel's failure to argue the defendant's version of the facts to a fact-finder constituted an "announcement" that counsel believed the defendant testified falsely. The court also ruled that the committing of perjury did not, in and of itself, deny the defendant the right to a fair trial.

As a result of this decision, and another handed down by the North Carolina Supreme Court in *State* v. *Robinson*—224 S.E.2d 1974 (1976)—the standing committee revised the perjury standard to allow an attorney to remain with his client, if the perjury is discovered once trial is under way. The revised standard still discourages an attorney from using perjured testimony to build a defense: "As to matters for which it is believed the defendant will offer perjurious testimony, the lawyer should seek to avoid direct examination of the defendant in the conventional manner."

The Council of the ABA Section on Criminal Justice, on the recommendations of an ad hoc committee on ethics and discipline, opposes both the current standard and the revisions, which it argues do not meet the *Lowery* or *State* tests. "The new proposal really doesn't change much, and it runs counter to the court decisions," said North Carolina Supreme Court Judge James Exxum, a member of the ad hoc committee and an author of the *State* v. *Robinson* opinion. Mr. Exxum said he strongly supports the council's alternative proposal, which would permit an attorney to treat perjured testimony "as any other evidence," once the attorney has made strong efforts to discourage the client from testifying falsely.

"Stay in There"

"In my experience, very few clients follow through on their threat to perjure themselves," Judge Exxum said. He added, "We're saying to the lawyer, 'stay in there with your client and keep counseling against perjury.' "

According to Judge Exxum, the council's alternative will do more to prevent perjury than the standing committee's proposal, which he says "is designed more to disassociate the legal profession from the perjury." He said that "given the dictates of the adversary system and the requirements of due process, there is little an attorney can do but use perjured testimony as evidence."

However, in its comments on the revised standards, the standing committee notes it is "not prepared to recommend adoption of a policy favoring the use of known perjured testimony by a lawyer." Asks revisions director Baker, "How can the ABA come out in favor of perjury?"

The perjury debate will not be the only controversy facing the House of Delegates as it considers the revised standards. Several other recommendations are sure to provoke strong opposition from parts of the ABA constituency.

The most far-reaching of the changes is a proposal to allow radio, television, and still photographic coverage of trial proceedings "subject to a number of constraints." The proposal was defeated last yeatr by the House of Delegates, but the committee is hoping it will reconsider.

"We're just trying to recognize the reality of the situation. Twenty-one states are already either experimenting with or allowing cameras in the courtroom," said Mr. Baker. He added, "We're just recommending that it be tried on a state-by-state basis. That's not exactly a radical suggestion."

The new standard would state that "television, radio and photographic coverage of judicial proceedings is not per se inconsistent with the right to a fair trial." It adds that "such coverage may be permitted if it would be unobtrusive and would not distract the attention of trial participants, demean the dignity of the proceedings or otherwise interfere with the fair administration of justice."

Plea Bargaining

Another proposal expected to draw opposition from the judiciary would allow judges a limited role in the plea negotiation process. The current ABA standard says bluntly that "the trial judge should not participate in plea discussions."

Again, Mr. Baker said, the revision was made to keep the standards in tune with present practices. "In many areas judges already participate in plea bargaining, even if they're not supposed to," he noted.

The revised standard would allow for judicial participation only at the request of either counsel, usually when an impasse in the negotiations has been reached. "There is value in having an objective third party step in and resolve differences when the defense counsel and the prosecutor can't reach an agreement. It's neutral arbitration," said Richard Kuh (of New York's Warshaw, Burstein, Cohen, Schlesinger & Kuh), the chairman of the ABA's Criminal Justice Section committee on plea negotiations. Mr. Kuh said some judges will oppose the revision because "they see their role as confined to particular cases and have little concern for the general administration of justice," which is better served by the new standard.

Defense Services

The standing committee has also "almost totally rewritten" the standards on provision of defense services, in order to "give defenders and assigned counsel independence of action," according to Mr. Baker. The recommendations include a suggestion that each judicial jurisdiction should provide both organized defense services and assignments to private attorneys for indigent defendants.

The revised standards also recommend that "the selection of public defense lawyers for specific cases should not normally be made by the judiciary or elected officials, but should be arranged by the administrator of the defender program." This change is designed to reduce defendants' suspicions that their court-appointed counsel are not fully committed to their defense.

In addition, under the revised standards, a case quota would be established for public defenders to limit the amount of work they can do. "Lawyers should not ethically take on more cases than they can handle," Mr. Baker said.

The final major revision in the criminal justice standards would allow prosecutors to make sentencing recommendations to a judge. Currently, only the defense counsel may make such a recommendation, and the original ABA standard supported that concept. According to Mr. Baker, many judges would like to hear the prosecutor's opinion on sentencing before making a decision, and the standing committee felt such an opinion, when requested by the court, is entirely appropriate.

Part III

Regulating Professional Ethics: The Alger Hiss Reinstatement Controversy

The Brief for the Petitioner, Alger Hiss

John F. Groden
Harold Rosenwald
John M. Reed

Issues Presented

1. Do *Matter of Keenan*—314 Mass. 544 (1943)—and *Centracchio, Petitioner*—345 Mass. 342 (1963)—establish any principle which leads to the conclusion that an unreversed, twenty-five year old conviction for perjury [a] precludes consideration of the evidence of present good character by an otherwise qualified applicant for readmission to the bar, [b] prevents such evidence from being entitled to any weight, and [c] compels denial of the petition?

2. Do the foregoing cases or the spirit of those cases prevent readmission of an attorney who, after such passage of time following the original disbarment, applies for readmission, satisfactorily demonstrates good character (aside from the conviction), and whose application is not opposed by the bar association which originally sought the disbarment?

3. In the circumstances set forth in the previous two questions, do the *Keenan* and *Centracchio* cases mean (a) that one who has constantly maintained his innocence of the original charge must, in order to show repentance and reform, either admit guilt of the original charge or be precluded forever from practicing the profession to which he is trained, or do they rather mean (b) that the twenty-five year old conviction is a judicial fact which must be weighed along with other facts in determining the outcome of the readmission proceeding?

Statement of the Case

This is a petition for readmission to the bar of Alger Hiss. The matter was reserved and reported by Mr. Justice Reardon on April 15, 1975—on the application for reinstatement; the affidavit of the applicant Mr. Hiss; the order of reference to the Board of Bar Overseers; the findings and recommendations of the Board of Bar Overseers; and the exhibits and transcript of the proceedings before the board (R. 121).

193

The application itself was filed on or about November 4, 1974. Mr. Hiss prayed that he be examined for reinstatement as an attorney and if found qualified, reinstated as such (R. 2). With the application, Mr. Hiss submitted an affidavit containing statements (many of which were later adopted by the board in its findings) (R. 4).

On November 11, 1974, the clerk of the Supreme Judicial Court for the County of Suffolk sent a copy of the petition for reinstatement (on the direction of the chief justice) to the Board of Bar Overseers. (Exhibit D, R.74). (A written order of reference was made on January 31, 1975 [R. 12]. We assume that such order, though subsequent to the board's hearing of the matter, is confirmatory of the original reference reflected in the letter of the clerk).

Pursuant to sec. 3.63, subsection F, of its rules of procedure, the board provided Mr. Hiss with a questionnaire on various aspects of his background, which is a part of the record in the present matter (Exhibit C, R. 60).

An evidentiary hearing took place before the board on January 7, 1975. The board's findings and recommendations were filed on April 4, 1975 (R. 13).

Factual Background

1.   Mr. Hiss was born in Baltimore, Maryland, in 1904, attended Baltimore City College, Powder Point Academy, and Johns Hopkins University, from which he graduated in 1926 with an A.B. degree (Findings, at 11, R. 23).

2.   He studied at the Harvard Law School, receiving an LL.B. degree in June of 1929, and was an editor of the *Harvard Law Review* during his second and third years. From October 1929 to October 1930, Mr. Hiss was secretary to Mr. Justice Holmes of the United States Supreme Court (Ibid.).

3.   After admission to the bar of Massachusetts, Mr. Hiss was employed by the firm of Choate, Hall & Stewart in Boston from October 1930 until April 1932 (Findings, at 11, R. 23).

4.   From April 1932 until May 1933, Mr. Hiss practiced law in a New York law firm, and then moved to Washington, D.C. in May 1933. From then until April 1935, he was employed as an assistant general counsel of the Agricultural Adjustment Administration. He served briefly as legal assistant to the United States Senate Committee Investigating the Munitions Industry (R. 24 and 54), and from August 1935 until August 1936 was a special attorney in the solicitor general's office. Mr. Hiss was employed by the State Department for over a decade, until about January 1947 (R. 24)

5.   In December 1946, having had much to do with the formation of the United Nations (Findings, at 12, R. 24), Mr. Hiss was elected president of the Carnegie Endowment for International Peace (Findings at 131, R. 25).

6.   In December 1948, Mr. Hiss was indicted by a grand jury of the United States in the Southern District of New York. The charge was that of perjury before the same grand jury. There were two trials on the indictment. The first resulted in a hung jury, but the second ended in a conviction on January 25, 1950. Mr. Hiss was sentenced for five years on each count, both sentences to run concurrently. The conviction was affirmed by the Court of Appeals for the Second Circuit on March 15, 1951. *See United States* v. *Hiss*, 185 F.2d 822, *certiorari denied*, 340 U.S. 948, the opinion being part of the record herein (R. 81).

7.   As a result of the conviction, Mr. Hiss was disbarred by the Appellate Division of the Supreme Judicial Court of New York on May 2, 1950, and was disbarred by this court on a petition of the Boston Bar Association on August 1, 1952. *See Matter of Hiss, Respondent* v. *Boston Bar Association, Petitioner*, Suffolk No. 49965, Law. Having been admitted in 1936 to the Bar of the United States Supreme Court, he was disbarred there (three justices not participating) on April 27, 1953. *See Re Disbarment of Hiss*, 97 L.Ed. 1946.

8.   A motion for new trial was *denied, United States* v. *Hiss*, 107 F.Supp. 128 (S.D. N.Y. 1952), *affirmed per curiam*, 201 F.2d 372 (2d Cir. 1953), *certiorari denied*, 345 U.S. 942.

9.   After his release from the Federal Penitentiary in late November of 1954, Mr. Hiss engaged in various activities set forth in his affidavit and further discussed below in this brief.

10.   Since his release from prison, Mr Hiss has not committed and has not been charged with the commission of any offense (except the minor one of playing ball with his son in the Washington Square Park) (R. 26).

11.   Immediately upon the filing of his application for reinstatement, Mr. Hiss (by his counsel) notified the Boston Bar Association, which had been the moving party on the original disbarment in this court. (Questionnaire, item 6, R. 62). In response to an inquiry by the board, the president of the Boston Bar Association addressed a letter to the board's chairman on December 30, 1974, as follows:

On December 17, 1974, notice was sent to all members of the Council of the Boston Bar Association and to all former presidents of the Association of a special meeting to be held on December 23 concerning the application of Alger Hiss. A copy of the notice is enclosed.

At the December 23 meeting of the Council, Mr. Hiss appeared with counsel. He was questioned fully by members of the Council. After deliberations, the

Council voted that I should communicate with the Board of Bar Overseers, in favor of the application, as follows:

It is the opinion of the Council of the Boston Bar Association that Mr. Hiss's "resumption of the practice of law will not be detrimental to the integrity and standing of the bar, the administration of justice, or to the public interest" (S.J.C. Rule 4:01, section 18 [4]).

In addition to the actual vote, set forth above, I think I should convey some information about the meeting and deliberations. The Council did not feel it was within their competence to pass judgment upon the other factors set forth in section 18(4) of Rule 4:01. They considered themselves bound by the criminal conviction of Mr. Hiss and were concerned that their vote not be construed in any sense as a "political" judgment concerning it. The attendance at the meeting was the largest I have ever seen. Some members had to stand. There was much discussion among the members of their individual views for voting in favor of Mr. Hiss, but it was decided to limit the actual vote as set forth above. Apart from the problems inherent in any application for readmission to the bar, there were no arguments presented against Mr. Hiss or his application.

(R. 93-94)

How the Board Dealt with the Matter

The findings and recommendations read as a whole show (a) that there was no opposition from those contacted by the board to the Hiss reinstatement, (b) that Mr. Hiss was candid in his responses to board questions, (c) that (the conviction to one side) his moral qualifications were not questioned, but (d) that these factors were not only outweighed, but destroyed, by the outstanding conviction. "*With Mr. Hiss's conviction outstanding, unreversed, not subject to attach, and necessary for us to consider, all the other evidence of his present character cannot be of any weight.*" (Findings, at 24, R. 36) (Emphasis supplied).

On such a basis and relying on the court's remarks in *Matter of Keenan*—314 Mass. 544 (1943)—the board reached these conclusions:

1. The present good character of the petitioner "in the sense in which the word seems to be used in the controlling case law, and in the light of the petitioner's disbarment and conviction," had not been established (Findings, at 28, R. 40).

2. Subject to evidence of completion of some court defined refresher study, the petitioner is competent and sufficiently learned in the law to be readmitted (Findings at 32, R. 44).

3. The readmission of the petitioner "would have an adverse effect on the administration of justice, the public interest and the standing of the Bar" (Findings, at 36, R. 48). The board added, however,

We believe ourselves bound by the decisions of this Court to make the findings above set forth.

The board then said that this case may call into question the interpretation and application of the stated principles of law which the board relied on (Findings, at 36, R. 48). The board further stated that the reconsideration of those principles, if appropriate, was not a matter for its action (Findings, at 36-37, R. 48-49). The board refrained from recommending or suggesting that such reconsideration was necessary, as it was not part of its function. The board therefore recommended, "in the present state of the law as we read it," that the petition be denied (Findings, at 37, R. 49).

Yet, the board had stated (at 27, R. 39):

> Nevertheless, the Board, if it were free to consider the matter in the absence of the only evidence to the contrary (the conviction), would unanimously find that Mr. Hiss is presently of good moral character and that he would almost certainly not commit any serious crime if readmitted to the bar.

And, in addition, the board had received a vote of the Council of the Boston Bar Association to the effect,

> It is the opinion of the Council of the Boston Bar Association that Mr. Hiss's "resumption of the practice of law will not be detrimental to the integrity and standing of the bar, the administration of justice, or to the public interest."

Summary of Argument

Rule 4:01 of the rules of this court, section 18(4), places the burden on the applicant to establish (a) his moral qualifications, competency and learning in law and (b) that his readmission will not be detrimental to the integrity and standing of the bar, the administration of justice, or the public interest (Page 12). This guideline calls for a case-by-case approach to the matter of reinstatement (Page 13).

The board, in reliance upon its reading of the *Keenan* and *Centracchio* cases, reasoned that, with Mr. Hiss's conviction outstanding, no other evidence of present character can be of any weight (Page 14). There was extensive evidence of Mr. Hiss's good character which the board accepted (Pages 15-19). *Keenan* was interpreted by the board, however, to require repentance and information, which (Mr. Hiss having always claimed his original innocence) creates an obvious dilemma.

In this situation the board misread *Keenan*. There the court confined its decision "to this case" (Page 24).

The present application differs from *Keenan* and *Centracchio* in that, unlike the situation in those cases, (a) the Hiss application is not opposed by the Boston Bar Association, which brought the original information, (b) the conviction arises in a vastly different context and Mr. Hiss gives clear assurance of his conduct in the future, and (c) a far more substantial period of time has elapsed since the time of the conviction. (Pages 28-34). We submit that the circumstances as a whole, the details of which are set forth in the board's findings, show that Mr. Hiss should be reinstated.

Argument

The Hiss reinstatement should be initially viewed in the light of the general standards of section 18(4) of Rule 4:01 rather than the mechanical approach adopted by the board derived from language of the Keenan opinion.

The present case is the first to arise under the new bar rules pertaining to reinstatement, and it is obvious that those rules should provide the initial guideline as to philosophy.

The rules suggest an approach which is consistent with the present reinstatement application:

> On any petition thus referred, the hearing committee shall promptly hear the respondent-attorney who shall have the burden of demonstrating that he has the moral qualifications, competency and learning in law required for admission to practice law in this commonwealth, and that his resumption of the practice of law will not be detrimental to the integrity and standing of the bar, the administration of justice, or to the public interest (Section 18[4]).

It is clear that the standard under section 18(4) permits a case-by-case approach to the reinstatement problem. In the following portions of the brief (section II), we contend that the *Keenan* case permits, and indeed calls for, such an approach, rather than the form of reasoning adopted by the board.

The Keenan case is inapplicable to the present facts

The board's findings and recommendations were made principally in reliance upon the board's reading of two decisions of this court denying petitions for readmission to practice law: *Matter of Keenan*—314 Mass. 544 (1944)—and *Centracchio, Petitioner*—345 Mass. 342 (1963).

In *Keenan*, the court said that disbarment for the offense there involved was "not only an adjudication of the original guilt, and therefore of lack of moral character at the time of the offense, but it also continues to be evidence of the most convincing kind against reinstatement" (314 Mass., at 549). *See also Matter of Keenan*—313 Mass. 186, 218-219 (1943). In *Centracchio,* this language was referred to (345 Mass., at 346), and the offenses of the petitioner upon which his disbarment had been based were held to outweigh the findings of his present good character in the proceedings for reinstatement.

If these words, taken as a categorical mandate, were to mean that a petitioner's proof of present good character can never overcome the incriminating effect of a serious offense upon which his disbarment was predicated, then his burden of proof would be tantamount to the hopeless task of Sisyphus. The board, bowing to its understanding of the authority of the *Keenan* and *Centracchio* cases, and adopting an extreme interpretation of the opinions, ruled that Mr. Hiss could not overcome the effect of his conviction. *See* Findings, at 24, R. 36, mentioned above, where the board said:

> With Mr. Hiss's conviction outstanding, unreversed, not subject to attach, and necessary for us to consider, all the other evidence of his present character cannot be of any weight.

We do not believe that the court intended that every disbarment for a serious offense should be definitive and permanent. The court further (314 Mass., at 551) made it clear that it was "confining its attention to this case as outlined above." Richard Wait, Esq., one of the participants in the drafting of the rules governing the hearings before the board (Tr. 35), spoke on behalf of the petitioner against any such doctrine of finality, as follows:

> Well, I think that the fact of conviction unquestionably justified the decision to disbar at the time. I think that it would be an awful thing, really awful, if an intelligent public felt that that was the absolute end of the road.

> I quite agree that the authority that would reinstate or is being asked to reinstate must be thoroughly satisfied that the taint, if you choose to call it that, left by a criminal conviction must be considered, but it cannot—in justice, fairness, decency—be absolutely final (Tr., at 32-33).

Indeed, in *Keenan* this court left open the clear possibility that the burden of proving the good character of a petitioner convicted of a serious offense can be met "through proof, for example, of long continued, unselfish, and outstanding service to mankind, or possibly in some other way . . . " (314 Mass., at 549).

As the board found (Findings, at 15-16), and the uncontradicted evidence proves, Mr. Hiss has lectured at many American schools, colleges, and universities, including Harvard, Princeton, Wesleyan, Trinity, Olivet, Cortland College of New York University, the New England School of Law, the New School for Social Research, University of Virginia, and Johns Hopkins; has conducted seminars at some of those institutions; had made three trips to England for similar purposes, including appearances on television; has authored a book on his case, and has written book reviews for legal periodicals; and has edited, at the request of the late Professor Mark deWolfe Howe, an abridged edition of the Holmes-Laski letters. He has lectured and written *inter alia* on subjects relating to the United Nations and to American foreign policy.

Thus, for a period in excess of twenty years, petitioner has engaged in scholarly, intellectual pursuits, lecturing to students and contributing to their education in the fields of his competence, and writing and editing books on legal or related subjects.

Furthermore, there was substantial uncontradicted additional evidence of petitioner's good moral character. While carrying on the above activities, he has earned a modest livelihood as an assistant to the president of a small manufacturing firm in New York City, and later as a salesman of stationery supplies and printing for Davison-Bluth of Nre York City. (Findings, at 14-15, R. 26-27). On the basis of the testimony of the petitioner's present employer (Tr. 45, et seq.), the board stated:

> We find that he is well regarded in the business he has last undertaken, and enjoys there an excellent reputation for honesty and integrity in the conduct of business affairs (Findings, at 25, R. 37).

The board found that petitioner, in testifying before the board, showed an "upright and persuasive bearing, humility and reasonableness" (Findings, at 22, R. 34); that he has conducted himself in a law-abiding manner since his release from prison, refraining from "any activity which might be considered the practice of law" and failing to engage in "criminal activity of any type" (Findings, at 14, R. 26); and that he has obeyed this court's order of disbarment (Findings, at 24, R. 36).

Finally there was persuasive evidence of the petitioner's past and present good moral character in the form of a letter from Mr. Justice Stanley Reed, retired, of the United States Supreme Court; an affidavit of Erwin N. Griswold, Esq., former solicitor general of the United States, former dean of the Harvard Law School and a member of this bar (Tr. 92-95); and testimony and affidavits of two law professors, also members of this bar, and of other prominent lawyers.

But for the supposed constraints of the *Keenan* language, the board would have found the petitioner to be of good moral character at the present time. Thus, the board stated (Findings, at 27, R. 39):

> Nevertheless, the Board, if it were free to consider the matter in the absence of the only evidence to the contrary (the conviction), would unanimously find that Mr. Hiss is presently of good moral character and that he would almost certainly not commit any serious crime if readmitted to the bar.

·

In *Keenan,* this court based its decision in part on the ground that the applicant for readmission had failed to establish the requisite complete change of moral character. On this point the court stated (314 Mass., at 50):

> There was little evidence of repentance or reform. The respondent's attitude seems to have been that he would recognize the binding character of the court's decision, but that he had never in fact been guilty as charged and could not repent for what he did not admit.

Alger Hiss does not challenge the *res judicata* effect of his conviction for perjury. Nevertheless, he has steadfastly denied that he was guilty of that offense. *See* Findings, at 18. Indeed, at the hearing before the board, he stated with complete candor (Tr. 148, Findings, at 26, R. 38):

> I have not had any complete change in moral character. I am the same person I have been, I believe, throughout my life. If that's the law of Massachusetts (referring to a quoted portion of the *Keenan* opinion), I am excluded.

In these circumstances the board concluded that "the task of a petitioner such as Mr. Hiss, who continues to assert his innocence (of a serious crime), to satisfy this board of his present good character, becomes logically impossible for him to meet under the law, as the board conceives the law to be" (Findings, at 17-18, R. 29-30).

Interpreting the *Keenan* holding in the way that the board applied it in the case at bar, the premise emerges that, since the petitioner has been disbarred because of his conviction of perjury, in order to be eligible for reinstatement to the bar he must provide "absolute assurance of a complete change of moral character" (*Keenan,* 314 Mass., at 549). He has at all times denied that he was guilty of the offense and cannot prove his repentance or contrition in respect of a crime which, as he insists, he never committed. Accordingly, he has failed to establish a complete change of his moral character. "Logic" then compels denial of his application for reinstatement.

If we assume that petitioner knows in his own mind and conscience that he was not guilty of the offense, the syllogism leaves him on the horns of a hopeless dilemma. He can either accept the finality of his disbarment and at least retain his own self-respect and personal integrity; or he can now falsely admit that he was guilty of the original charge, and claim that he has since repented and has undergone the required complete change of his moral character.

The injustice of such a syllogism is apparent when it is realized that it gives a preference to one who admits the commission of an offense over one who denies his guilt. We respectfully submit that a syllogistic rule which may result in a gross miscarriage of justice if a denial of guilt is truthfully made, and which encourages a confession of guilt by an innocent person, creates a distortion in the law which requires correction.

The very nature of applications for admission compels an *ad hoc* determination with respect to each individual. *See* Rule 4:01, section 18(4), quoted in section I of this brief. The tests are clear—(a) legal qualifications, (b) moral character, and (c) integrity of the bar in the eyes of the public.

Applying these tests, all the evidence must be considered and weighed as a whole—testimony of knowledgeable witnesses, life record, including the prior conviction, disbarment, protestations of innocence.

The error of the board was in concluding that everything else was entitled to no weight in the face of nonrepentance as suggested by the *Keenan* case.

The effect was to deny the availability of material evidence to the court, which encroaches on the court's jurisdiction to determine the matter on the basis of all the factors.

A judicially foreclosed fact is not necessarily an actual fact. Mr. Hiss may not be able to retry the conviction, but a protestation of innocence should be weighed like any other testimony. The view that *Keenan* established an immutable principle of compelled repentance, applicable to all cases, means that the bar applicant, however innocent in fact if not in law, must make the same painful choice as when offered a pardon.

> Circumstances may be made to bring innocence under the penalties of the law. If so brought, escape by confession of guilt implied in the acceptance of a pardon may be rejected—preferring to be the victim of the law rather than its acknowledged transgressor—preferring death even to such certain infamy. *(Burdick* v. *United States,* 236 U.S. 79, 90-91, 59 L.Ed. 476,480 [1915]).

Finally, *Keenan* does not purport to stand for any such principle. At page 551, the court expressly states that it confines its decision "to this case."

The following, from *Swan* v. *Justices of the Superior Court*—222 Mass. 542,545 (1915)—has been stated may times in many ways:

> Every opinion must be read in the light of the facts then presented. Statements of rules as applicable to that case cannot be taken out of their context and stretched to different circumstances not before the mind of the court. *Cawley* v. *Jean,* 218 Mass. 263,270; *Carroll* v. *Carroll,* 16 How. 275,286; *Pollock* v. *Farmers' Loan & Trust Co.,* 157 U.S. 429,574; *Quinn* v. *Leathem* (1901) A.C. 495,506. The reason for this rule is plain. As was said by Chief Justice Marshall in *Cohens* v. *Virginia*—6 Wheat 264,399—"The question actually before the court is investigated with care, and considered in its full extent. Other principles, which may serve to illustrate it, are considered in their relation to the case decided, but their possible bearing on all other cases is seldom completely investigated."

The issue raised by the *Keenan* language quoted by the board was presented to the Maryland Supreme Court in *In re Braverman*—271 Md. 196,316 A.2d 246 (1974). Braverman was convicted in 1952 of a conspiracy to teach and advocate the violent overthrow of the government in violation of the Smith Act. He was fined $1,000 and sentenced to imprisonment for three years. As a result of this conviction, he was disbarred in 1955. Eighteen years later, Braverman filed a petition for reinstatement to the Maryland bar in the Maryland Supreme Court. The supreme court referred the petition for an evidentiary hearing to a panel of three Maryland lower court judges. *In re Braverman*—269 Md. 661,309 A.2d 468 (1973). The Maryland State Bar Association of Baltimore City informed the panel that there had been no evidence presented to its executive council of anything contrary to Braverman's good character.

The three-judge panel concluded that Braverman had established his fitness to practice law and recommended his reinstatement. In its report to the supreme court, the panel dealt with the dilemma of Braverman in his refusal to acknowledge his guilt of the offense for which he had been disbarred as follows:

> As to Petitioner's reformation, the Baltimore Bar Association raises the philosophical question of how petitioner has proven his reformation when he refuses to recognize the existence of any misconduct from which to reform. Since petitioner is adamant in his belief in his innocence, he is consistent in not expressing any repentance. While he seems to hinder his cause by not taking what might be the easier way of confession and contrition, the intellectual honesty of his position must be recognized. Reform has been defined as: to change from worse to better, to bring from a bad to a good state. We believe petitioner has demonstrated his reformation without an expression of contrition from him. Starting from the premise that his guilt was conclusively proven, we find his conduct since conviction to be a complete turnabout from that which resulted in his conviction. We find his conduct since conviction to be totally inconsistent with the probability of repetition of his previous misconduct. We believe this constitutes reformation as this term is used in the present proceedings (271 Md., at 201-202).

The supreme court accepted the recommendation of the panel of judges and reinstated Braverman to the bar, with two of the seven judges dissenting.

The instant case is similar in important respects to the *Braverman* case. It is vastly different from the *Keenan* and *Contracchio* cases.

First: The positions of the bar associations as taken in these cases differed. The bar associations were the disciplinary agencies at the relevant times of disbarment. The opinions of bar associations in cases like the present are entitled to consideration. The Board of Bar Overseers in this case, believing it was constrained by a rule of law, gave no weight to such opinion.

In the case at bar, the Boston Bar Association had originally initiated the proceedings for the disbarment of petitioner by filing an information in this court (Findings, at 5; Exhibit E); but, in the present proceedings, after its council had heard, observed and interrogated petitioner, that association reported nothing derogatory concerning petitioner, voted that petitioner's "resumption of the practice of law will not be detrimental to the integrity and standing of the bar, the administration of justice, or to the public interest," and declined the board's invitation to participate in its hearing (Findings, at 8,32-33; Exhibits J, J-1). The Association of the Bar of the City of New York, which had instituted the proceedings for petitioner's removal from the New York bar in the appellate division (first department) of the supreme court, and the Massachusetts Bar Association, which had no part in the proceedings for petitioner's disbarment in this court, each informed the board, in response to its inquiries, that it did not wish to be heard in the board's proceedings. Similarly, in *Braverman,* as stated above, the Maryland State Bar Association recommended the readmission of Braverman after conducting its own investigation, and the Baltimore Bar Association reported that there was no derogatory evidence against him.

To the contrary, in *Keenan,* the Boston Bar Association opposed the petition for readmission in lengthy proceedings in the superior court, and, after the petition was granted by that court, the Boston Bar Association and the Massachusetts Bar Association, as well as the attorney general, filed separate informations in this court, each of which "called the attention of this Court to the situation created by Keenan's reinstatement by the Superior Court and to the question whether a mistake had been made affecting public confidence in the administration of justice" (314 Mass., at 546). Again, in *Centracchio* the petition for readmission was opposed by the Boston Bar Association in this court.

Second: Petitioner's conviction for perjury was based on two related statements to a federal grand jury, which were found to be false. Although we cannot challenge the conviction as a judicial fact, it was the result of a verdict based on complicated strands of evidence not yet untangled. The offense was *totally inconsistent* with Mr. Hiss' professional and personal conduct prior and subsequent thereto. Such was not the situation in the *Keenan* case. Keenan was one of a number of lawyers disciplined after a citizens' petition was filed in this court concerning widespread abuses in the practice of tort litigation. Nineteen lawyers, some of who were prominent in trial work, were disbarred (314 Mass., at 547-8). The court could not have let Keenan be reinstated five years after disbarment—*all* the factors were against it.

It is difficult to see why the other attorneys who have been disbarred since the petition was filed by the committee of citizens, or at least many of those attorneys, could not produce evidence in their own behalf similar to that produced by Keenan . . . Are we to include in this process an attorney disbarred for one of the most serious offenses of which an attorney can be guilty, and is he to be reinstated upon evidence which falls far short of a guaranty against its repetition? Without attempting to assert that all the other instances are necessarily to be classed with this one, and that there may not be substantial differences growing out of the nature of the offenses committed or of the evidence offered, but confining our decision to this case as outlined above, the answer is plain . . . "

Although Keenan's actual conviction was based on a single incident of bribing three jurors, his offense was discovered in the context of a ten-year investigation of widespread professional misconduct on the part of tort lawyers. Centracchio had engaged in a continuous course of misconduct of splitting fees with doctors and evading federal income taxes over a period of years, during most of which time, if not at all, he had been a judge of a court of record in this commonwealth.

Third: There are significant differences in the periods of time separating the disbarments from the respective petitions for readmission in these cases. The present petition was filed on November 4, 1974, more than twenty-one years after petitioner was disbarred on August 1, 1952 (Findings, at 1, 5; Exhibit H). Braverman applied for readmission to the Maryland bar eighteen years after his disbarment (271 Md., at 198). On the other hand, Keenan applied for reinstatement barely five years after his disbarment (314 Mass., at 545); and Centracchio sought reinstatement "after an interval of eight or nine years" (345 Mass., at 348).

This long period has afforded ample opportunity for the court to be satisfied that the petitioner has at least the equivalent of reformation of character, as such reformation is formulated in *Braverman,* and that this has been established by the proof of his exemplary behavior since his release from prison, the impressive evidence of his present good moral character, and the lack of any evidence to the contrary (other than the conviction). The board noted (Findings, at 27, R. 39):

> Nevertheless, the Board, if it were free to consider the matter in the absence of the only evidence to the contrary (the conviction), would unanimously find that Mr. Hiss is presently of good moral character and that he would almost certainly not commit any serious crime if admitted to the bar.

In *Keenan* and *Centracchio,* the adversary positions of the bar associations, the extreme characteristics and apparently continuing nature of the offenses involved, and the relatively brief periods of time that elapsed between the disbarments and requested reinstatements justified the harsh doctrines that were announced by this court. However, those doctrines, in their rigid and inflexible aspects, should not be applied indiscriminately in all cases where disbarment has resulted from the conviction of a serious crime.

Although the board might have distinguished the *Keenan* and *Centracchio* cases on the grounds suggested above, it ruled that those cases controlled its decision, and that any reconsideration of the principles established by those cases was within the sole jurisdiction of this court (Findings, at 35-36 and *passim*). Accordingly, we urge this court to deal with those cases in their entirety and not to draw principles from particular sentences of the *Keenan* opinion.

In particular, the appropriate principle should be that, in proceedings for readmission to the bar brought by an attorney who has been disbarred because of his conviction of a serious crime, such conviction should properly be evidence against the petitioner; but that the effect of the conviction as a judicial fact can be overcome, after passage of time, and particularly where the bar association involved in the original disbarment does not oppose, by clear and convincing proof of his present good moral character. The subsidiary findings of the board show that this standard is abundantly met.

Conclusion

For the reasons stated, the petition should be granted.

Notes

1. The statements were (a) that Mr. Hiss had never, nor had his wife in his presence, turned over any documents of the State Department or of any other government organization, or copies of such documents, to Whittaker Chambers or to any other unauthorized person and (b) that he did not see Mr. Chambers after January 1, 1937 (185 F.2d, at 824).
2. *Compare* In re May, 249 S.W.2d 798 (1952):

   The Bar Commissioners based their refusal to reinstate Mr. May on the ground that restoration of a lawyer to citizenship after a felony conviction, or his pardon, does not restore his good character and make him fit to practice law. We readily agree that it does not. But the fact that one has transgressed does not forever place him beyond the pale of respectability. Such a conception of morality is not in keeping with Christian principles. The sole question before the Bar Commissioners was whether Mr. May's conduct since his conviction practically five years ago, and since his release from prison almost two years ago, has been such as to prove he is now a man of good moral character and entitled to confidence.

For cases where applicants for admission to the bar had given false statements in connection with communist activities but have been nevertheless ordered admitted to practice, *see* March v. Committee of Bar Examiners, 67 Cal. 2d 718, 43 P. 2d 191 (1967) (false sworn statements to Dies Committee in 1939; assumed that this constituted "moral turpitude"; *held:* (admitted to practice in 1967); Application of Jolles, 235 Ore. 262, 383 P.2d 388 (Oregon, 1963) (false information as to Communist party membership).

Judgment of the Massachusetts Supreme Judicial Court

Argued May 9, 1975
Decided August 5, 1975

Petition was filed for reinstatement to the bar. The matter was referred to the Board of Bar Overseers, which filed a report, and the case was reserved and reported by Reardon, J. The Supreme Judicial Court, Tauro, C.J., held that petitioner was was disqualified for reinstatement solely becuase he continued to deny that he had committed the crime on which his disbarment had been based; and that where it appeared that petitioner was of good moral character, that he would almost certainly not commit any serious crime if readmitted to the bar; and that granting of petition for reinstatement would clearly have not actual adverse effect upon the integrity of the bar; reinstatement was warranted. Petition granted.

Before Taura, C.J., and Reardon, Quirico, Braucher, Hennessey, Kaplan, and Wilkins, JJ.

Alger Hiss was struck from the roll of Massachusetts lawyers on August 1, 1952, and now seeks reinstatement. The facts, as disclosed by the record before us, are as follows. On January 25, 1950, Alger Hiss was convicted of two counts of perjury in his testimony before a federal grand jury. A previous trial had resulted in a jury disagreement, and a mistrial has been declared. In particular, Hiss was found to have testified falsely (1) that he had never, nor had his wife in his presence, turned over documents or copies of documents of the United States Department of State or of any other organization of the federal government to one Whittaker Chambers or to any other unauthorized person and (2) that he thought he could say definitely that he had not seen Chambers after January 1, 1937. Chambers was the principal witness against Hiss and had been his principal accuser during hearings held prior to the grand jury investigation by the Committee on Un-American Activities of the House of Representatives.[1] After Hiss had exhausted his rights of appeal (*United States* v. *Hiss,* 185 F.2d 822 [2d Cir. 1950], *cert. den.* 340 U.S. 948, 71 S.Ct. 532, 95 L.Ed. 683 [1951]; *see also United States* v. *Hiss,* 107 F.Supp. 128 [S.D.N.Y. 1952], *affd. per curiam,* 201 F.2d 372 [2d Cir. 1953], *cert. den.* 345 U.S. 942, 73 S.Ct. 830, 97 L.Ed. 1368 [1953] [motion for a new trial]), he was committed tot he United States penitentiary at Lewisburg, Pennsylvania, where he served some three and one-half years.

Following affirmance of the conviction, the Boston Bar Association filed an information with this court, setting forth the circumstances and a prayer for "such action as the Court may deem fit." The matter was duly set down for hearing before a single justice of this court, but, though given due notice of the hearing, Hiss, on the advice of counsel, failed to enter an appearance. On November 2, 1951, the single justice ordered Hiss defaulted and found the bar association's allegations to be true. On August 1, 1952, after arguments by counsel, judgment was entered by the single justice removing Hiss "from the Office of Attorney-at-Law in the Courts of this Commonwealth."

On November 4, 1974, for the first time, Hiss, then age sixty-nine, filed a petition for reinstatement as an attorney and an accompanying affidavit which detailed his activities since his release from prison. The matter was referred to the Board of Bar Overseers (the board) pursuant to S.J.C. Rule 4:01, § 18(4), Mass. (1974). The board members[2] heard evidence and filed a report, consisting of findings and recommendations for disposition. The matter is before us now on reservation and report without decision of the single justice. Three fundamental questions are presented for our determination: (1) Were the crimes of which Hiss was convicted and for which he was disbarred so serious in nature that he is forever precluded from seeking reinstatement? (2) Are statements of repentance and recognition of guilt necessary prerequisites to reinstatement? (3) Has Hiss demonstrated his fitness to practice law in the Commonwealth?

[1] 1. At the outset, we stress that we are not here concerned with a review of the criminal case in which Hiss was tried, convicted and sentenced.[3] In his trial, he received the full measure of due process rights and opportunities to contest allegations of guilt: a trial before a jury of his peers supplemented by ample avenues of appeal. Basic respect for the integrity and finality of a prior unreversed criminal judgment demands that it be conclusive on the issue of guilt and that an attorney not be permitted to retry the result at a much later date in his reinstatement proceedings. (Cf. In the Matter of Braverman, 271 Md. 196, 316 A.2d 246[1974]). Hiss does not contend otherwise. While, in some civil proceedings, we permit retrial of factual issues adjudicated previously in criminal cases (see, e.g., Silva v. Silva, 297 Mass. 217, 218, 7 N.E.2d 601 [1937]), "[s]omething different is involved . . . [here]. . . . A member of the bar whose name remains on the roll is in a sense held out by the Commonwealth, through the judicial department, as still entitled to confidence. A conviction of crime, especially of serious crime, undermines public confidence in him. The average

citizen would find it incongruous for the . . . [Federal government] on the one hand to adjudicate him guilty and deserving of punishment, and then, on the other hand, while his conviction and liability to punishment still stand [for the Commonwealth] to adjudicate him innocent and entitled to retain his membership in the bar." *Matter of Welansky,* 319 Mass. 205, 208-209, 65 N.E.2d 202, 204, (1946).[4] Accord, American Bar Association Special Committee on Evaluation of Disciplinary Enforcement, Problems and Recommendations in Disciplinary Enforcement 131 (Final Draft 1970).[5] Thus, Hiss comes before us now as a convicted perjuror, whose crime, a direct and reprehensible attack on the foundations of our judicial system, is further tainted by the breach of confidence and trust which underlay his conviction. His conviction and subsequent disbarment are "conclusive evidence of his lack of moral character *at the time of his removal from office.*" *(emphasis supplied). Matter of Keenan,* 313 Mass. 186,219, 47 N.E.2d 12,32 (1943).

[2] 2. Nevertheless, the serious nature of the crime and the conclusive evidence of past unfitness to serve as an attorney do not *necessarily* disqualify Hiss at the present time. We cannot subscribe to the arguments advanced by the chief bar counsel (Bar Counsel)[6] that, because the offenses committed by Hiss are so serious, they forever bar reinstatement[7] irrespective of good conduct or reform.[8] Though in previous cases we intimated by way of dicta that there may be "offenses so serious that the attorney committing them can never again satisfy the court that he has become trustworthy" (*Matter of Keenan,* 314 Mass. 544, 548-549, 50 N.E. 2d 785, 788 [1943]; *see, e.g., Matter of Keenan,* 313 Mass. 186,219, 47 N.E.2d 12 [1943;]*Centracchio, petitioner,* 345 Mass. 342, 346-347, 187 N.E.2d 383 [1963)]we cannot now say that any offense is so grave that a disbarred attorney is automatically precluded for attempting to demonstrate through ample and adequate proofs, drawn from conduct and social interactions, that he has achieved a "present fitness" (*In re Kone, 90 Conn. 440,442, 97 A. 307* [1916]) to serve as an attorney and has led a sufficiently exemplary life to inspire public confidence once again, in spite of his previous action.[9]

[3] Disbarment is not a permanent punishment imposed on delinquent attorneys as a supplement to the sanctions of the criminal law—"though it may have that practical effect. Its purpose is to exclude from the office of an attorney in the courts, for the preservation of the purity of the courts and the protection of the public, one who has demonstrated that he is not a proper person to hold such office." *Keenan, petitioner, 310 Mass. 166,169, 37 N.E.2d 516,519 (1941). Accord*[10] *Bar Assn. of the City of Boston* v. *Greenhood,* 168 Mass. 169,183, 46 N.E. 568,575 (1897) ("protection of the public from attorneys who disregard their oath of office"); *Bar Assn. of the*

City of Boston v. *Casey,* 211 Mass. 187,192, 97 N.E. 751 (1912); *Matter of Keenan,* 314 Mass. 544,546-547, 50 N.E.2d 785 (1943). The position of the Bar Counsel presupposes that certain disbarred attorneys, guilty of particularly heinous offenses against the judicial system, are incapable of meaningful reform which would qualify them to be attorneys and, further, that the public will never be willing to revise an earlier opinion that the offender was not a proper person to function as an attorney. If adopted the rule would provide that "no matter what a disbarred attorney's subsequent conduct may be; no matter how hard and successfully he has tried to live down his past and atone for his offense; no matter how complete his reformation—the door to restoration is forever sealed against him." *In re Stump,* 272 Ky. 593,597-598, 114 S.W.2d 1094,1097 (1938). Such a harsh, unforgiving position is foreign to our system of reasonable, merciful justice. It denies any potentiality for reform of character. A fundamental precept of our system (particularly our correctional system[11]) is that men can be rehabilitated. "Rehabilitation . . . is a 'state of mind' and the law looks with favor upon rewarding with the opportunity to serve, one who has achieved 'reformation and regeneration.' " *March* v. *Committee of Bar Examrs.,* 67 Cal.2d 718,732, 63 Cal.Reptr. 399,408,433, P.2d 191,200 (1967). Time and experience may mend flaws of character which allowed the immature man to err. The chastening effect of a severe sanction such as disbarment may redirect the energies and reform the values of even the mature miscreant. There is always that potentiality for reform, and fundamental fairness demands that the disbarred attorney have opportunity to adduce proofs.

[4] The public welfare, "the true test" in all proceedings for reinstatement (*Matter of Keenan,* 314 Mass. 544,547, 50 N.E. 2d 785 [1943]), calls for no different result. There can be no harm in permitting any disbarred attorney to adduce proofs of his changed character. Certainly, the proceeding itself poses no threat to the public interest.[12] It does not guarantee readmission. Before he again will be entered on the rolls as an attorney eligible to practice, the disbarred attorney who has committed the grave offenses to which the Bar Counsel directs attention must bear a heavy burden of proof (*see, infra,* at 438) and pass the close scrutiny to which reviewing courts subject petitions for reinstatement. Indeed, the proceeding may ultimately redound to the public benefit, for the attorney who can attain reinstatement in such a proceeding after having committed a grave offense could become a credit to the bar and an asset to those he serves.

3.   In assessing Hiss's fitness for reinstatement to the bar, the Board of Bar Overseers considered itself bound by our decision in *Matter of Keenan*—314 Mass. 544, 50 N.E.2d 785 (1943)—to require admission of guilt and repentance as part of the proof of Hiss's present good moral char-

acter and rehabilitation. Accordingly, because Hiss continues to insist on his innocence, the board recommended that his petition for reinstatement be denied. The board wrote: "When the disbarment is wholly based upon the conviction of the petitioner of an offense which is clearly a 'serious crime' (perjury), which conviction has not been reversed, and the petitioner has not been pardoned, the task of a petitioner such as Mr. Hiss, who continues to assert his innocence; to satisfy this Board of his present good character, becomes logically impossible for him to meet under the law, as the Board conceives the law to be. . . . [S]o long as Mr. Hiss's conviction stands, and so long as he continues to deny his guilt of an offense of which he was convicted, after what was ruled to be a fair trial, the Board finds, *under the decisions by which it is bound,* that the petitioner has not satisfied us that his readmission would not be detrimental to the standing of the Bar, the administration of justice or to the public interest" (emphasis supplied).

Neither the controlling case law nor the legal standard for reinstatement to the bar requires that one who petitions for reinstatement must proclaim his repentance and affirm his adjudicated guilt. *Matter of Keenen,* 314 Mass. 544, 50 N.E.2d 785 (1943), cited by the board as dispositive, does not hold that repentance and admission of guilt are mandatory. In *Keenan, supra,* we considered a variety of factors relevant to reinstatement; repentance was but one of them. After a full review of the evidence presented, we concluded that "in view of all the factors which must be taken into account" (*id.,* at 350, 50 N.E.2d, at 788) Keenan should not be reinstated. The evidence held "forth no certainty that . . . [the petitioner] would not again fall a victim to the same weakness that was his first undoing." (*Ibid*). Particular emphasis was placed on the "unusual history and background" (*id.,* at 547, 50 N.E.2d 785) of the case—the sweeping public investigation into abuses and unprofessional conduct of the tort bar—and on the precedent that the case would be for similar petitions by others exposed in the same investigation. The failure of Keenan to admit guilt or repent[13] did not, any more than the other factors considered, determine the outcome. *Centracchio, petitioner*—345 Mass. 342, 187 N.E.2d 383 (1963)—the other case from this jurisdiction cited by the board, contains no explicit holding with respect to repentance. In fact, the petitioner was denied reinstatement though, through his conduct, he had given evidence of repentance.

[5,6] The legal standard for reinstatement to the bar is set forth in S.J.C. Rule 4:01, § 18(4), Mass. (1974). There is no mention of repentance as a prerequisite to admission: "The respondent-attorney . . . shall have the burden of demonstrating that he has the moral qualifications, competency and learning in law required for admission to practice law in this Commonwealth, and that his resumption of the practice of law will not be detrimen-

tal to the integrity and standing of the bar, the administration of justice, or to the public interest." In proceedings on petitions for reinstatement, we must ascertain that the prospective members of the bar are presently "trustworthy" (see *Bar Assn. of the City of Boston* v. *Greenhood*, 168 Mass. 169, 183, 46 N.E. 568 [1897]; *Keenan, petitioner,* 310 Mass. 166,168, 37 N.E.2d 516 [1941]; *Kepler* v. *State Bar of Cal.*, 216 Cal. 52, 55, 13 P.2d 509 [1932]; *In re Application of Smith,* 220 Minn. 197,200, 19 N.W.2d 324 [1945)]and upright of character, not that they are willing to admit past mistakes. Statements of guilt and repentance may be desirable as evidence that the disbarred attorney recognizes his past wrongdoing and will attempt to avoid repetition in the future. However, to satisfy the requirements of present good moral character in the tests for reinstatement noted above, it is sufficient[14] that the petitioner adduce substantial proof that he has "such an appreciation of the distinctions between right and wrong in the conduct of men toward each other as will make him a fit and safe person to engage in the practice of law." *In re Koenig,* 152 Conn. 125,132, 204 A.2d 33,36 (1964). *See In re Stump,* 272 Ky. 593,598-599, 114 S.W.2d 1094 (1938). Such an appreciation, if deeply felt and strongly anchored, will serve as a firm foundation and justification for the order of reinstatement. Mere words of repentance are easily uttered and just as easily forgotten.

[7]The continued assertion of innocence in the face of prior conviction does not, as might be argued, constitute *conclusive* proof of lack of the necessary moral character to merit reinstatement.[15] Though we deem prior judgments dispositive of all factual issues and deny attorneys subject to disciplinary proceedings the right to relitigate issues of guilt, we recognize that a convicted person may on sincere reasoning believe himself to be innocent. We also take cognizance of Hiss's argument[16] that miscarriages of justice are possible. Basically, his underlying theory is that innocent men conceivably could be convicted, that a contrary view would place a mantle of absolute and inviolate perfection on our system of justice, and that this is an attribute that cannot be claimed for any human institution or activity. We do not believe we can say with certainty in this case, or perhaps any case, what is the true state of mind of the petitioner. Thus, we cannot say that every person who, under oath, protests his innocence after conviction and refuses to repent is committing perjury.

Simple fairness and fundamental justice demand that the person who believes he is innocent though convicted should not be required to confess guilt to a criminal *act* he honestly believes he did not commit. For him, a rule requiring admission of guilt and repentance creates a cruel quandary: he may stand mute and lose his opportunity; or he may cast aside his hard-retained scruples and, paradoxically, commit what he regards as perjury to prove his worthiness to practice law. Men who are honest would prefer to relinquish the opportunity conditioned by this rule: "Circumstances may be made to bring innocence under the penalties of the law. If so brought, escape by confession of guilt . . . may be rejected—preferring to be the victim of the law rather than its acknowledged transgressor—preferring death even to such certain infamy."[17] *Burdick* v. *United States,* 236 U.S. 79,90-91, 35 S.Ct. 267,269, 59 L.Ed. 476 (1915). Honest men would suffer permanent disbarment under such a rule. Others, less sure of their moral positions, would be tempted to commit perjury be admitting to a nonexistent offense (or to an offense they believe is nonexistent) to secure reinstatement. So regarded, this rule, intended to maintain the integrity of the bar, would encourage corruption in these latter petitioners for reinstatement and, again paradoxically, might permit reinstatement of those least fit to serve. We do not consider in this context the person who admits committing the alleged criminal act but honestly believes it is not unlawful.

[8,9] Accordingly, we refuse to disqualify a petitioner for reinstatement *solely* because he continues to protest his innocence of the crime of which he was convicted. Repentance[18] or lack of repentance is evidence, like any other, to be considered in the evaluation of a petitioner's character and of the likely repercussions of his requested reinstatement. However, nothing we have said here should be construed as detracting one iota from the fact that in considering Hiss's petition we consider him to be guilty as charged. Our discussion relates only to the issue of whether Hiss must admit his guilt as condition to reinstatement.

[10-12] 4. Having resolved these preliminary questions of law, we pass now to consideration of Hiss's present fitness to serve as an attorney. The standards for reinstatement drawn from the rules of this court have been set forth (*see* p. 436, *supra*). In judging whether a petitioner satisfies these standards and has demonstrated the requisite rehabilitation since disbarment, it is necessary to look to (1) the nature of the original offense for which the petitioner was disbarred, (2) the petitioner's character, maturity, and experience at the time of his disbarment, (3) the petitioner's occupations and conduct in the time since his disbarment, (4) the time elapsed since the disbarment,[19] and (5) the petitioner's present competence in legal skills. *See Application of Spriggs,* 90 Ariz. 387,388, n. 1, 368 P.2d 456 (1962); *In re Barton,* 273 Md. 377,379, 329 A.2d 102 (1974); *In re Application of Strand,* 259 Minn. 379,381 107 N.W.2d 518 (1961); *In the Matter of the Petition of Seijas,* 63 Wash. 2d 865,868-869, 389 P.2d 652 (1964). (*Cf. In re Petition of Dawson,* 131 So.2d 472,474 [Fla.1961]). The judgment of disbarment "continues to be evidence against . . . [the petitioner] with respect to lack of moral character at later times in accordance with the principle that 'a state of things once proved to exist may generally be found to continue.' *Galdson* v. *McCarthy,* 302 Mass. 36,37, 18 N.E.2d 331,332

[1938.]Whatever the offense for which a judgment of disbarment was entered, the person disbarred has a heavy burden on a subsequent petition for admission to the bar to overcome by evidence the weight of the facts adjudicated by such judgment and to establish affirmatively[20] that since his disbarment he has become 'a person proper to be held out by the court to the public as trustworthy'" (footnote added). *Matter of Keenan,* 313 Mass. 186,219, 47 N.E.2d 12,32 (1943). *See McArthur* v. *State Bar of Cal.,* 28 Cal.2d 779,788, 172 P.2d 55 (1946). While the courts are slow to disbar, they are justifiably slower to reinstate and "to put into the hands of an unworthy petitioner that almost unlimited opportunity to inflict wrongs upon society possessed by a practicing lawyer." *In re Petition of Morrison,* 45 S.D. 123,126, 186 N.W. 556,557 (1922). Accord, *In re Application of Smith,* 220 Minn. 197,200, 19 N.W.2d 324 (1945).

[13-15]In any disciplinary proceeding the findings and recommendations of the boards, though not binding on this court, are entitled to great weight.[21] *See March* v. *Committee of Bar Examrs.,* 67 Cal.2d 718,720, 63 Cal. Rptr. 399, 433 P.2d 191 (1967); *In the Matter of Bennethum,* 278 A.2d 831,833 (Del.1971); *Petition of Eddleman,* 77 Wash.2d 42,43, 459 P.2d 387 (1969). *(Cf.) In re Application of Strand,* 259 Minn. 379,381, 107 N.W.2d 518 (1961). The board has heard testimony and observed witnesses and, by virtue of this firsthand observation, is better able than a reviewing court to judge the relative credibilities of witnesses and to assign weight to the evidence they give. In the instant case, the failure of Hiss to repent aside,[22] the board found (1) "that Mr. Hiss is presently of good moral character and that he would almost certainly not commit any serious crime if readmitted to the bar" and (2) "that the granting of the petition will clearly have no actual adverse effect upon the integrity of the Bar, as it would be evidenced by the conduct of any other attorney." These findings are supported by substantial evidence and warrant Hiss's reinstatement as a member of the bar. In the light of these findings, we believe that, absent the issue of repentance, the board would have recommended Hiss's reinstatement.

Considerable time (approximately twenty-three years) has elapsed since the original disbarment of Hiss. His activities since his disbarment reflect the efforts of a man who wished to abide by the court's decree of disbarment and to earn a living in other fields of endeavor while he maintained the scholarly interests he had held prior to his disbarment. In the interval between his disbarment and the present, he has scrupulously refrained from the practice of law. He has not been convicted of any crime[23] and has not been implicated in any activities which contained the slightest hint of dishonesty or moral turpitude. As the board found on ample evidence, "he has courageously and industriously set himself to earn an honest living and to support his family, without bewailing the financial loss caused by his conviction and disbarment."[24] He has pursued his scholarly interests through a program of diverse lectures and the publication of articles and books. In his lectures, delivered at a wide variety of colleges, universities, and other public forums, in this country and abroad, he has generally avoided the subject of his personal tribulations in order to concentrate on subjects relating to the United Nations and American foreign policy. He has written two books and has contributed a number of book reviews to periodicals. At the request of the late Professor Mark deWolfe Howe of Harvard Law School, he edited the abridged edition of the Holmes-Laski letters.

The evidence regarding character supplied by Hiss's gainful employment in the business world is uniformly good. From 1956 to 1959, he was the assistant to the president of a small manufacturing concern, presumably a position of confidence. His employment was terminated by the financial difficulties suffered by his employer. After a brief period of unemployment, he obtained his current job as a salesman of stationery supplies and printing. The board found that "he has earned an excellent business reputation both for industry and honesty in this occupation." A representative of the company which employs Hiss testified that he had achieved a very close relationship with his customers and that they insisted that he alone service their accounts. She testified further that "[i]n the preparation of his billing" he had "always been very, very fair and equitable and [had] never taken himself into consideration." Specifically, he had not availed himself of a bonus system through which he could have expanded his own commissions by charging a higher markup on sales. As additional proof of the high regard in which Hiss is held by his business colleagues, there is in evidence a letter from the president of the corporation which is his employer's controlling stockholder. The president writes that in the event Hiss were to become a member of the Massachusetts bar, the firm "would be glad" to engage Hiss as a legal consultant to explore the legal requirements for doing business in Massachusetts.

At the hearing before the board, a number of talented and eminent attorneys came forward to attest to Hiss's good character.[26] Others, including a retired Justice of the United States Supreme Court and a former solicitor general of the United States, submitted complimentary affidavits and letters.[27] We[28] have had to discount a part of this evidence because some of those giving evidence did not accept Hiss's guilt of the crime for which he had been disbarred and, thus, spoke of his good character without distinguishing the period before his conviction and disbarment from that which succeeded it.[29] *See Matter of Keenan,* 314 Mass. 544,550, 50 N.E.2d 785 (1943).

However, several witnesses provided solid evidence of fitness for reinstatement. Professor Victor Brudney of the Harvard Law School met Hiss after his release from prison and has had regular social contacts with Hiss throughout the years. In the course of their acquaintanceship, Professor Brudney testified, they have had numerous conversations on law and law-related subjects. In those conversation, Professor Brudney found Hiss to be quite competent ("a first-rate mind") in dealing with legal problems and aware of trends and events in the law. According to Professor Brudney, "the attitudes . . . [Hiss] revealed in discussion disclosed a perception and a sensitivity for the interests of others in controversial situations." Hiss was candid and direct in his dealings with people, and Professor Brudney said that he would "feel comfortable" if he received the first draft of a contract from Hiss, if Hiss were acting for the other side. When asked if he would consult and confide in Hiss as a lawyer, Professor Brudney's response was enthusiastic and affirmative. Of a similar tenor was the testimony of Professor Richard Field, also of the Harvard Law School faculty. Professor Field, a noted scholar and pedagogue, currently teaches a course in "professional responsibility." His contacts with Hiss subsequent to the perjury convictions appear to have been less frequent than those of Professor Brudney, but were sufficiently numerous to provide ample basis for judgment. Professor Field testified that Hiss had retained his "deep interest" in the law and that, from their discussion, it was manifest that Hiss had "kept himself well abreast of developments" in the field of international law, his specialty. Professor Field stated further that he would have no hesitancy in employing Hiss as a legal consultant in the areas of Hiss's specialty.[30]

The testimony of Helen Buttenwieser, a member of the New York bar and a good friend of Hiss, who on occasion had counseled Hiss on legal matters, also provides substantial support for the board's findings. According to her testimony, she has had frequent and fairly regular contacts with Hiss during the period subsequent ot his disbarment. In the course of their relationship, both professional and social, she has found him to be a man of the "highest" integrity. She testified: "If he has a fault, it is that he tends to bend over backwards for fear he might possibly be trying to persuade somebody to do something which was beyond what he wanted to do." She testified further that she and one of her partners had often met with Hiss for lunch and that, during their luncheon conversation, they had had occasion to discuss legal cases of mutual interest. The discussions had ranged over questions of constitutional and civil liberties law and had accorded particular emphasis to issues from cases which her partner had pending before the United States Supreme Court. In these discussions, the witness had found Hiss both "capable" and "stimulating." Hiss has not, to her knowledge, shown any anger or rancor regarding the outcome of his trial. She testified: "[H]is attitude is that this is our system of justice and he will take his chances with it again and again and again."

Finally,[31] Hiss's own testimony must be mentioned in support of the board's finding of fitness. His testimony was both forthright and principled. He stated that he found the charge of perjury "abhorrent and that the perjury charge had included two other charges worse than perjury, which I regard as absolutely reprehensible in a lawyer—failure of trust and failure of confidence." He candidly gave his own impression of the development of his moral character, though that candid impression might have thwarted his reintatement: "I have not had any complete change in moral character. I am the same person I have been, I believe, throughout my life. If that's the law of Massachusetts [requiring repentance and complete change of moral character], I am excluded." His testimony contained no hint of present animosity or grudge against those who had prosecuted and convicted him. The conviction itself had not shaken his faith in the judicial system: "[A]s far as the courts are concerned . . . I have never had the slightest doubt that ours is the finest judicial system there is, and I don't just mean in the Churchill sense . . . [i.e., that it's] better than any he knows about. It's good; it's fine. I think it makes mistakes, and I know it made a mistake in my case, but there is no human institution that doesn't sometimes make mistakes."

The testimony detailed above provides abundant support for the board's conclusion that Hiss is presently of good character. Though Hiss, himself, in holding fast to his contention of innocence, admits no rehabilitation of character, we believe that the evidence amply warrants the board's finding that he would not now commit the crime of which he was convicted. The considerable evidence of his present good character, his exemplary behavior over a substantial time span, and the tributes paid him by eminent practitioners who have known him well during the period convince us that, despite the gravity of the crime and his maturity at the time of its commission, "his resumption of the practice of law will not be detrimental to the integrity and standing of the bar, the administration of justice, or to the public interest." S.J.C. Rule 4:01, § 18(4), Mass. (1974). It is notable in this regard that the record contains no testimony in opposition to reinstatement. Indeed, the Council of the Boston Bar Association, the organization which filed the information leading to disbarment, voted to communicate the opinion to the board that Hiss's resumption of practice would not adversely affect the standing and integrity of the bar or the public interest. The board could correctly find that Hiss has sustained the heavy burden of showing moral and intellectual fitness by good and sufficient proofs.

The petition for reinstatement to the bar is to be granted. On subscription to the required oaths, Hiss is to be readmitted to the practice of law in the Commonwealth. So ordered.

Notes

1. A more detailed history of events surrounding the trial and conviction may be found in United States v. Hiss, 185 F.2d 822 (2d Cir. 1950), *cert. den.* 340 U.S. 948, 71 S.Ct. 532, 95 L.Ed. 683 (1951).
2. Pursuant to S.J.C. Rule 4:01, § 18(4), the board could have referred the matter to a hearing committee, but the members chose to hear the evidence themselves.
3. Hiss seeks reinstatement and not vindication.
4. In Welansky, we were concerned with retrial of criminal convictions in disbarment proceedings. The result follows a fortiori in reinstatement proceedings.
5. This special committee report addressed the problem of "[n]o provision making conviction of crime conclusive evidence of guilt for purposes of the disciplinary proceeding based on the conviction."
6. The Bar Counsel and assistants are appointed by the board with the approval of this court pursuant to S.J.C. Rule 4:01, § 5(3)(b), Mass. (1974). The Bar Counsel is charged with the responsibility of "[investigating] all matters involving alleged misconduct by an attorney" and "[prosecuting] all disciplinary proceedings before hearing committees, the [b]oard and this court." S.J.C. Rule 4:01, §7(1), (3), Mass. (1974). The rules of this court provide that "at hearings conducted with respect to motions for reinstatement" the Bar Counsel "shall appear with full rights to participate as a party." S.J.C. Rule 4:01, §7(4), Mass. (1974).
7. Some aspects of the board's findings and recommendations may be read to embrace this position: "With Mr. Hiss's conviction outstanding, unreversed, not subject to attack, and necessary for us to consider, all the other evidence of his present character cannot be of any weight." However, the context and remainder of the board's report make clear that the board does not subscribe to the full measure of its counsel's position.
8. In view of what we say in the opinion, we need not consider or decide whether such a ruling would amount to a *conclusive* presumption frowned on by many courts. (*Compare* Vlandis v. Kline, 412 U.S. 441,446, 93 S.Ct. 2230, 37 L.Ed.2d 63 [1973]; Leary v. United States, 395 U.S. 6, 89 S.Ct. 1532, 23 L.Ed.2d 57 [1969]; and Barnes v. United States, 412 U.S. 837, 93 S.Ct. 2357, 37 L.Ed.2d 380 [1973]; *with* Weinberger v. Salfi, U.S., 95 S.Ct. 2457, 45 L. Ed.2d 522 [1975]).
9. Other jurisdiction appear split on whether conviction for particularly heinous crimes will necessarily result in permanent disbarment. *See generally* American Bar Association Special Committee on Evaluation of Disciplinary Enforcement. Problems and Recommendations in Disciplinary Enforcement, 150 (Final Draft 1970); anno. 70 A.L.R.2d 268,276-279 (1960). A number of states permit reinstatement on a showing of rehabilitation despite conviction for serious crimes involving moral turpitude or breaches of trust. *See, e.g.,* Allen v. State Bar of Cal., 58 Cal.2d 912, 26 Cal.Rptr. 771,

376 P.2d 835 (1962)(perjury); In re May, 249 S.W.2d 798 (Ky.Ct.App. 1952) ("not forever... beyond the pale of respectability"). In re Taylor, 330 S.W.2d 393 (Ky.Ct.App.1959) (fraud on the court); Ex Parte Marshall, 165 Miss. 523, 147 So. 791 (1933)(blackmail). (*Cf.* March v. Committee of Bar Examrs., 67 Cal.2d 718, 63 Cal. Rptr. 399, 433 P.2d 191 [1967] [first admission to bar; no conviction but false testimony before Congressional committee]; Williams v. Governors of the Fla. Bar, 173 So.2d 686 [Fla.1965] [reinstatement considered and denied; conspiracy to thwart prosecution]; In re Sympson, 322 S.W.2d 808 [Mo.1959] [criminal contempt for suborning perjury; not reinstated]). Other states make conviction of certain serious crimes a ground for permanent disbarment. See, e.g., People v. Buckles, 167 Colo. 64, 453 P.2d 404 (1969) (statute); In the Matter of Bennethum, 278 A.2d 831,833 (Del. 1971); People ex rel. Chicago Bar Assn. v. Reed, 341 Ill. 573,577, 173 N.E. 772 (1930); In re Application of Van Wyck, 225 Minn. 90, 29 N.W.2d 654 (1947); Tenn.Code Anno. § 29-310 (1955 and Supp. 1974); (*Cf.* Cantor v. Grievance Comms., 189 Tenn. 536, 226 S.W.2d 283 [1949]).

10. In re Kone, 90 Conn. 440442, 97 A. 307 (1916). In re Barton, 273 Md. 377,381, 329 A.2d 102 (1974). In re Application of Smith, 220 Minn. 197,199, 19 N.W.2d 324 (1945). In re Sympson, 322 S.W.2d 808,812 (Mo. 1959). In re Petition of Morrison, 45 S.D. 123,129, 186 N.W. 556 (1922). In re Enright, 69 Vt. 317,319, 37 A. 1046 (1897).

11. "Even wrongdoers convicted of crime are given another chance." In re Stump, 272 Ky. 593,598, 114 S.W.2d 1094, 1097 (1938).

12. It is appropriate to observe that a proceeding which fairly provides an opportunity to demonstrate good moral character cannot lower the standing of the bar or bring it into disrepute.

13. Note also that the court wrote that "[t]here was little evidence of repentance or reform" (emphasis supplied). Matter of Keenan, 314 Mass., at 550, 50 N.E.2d, at 788 (1943). Ample evidence of character reform would have been sufficient, in and of itself, to support reinstatement (though repentance alone would not have been).

14. A number of jurisdictions do not require an avoval of repentance as a prerequisite to reinstatement. *See, e.g.,* In re Barton, 273 Md. 377,382, 329 A.2d 102 (1974); Ex Parte Marshall, 165 Miss. 523,551-552, 147 So. 791 (1933); In re Eddleman, 77 Wash. 2d 42, 45, n. 1, 459 P.2d 387 (1969). (*But cf.* In the Matter of Bennethum, 278 A.2d 831,833 [Del. 1971]; In re Application of Smith, 220 Minn. 197,202, 19 N.W. 324 [1945]).

15. The contrary position seems to have been adopted by the board: "Strict application of logical principles might, in fact, lead to the conclusion that the petitioner gives evidence of his present lack of moral character when he again testifies to his innocence of the original charge, in the face of a conviction which this Board, for purposes of its deliberations, must accept as establishing the fact of his guilt."

16. The Bar Counsel in his brief agrees that repentance and admission of guilt should not be conditions of reinstatement: "While an adjudication of guilt must stand as a determination of that fact, legally and judicially, binding upon the accused and all the world, all that is or can be demanded of the accused is that he shall accord full respect to and acquiescence in that finding and judgement. *It cannot be demanded that he deny his own conscience or his own knowledge, and that he assert a guilt which for him does not exist.* The Keenan case does not make such a demand. Repentance is only one of

many factors that may be considered" (emphasis supplied). The Boston Bar Association, in its amicus brief, took a similar position.

17. The quotation refers to confession of guilt through acceptance of a pardon.

18. Different principles may apply to cases in which the delinquent attorney should make restitution of misappropriated funds. We do not here decide what effect failure to make restitution should have on a petitions for restatement.

19. Since disbarment is not primarily a punishment for the offending lawyer, passage of time alone is insufficient to warrant restatement. *See* In the Matter of Bennethum, 278 A.2d 831,834 (Del. 1971); Williams v. Governors of the Fla. Bar, 173 So.2d 686 (Fla. 1965). (*Cf.* Centracchio, petitioner, 345 Mass. 342,348, 187 N.E.2d 383 [1965]). Length of time disbarred should not be treated as an additional penalty. The petitioner must demonstrate that his reinstatement would not be detrimental to the public welfare. In this regard, a long time span between disbarment and petition for reinstatement, during which the petitioner's conduct was exemplary, reinforces his claim to rehabilitation.

20. In Matter of Keenan—314 Mass. 544,548,549, 50 N.E.2d 785, 788 (1943)—we employed a more exacting standard: "To overcome it [the crime of 'corruptly influencing three jurymen'] and to prove that the guilty person can again inspire the public confidence necessary to the proper performance of the duties of an attorney at law requires little less than absolute assurance of a complete change of moral character."

21. In Centracchio, petitioner—345 Mass. 342, 187 N.E.2d 383 (1963)—we had before us a report of the Board of Bar Examiners, the board's predecessor in the position of oversight over disciplinary matters. We applied the standard for use of such reports which was prescribed in Rule 1(7) of the General Rules (1952), 328 Mass. 732-733 (1952). "'At such hearing [before a single justice of this court] the report shall have the weight and effect of an auditor's report in an action of law.' This means 'prima facie evidence.' G.L. (Ter.Ed.) c.221, § 56." Centracchio, petitioner, *supra,* at 346, 187 N.E.2d at 385.

22. The board prefaced the first the first of these findings as follows: "Nevertheless, the Board, if it were free to consider the matter in the absence of the only evidence to the contrary (the conviction), would unanimously find. . . ." The context makes clear that the board referred to the conviction only in so far as the conviction compels reference to evidence of repentance and rehabilitation. We have previously dealt with the issue of repentance. We believe that the finding of present good moral character demonstrates rehabilitation.

23. To be precise, he was once fined $5 for playing baseball with his son in Washington Square Park.

24. Because of restrictions on his activities, his earnings over the years have been quite modest. Since 1966, Hiss's yearly earnings from his job as a salesman have not exceeded $14,000 and have averaged only about $10,400.

25. The witness had worked with Hiss in the billing and credit aspects of the business.

26. No witnesses came forward to oppose reinstatement. When duly notified, the Attorney General of the United States indicated that he did not "wish to be heard or to be represented at the hearing." Similar communications were received from the Massachusetts Bar Association, the Committee on Grievances of the Association of the Bar of the City of New York and the

clerk of the United States Supreme Court. The prosecutor of the Hiss perjury case, the Honorable Thomas F. Murphy, did not respond to the communication of the board's counsel.

27. Erwin N. Griswold (former solicitor general of the United States and dean of the Harvard Law School), Eli Whitney Debevoise, Benjamin V. Cohen, Charles A. Horsky and Joseph A. Fanelli, submitted sworn affidavits recommending reinstatement. Mr. Justice Stanley Reed submitted a letter to the same effect.

28. The board did as well.

29. As noted above, some of the witnesses based their recommendations for Hiss's reinstatement on the belief that Hiss was innocent. it is true that the petitioner's record prior to the incident in question was outstanding and without blemish and that his life for the past two decades since his release from prison has been impeccable. It is equally true that nothing in the record corroborates in any way the fact of guilt and, further, that the Department of Justice, although invited, has declined to appear in these proceedings. Nonetheless, we emphasized that whether Hiss was innocent is not an issue in this matter and can receive no consideration. The record of conviction must stand without question.

30. The force of Professor Field's testimony is vitiated to an extent by his admission that he has never believed that Hiss was guilty of the crimes charged and that his opinion of Hiss's moral character was not changed by his conviction and disbarment.

31. In the interests of brevity, we omit description of the supporting testimony of Robert Von Mehren of the New York bar and Richard Wait of this bar.

Reinstatement Dilemma:
The Hiss Decision and Its Effects
Upon Disciplinary Enforcement

Barry Brown

In September 1974, by order of the Supreme Judicial Court of the Commonwealth of Massachusetts, a disciplinary agency known as the Board of Bar Overseers (hereafter the Board) was established in the commonwealth to ensure the unified registration and discipline of attorneys.[1] The Board is empowered to appoint staff members to a prosecutorial office—the office of the bar counsel[2]—whose function is to investigate complaints alleging misconduct[3] by attorneys and prosecute disciplinary proceedings before hearing committees, the Board, and the Supreme Judicial Court of Massachusetts.[4]

In order to facilitate this task, Massachusetts was divided into six disciplinary districts containing two or more hearing committees in each district. The hearing committees, made up of local lawyers chosen by the court, sit as trial masters to determine the facts in each particular instance of alleged misconduct. A record (which includes a transcript of witness testimony) made of the proceedings is the basis upon which appeal of a recommendation made by a local hearing committee is taken; first to the Board, and then to the Supreme Judicial Court of Massachusetts. The functioning of the administrative trial and appeal process allows for complete presentation of evidence and cross-examination of witnesses by both the bar counsel and the accused. The Administrative Procedure Act[5] (under which the proceedings are conducted prior to presentation to the supreme judicial court) permits the introduction of all relevant testimony, including that which would normally be hearsay under the rules of evidence.[6]

The Massachusetts system, embodying new rules of disciplinary procedure, appears to have corrected the anomalous aspects of the prior regulatory system[7], while providing for both requisite due process safeguards and consistent application of the law. The approach of the new court rules and the Board is consistent with the report of the Special Committee on Disciplinary Enforcement of the American Bar Association made in June 1970. This report indicated that the disciplinary organizations within various states were largely inefficient, without funding or professional staffs, and had caused, to some extent, public distrust for, and dissatisfaction with, the legal profession. During the past four years, the Board has sought to correct the apparent decline of public trust and confidence in attorneys by policing the legal profession.

The task of the Board as directed by the court, however, is not simply to consider allegations of, or make recommendations concerning, professional misconduct. The Board must also consider and report to the supreme judicial court concerning the applications of those attorneys who, having been suspended or disbarred for more than five years, desire reinstatement to the profession.

Ironically, in its first year of operation, the Board was faced with two cases of public note which tested both the disciplinary and reinstatement mechanisms almost as soon as the rules had been effected. Both cases involved public figures who were related, by prior association, to Richard M. Nixon. The two cases, *Matter of Alger Hiss*[8] and the *Petition for Discipline of Charles W. Colson,* involved remarkably similar problems, even though one involved the reinstatement of a disbarred attorney, and the other involved the removal of an attorney from the practice of law. Both men stood before the court as convicted felons. Hiss was convicted (on January 25, 1950) of having committed two counts of perjury in his testimony before a federal grand jury. The court determined that Hiss lied when he testified under oath:

> . . . (1) that he had never, nor had his wife in his presence, turned over documents or copies of documents of the United States Department of State or of any other organization of the Federal government to one Whittaker Chambers or any other unauthorized person and (2) that he thought he could say definitely that he had not seen Chambers after January 1, 1937.[9]

Chambers, an admitted communist agent, testified against Hiss at hearings conducted by the House Committee on Un-American Activities, in which Richard M. Nixon sat as the congressman from California. Hiss was sentenced and committed to federal prison where he served three and one half years before release.

Charles Colson, former counsel to Richard M. Nixon, was charged with obstructing justice[10] by devising and implementing a scheme to destroy the public image and credibility of Daniel Ellsberg and his attorney, Leonard Boudin, and by releasing to the news media defamatory information from confidential files with the intent to influence the outcome of Ellsberg's criminal trial. Colson pleaded guilty to the charge, and was sentenced by Judge Giselle to a one to three year term of imprisonment and fined $5,000. Colson served seven months of his sentence and was then released. During that period he was disbarred in the Commonwealth of Virginia and by the United States District Court for the District of Columbia. It is ironic that both cases, uniquely tied to the rise and decline of Richard M. Nixon, were ready and waiting for disposition on their disciplinary issues upon the establishment of the Board.

Alger Hiss, who was disbarred by the commonwealth on August 1, 1952, filed a petition for reinstatement on November 4, 1974. At that time, Hiss was 69 years of age. The petition was referred to the Board[11] which received evidence and filed a report recommending a denial of the petition for reinstatement. The case was then referred for final disposition to the Supreme Judicial Court of Massachusetts.

Under Massachusetts law, an attorney requesting reinstatement has ". . . the burden of demonstrating that he has the moral qualifications, competency and learning in law required for admission to practice law in the Commonwealth, and that his resumption of the practice of law will not be detrimental to the integrity and standing of the bar, the administration of justice, or to public interest."[12]

The weight of precedent was against an attorney's reinstatement to the bar prior to the *Hiss* decision. Two cases, resulting from the reinstatement attempts of two former Massachusetts attorneys, had produced the most authoritative criteria to date regarding the requirements for reinstatement in the commonwealth. The first series of holdings concerned the disbarment and attempted reinstatement of Wilfred Keenan.[13] The Keenan decisions, which involved petitions for reinstatement of an attorney who had been found guilty of bribing jurors, established a standard requiring ". . . little less than absolute assurance of a complete change of moral character" to sustain the petitioner's burden of proof.[14] At that time, the act of reinstating a disbarred attorney in Massachusetts appeared to involve certification to the public that the petitioner was one in whom the utmost faith and absolute trust could be placed. As the court stated in the final Keenan decision:

> [I]n deciding a case of this kind considerations of public welfare are wholly dominant. The question is not whether the respondent has been 'punished' enough. To make that a test would be to give undue weight to his private interests, whereas the true test must always be the public welfare. Where any clash of interest occurs, whatever is good for the individual must give way to whatever tends to the security and advancement of the public justice.[15]

Thus, the burden upon an applicant for reinstatement appeared to be heavier under the *Keenan* view than upon applicants for initial admission to the bar.[16] As a component of this burden, the applicant was required to go beyond the mere presentation of testimonials from friends and associates to the effect that he was a changed man, or of good moral character. He must demonstrate that he woiuld be a credit to the bar if reinstated, and that his readmission would not damage the public view of the profession or the administration of justice.

This view was later adopted by the Massachusetts court in the case of *Centracchio, petitioner,*[17] which involved an attorney who was found guilty of fee splitting while serving as a special justice of a district court. There the court focused largely upon the fact that the conduct which caused the disbarment had occurred while the petitioner was serving as a justice, and was, therefore, a matter of public knowledge. In denying the petition, the court adopted that portion of the Keenan decision which stated:

> [T]here may be an offense so serious that the attorney committing it can never again satisfy the court that he has become trustworthy. . . [t]o prove that the guilty person can again inspire the public confidence necessary to proper performance of the duties of an attorney-at-law requires little less than the absolute assurance of complete change of moral character.[18]

Thus, the fundamental problem for an applicant desiring reinstatement in Massachusetts prior to the *Hiss* case lay in proving that public trust in the applicant had been (or could be) restored to the extent that a decision favoring reinstatement would be in the interest of the public welfare, as well as the integrity of the court and the bar.

In both *Keenan* and *Centracchio*, the court had refused to reinstate a disbarred attorney. In contrast to Massachusetts, several jurisdictions had reinstated disbarred attorneys with less than a full showing of absolute public trust, where there had been found a genuine rehabilitation of the normal character of the applicant.

After the *Centracchio* case, however, the Supreme Judicial Court of Massachusetts did not exercise its prerogative to reinstate a disbarred attorney. Consequently, there was no further clarification of the court's standards for reinstatement prior to the petition of Hiss. In the interim, other jurisdictions, most notably Ohio and New York, had established clear and rather strict guidelines for readmission of disbarred attorneys. Massachusetts, however, retained its amorphous standards which, in the particular case presented by Hiss, appeared to be so vague as to raise the question of whether Hiss would be afforded proper process of law.

The issue of due process was particularly relevant in light of a comparison between the facts involved in the *Hiss* case and two landmark decisions by the United States Supreme Court—*Schware* v. *Board of Bar Examiners of New Mexico,*[19] and *Konigsberg* v. *State Bar of California.*[20] Both the *Konigsberg* and *Schware* decisions, although not concerned with the issue of reinstatement, raise questions of the due process standards to be used in determining whether an individual possesses the proper qualifications for admission to the bar, and are therefore relevant in readmission proceedings.

Both Schware and Konigsberg were members of the Communist Party at various points in their lives. In each case, as applicants to the bars of their respective states, they failed to properly disclose their activities as members of the party. Failure to disclose their membership activities (as well as membership itself) resulted in recommendations by the boards of bar examiners of California and New Mexico, respectively, that Konigsberg and Schware did not possess the "good moral character" and loyalty to the state and federal governments required for admission.

After examining the decisional process undertaken by the respective boards of bar examiners, Mr. Justice Black, in writing for a majority of the U.S. Supreme Court, held that:

> A state can require high standards of qualification such as good moral character or proficiency in its law, before it admits an applicant to the bar, but any qualification must have a rational connection with the applicant's fitness or capacity to practice law.

Schware and Konigsberg were admittedly intellectually qualified for admission. The question, therefore, was whether the supreme courts of California and New Mexico could reasonably find a lack of "good moral character." The focus of Justice Black's analysis bears particular relevance to the vague criteria set forth in the *Keenan* and *Centracchio* decisions, and is, therefore, germane to the application of those cases to the Hiss petition. While the United States Supreme Court recognized the importance of leaving the states free to select members of their own bars, it found that it was equally important for the states not to exercise this power in an arbitrary or discrimanatory manner. Examined in this context, the standard of admission defined by the expression "good moral character" was held by the supreme court to be too ambiguous to satisfy the constitutional requirements of due process:

> [Good moral character] can be defined in an almost unlimited number of ways, for any definition will necessarily reflect the attitudes, experiences, and prejudices of the definer. Such a vague qualification, which is easily adapted to fit personal views and predilections, can be a dangerous instrument for arbitrary and discriminatory denial of the right to practice law.

Due process, the court said, requires more than defining ". . . 'good moral character' in terms of an absence of proven conduct or acts which have been historically considered as manifestations of 'moral turpitude'."

It is not that a standard of "good moral character" is itself unworkable in constitutional terms, but rather that it must be precisely defined to permit consistency and fairness in its application.

In light of the *Schware* and *Konigsberg* decisions, it was apparent that the Board and the Supreme Judicial Court of Massachusetts had to avoid the generalities and vague standards of "public trust and confidence" that marked the *Keenan* and *Centracchio* cases. Predictability and rationality are essential elements of the administrative and judicial process which the Fourteenth Amendment was designed to protect. Taken within this context, the standard for reinstatement based on "public trust and confidence" is one which defies consistency of application. Consequently, if Hiss showed himself to be of the intellectual capacity and present "good moral character" to be a candidate for readmission, the Board and the Supreme Judicial Court had no choice but to confront the issue of his crime and its ultimate effect upon the reinstatement process.

On this issue the court was faced with the recent decision of *In re Braverman*,[21] in which a respondent applying for readmission to the Maryland bar had been convicted (under the Smith Act) of crimes which were largely political in nature, and which the Maryland court chose to view in light of present realities:

> Although we do not consider court decisions rendered after Petitioner's conviction as undermining the conclusive truth of his guilt, we do consider as relevant the change in attitude which is evident by such decisions. We find that it amply demonstrated that developments in the law have necessitated a change in judicial and prosecutorial attitudes. We also believe that since Petitioner's disbarment, public acceptance of the change in legal attitude, public attention to civil rights generally, and the right of dissent particularly, and public emphasis on detente with communist nations in our foreign affairs all have tempered the attitude of the public toward one in the Petitioner's position.

Braverman was readmitted to the Maryland bar, in spite of his conviction of a felony. Hiss requested the same treatment from the Commonwealth of Massachusetts. However, the crime of perjury raised more serious questions than those presented to the Maryland court, namely, whether an attorney—an officer of the court—found guilty of willful deceit, before the very tribunal of which he is an officer, can ever be trusted not to commit the same offense again.

The Board reported three issues for consideration by the supreme judicial court: (1) whether the crimes for which Hiss was convicted (and for which he was disbarred) were of such a serious nature that he was forever precluded from seeking reinstatement; (2) whether statements of repentance and recognition of guilt were necessary prerequisites for reinstatement; and (3) whether Hiss had demonstrated his fitness to practice law in the commonwealth.

With respect to the third issue, the court arrived at its quickest decision. Hiss was clearly an intelligent and competent individual, who, in the absence of present difficulties, would be considered by the court to be a welcome addition to the bar of Massachusetts. At age sixty-nine, he had apparently retained all of his intellectual faculties and had kept abreast of current developments in the law. The court found, therefore, that he had retained the requisite intellectual basis for returning to the profession.

As to the first and second issues, however, there was a split between the Board and the bar counsel in the arguments presented by each to the court. In testifying before the Board, Hiss had stated that he had not ". . . had any complete change in moral character. I am the same person I have been, I believe, throughout my life." By making this statement, Hiss put himself squarely in conflict with the *Keenan* case, which required little less than an absolute assurance of complete change in moral character prior to reinstatement. In effect, Hiss argued that although he respected the system, he could not repent of acts for which he was convicted (and subsequently disbarred), because he had not committed them, and therefore, his original good moral character had not changed. Upon this syllogistic argument, the Board found that it would be impossible to recommend the reinstatement of Hiss so long as *Keenan* and *Centracchio* stood as law in Massachusetts.

The bar counsel, however, took the position that to retain this view would be to interpret *Keenan* as demanding personal affirmation of proven guilt. The loss of basic human dignity implicit in such a demand prompted bar counsel to take a position different from that of the Board.

In fact, the court in *Keenan* did not apply the notion of repentance so mechanistically. It was one of several factors of relevance in determining whether there was sufficient proof of reformation in the years after disbarment to overcome the presumption of bad character established by the adjudication of disbarment. In Massachusetts, as well as other states, a combination of factors affect a court's decision with respect to reinstatement. Repentance can, indeed, be evidence in favor of an applicant, and can provide support for his claim of good moral character. On the other hand, the *Keenan* case did not demand, as the Board asserted, that a respondent deny his own conscience or his own knowledge, and that he assert a guilt which for him did not exist.

In contrast to the Board, the bar counsel was more concerned with determining whether (by their nature) some offenses are so serious, that the individual convicted of them is forever precluded from reinstatement. This appeared to be the case with Hiss. He stood before the court, convicted of perjury. That conviction was binding upon the court as a matter of law, and there could be no search behind the record to determine the factual truth of the crime. In the *Keenan* decision, the court had stated that there may be crimes so severe as to forever preclude reinstatement to the bar. The bar counsel essentially took the position of the American Bar Association's Special Committee on the Evaluation of Disciplinary Enforcement: the more serious the offense and the nearer it strikes to the heart of the administration of justice, the greater the affirmative proof that should be required of the applicant for readmission. Hiss had stated in his own testimony before the Board that:

> In my case, the charge was far worse than perjury... I had two other charges
> ... which I regard as absolutely reprehensible in a lawyer—failure of trust
> and failure of confidence ...

Based on such an admission by the petitioner himself, could there ever be certification to the public that he was one in whom the utmost faith and trust could be placed?

In its review of the issue of repentance presented by the Board, and the issue of a crime so serious as to forever bar reinstatement presented by the bar counsel, the court found in favor of Hiss. In doing so Chief Justice Tauro, writing for the court, in effect rejected both of the stated theories and injected a new principle into the law of disciplinary enforcement—the qualitative passage of time.

The court recognized that Hiss, convicted of perjury, had commited a crime which was a direct and reprehensible attack upon the foundations of the judicial system. Such a crime was "... conclusive evidence of his lack of moral character at the time of his removal from the bar." Nevertheless, the court ruled that the serious nature of the crime, though conclusive evidence of past unfitness to serve as an attorney, did not necessarily disqualify Hiss from present consideration for reinstatement. Accordingly, the court summarily rejected the arguments of the bar counsel that there could be offenses so serious that they would forever bar reinstatement, irrespective of good conduct or reform. The view presented in the *Keenan* case—that there may be "... offenses so serious that the attorney committing them can never again satisfy the Court that he has become trustworthy,"—was held to be dicta which the court would not interpret as meaning that there was an offense so grave that a disbarred attorney was automatically precluded from attempting to demonstrate through ample and adequate proof, "... drawn from conduct and social interactions, that he had achieved a present fitness to serve as an attorney and has a sufficiently exemplary life to inspire public confidence once again in spite of his previous action."

Similarly, with respect to the argument presented by the Board, the court held that the continued assertion of innocence in the face of a prior conviction does not constitute conclusive proof of lack of the "present good moral character" necessary to merit reinstatement. The court recognized that miscarriages of justice were possible and that an innocent man could conceivably be convicted. It reasoned that if this did happen, a rule that the man must repent of his wrongs when he believed himself to be innocent, would place ". . . a mantle of absolute and inviolate perfection on our system of justice . . . [and that] . . . this is an attribute that cannot be claimed for any institution or activity." For an attorney, an individual sworn to uphold the decisions of the various tribunals to which he is admitted as an officer of the court, the protestation of innocence after conviction would appear itself to be perjury. However, Chief Justice Tauro, in his review of this issue, would not permit the court to fall into this syllogism:

> Simple fairness and fundamental justice demand that a person who believes he is innocent though convicted should not be required to confess guilt to a criminal act he honestly believes he did not commit. For him, a rule requiring admission of guilt and repentance creates a cruel quandary; he may stand mute and lose his opportunity; or he may cast aside his hard retained scruples and, paradoxically, commit what he regards as perjury to prove his worthiness to practice law.

What, then, is the purpose of disbarring an individual convicted of a crime? According to the court, it is not a permanent punishment. In fact, it may not be punishment at all, though it appears to the public to generally have that effect. It is a condition which invites rehabilitation. As the court stated: "Time and experience may mend flaws of character which allowed the immature man to err." The "chastening effect" of disbarment may ultimately ". . . redirect the energy and reform the values of even the mature miscreant. There is always the potential for reform . . . "

In the case of Hiss, the passage of time was a testimonial to this principle. During the years following his disbarment he lived a simple and honorable life, maintaining a good reputation, writing and teaching. In this humble position, he maintained his intellectual competency and earned the respect of his employers and former peers in the profession. Based upon these facts, the Supreme Judicial Court of Massachusetts found no reason to question the impact that his readmission would have upon the public trust and confidence in the legal profession, and therefore, reinstated the name of Alger Hiss to the roll of those entitled to practice law in the commonwealth.

What effect does the decision of the court have with respect to the modern trend in disciplinary enforcement? Certainly, for those attorneys disbarred in Massachusetts, and perhaps in other states, the decision suggests that the passage of time may itself be a factor in determining whether past evidence of bad moral character may be erased, and sufficient rehabilitation established to warrant readmission of an attorney, even after his conviction of a serious crime. More significantly, in emphasizing the time factor, the court, in effect, suggested that disbarment is merely a severe form of suspension; not a permanent disability, but one which can always be corrected by living an exemplary life after the imposition of discipline.

It is this implicit view of the court which raises the greatest problem for those entrusted with disciplinary enforcement. If disbarment is merely a severe form of suspension, one which increases the burden upon the petitioner to establish the requisite (present) good moral character to permit reinstatement, then in what instances is such a recommendation warranted? This was the question before the bar counsel in the *Matter of Charles W. Colson,* a case which presented the first instance in which the underlying theory of the *Hiss* case would have to be implemented.

By the time Colson appeared before the Supreme Judicial Court of Massachusetts, he had served his prison term and had been released. His crime, a felony under federal law, was not recognized under Massachusetts law. It appeared from the evidence presented on his behalf, that Colson had undergone some degree of rehabilitation in terms of his personal and professional life prior to judicial review of the disciplinary issue. As such, the bar counsel did not recommend disbarment, but rather an indefinite suspension, from which readmission would be predicated upon a showing of Colson's continued effort to establish the requisite public trust and confidence in him as an individual and as a lawyer. In an approach apparently consistent with that taken by the court en banc in *Hiss,* Justice Wilkins, the single justice sitting to determine the extent of discipline required in the *Colson* matter, decided to accept the recommendation of the bar counsel and suspend Colson rather than disbar him from the practice of law.

Taken together, both decisions suggest that in Massachusetts, disbarment will be imposed only in the most severe cases of misconduct, and that the trend in disciplinary enforcement will focus on indefinite suspensions, in which the court will retain, through the Board and bar counsel, a supervisory role in the rehabilitative process of attorneys found to be guilty of unprofessional activity. Whether this imposes too much of a burden on the administrative process, and whether, in fact, an absolute rule with respect to disbarment would be more favorable to creating a climate of public trust and confidence in the bar are questions which the Supreme Judicial Court of Massachusetts has chosen to ignore. It remains to be seen whether the effect of this policy of continued and prolonged supervision will result in a legal community whose members maintain respect for their own Code of Professional Responsibility, while at the same time achieving the trust and confidence of laymen who have long condemned the morality of the profession whose task is to speak for others in the name of justice.

Notes

1. Prior to the establishment of the Board, the disciplinary function in Massachusetts, as in many other states, had been carried out on a voluntary basis by local bar associations which took upon themselves the task of investigating complaints and reporting alleged acts of misconduct on the part of practicing attorneys to the supreme judicial court. In Massachusetts, as in several other states including California, Illinois, Michigan and Pennsylvania, the establishment of a centralized disciplinary agency by the court was an attempt to unify and strengthen a rather haphazard and impressionistic system of self-regulation by the legal profession.
2. Board appointments to the office of the bar counsel are made, subject to final approval by the Supreme Judicial Court of Massachusetts, pursuant to S.J.C. Rule 4:01, § 5(3)(b) _____ Mass. _____ (1974).
3. "Misconduct" is construed by the bar counsel as any act which violates the canons of legal ethics, or the disciplinary rules regulating the practice of law, which have been adopted by the Supreme Judicial Court of Massachusetts.
4. S.J.C. Rule 4:01,§ 7(1)(3) _____ Mass _____ (1974).
5. U.S.C.A. §§ 551 et seq., 3105, 3344, 5371, 7521.
6. The act provides for the admission of:"Any oral or documentary evidence.. but the agency as a matter of policy shall provide for the exclusion of irrelevant, immaterial or unduly repetitious evidence." 5 U.S.C.A. §556(d).
7. *See* note 1, *supra.*
8. Mass., 333 N.E.2d 429 (1975).
9. Matter of Hiss, *supra* note 14, 333 N.E.2d at 431.
10. 18 U.S.C.A. § 1503 prohibits individuals from intentionally acting to obstruct justice. [Ed.] Penalties included under this section include a fine of $5,000, or imprisonment for a term not to exceed five years, or both.
11. [Ed.] The case was transferred pursuant to S.J.C. Rule 4:01, § 18(4) _____ Mass. _____ (1974).
12. *In re* Hiss, *supra* note 14, 333 N.E.2d, at 436.
13. Matter of Keenan, 287 Mass. 577, 197 N.E. 65 (1934); Keenan, Petitioner, 310 Mass. 166, 37 N.E.2d 516 (1941); Matter of Keenan, 313 Mass. 186, 47 N.E.2d 12 (1943); Matter of Keenan, 314 Mass. 544, 50 N.E.2d 785 (1943).
14. Keenan, *supra* note 21, 314 Mass., at 549, 50 N.E.2d, at 788.
15. *Id,* at 547, 50 N.E.2d, at 787.
16. [Ed.] With respect to this point the court stated: "But a person who has been disbarred does not come into court upon his subsequent petition for admission to the bar upon the same level as does a person who has no record of misconduct." Keenan, *supra* note 21, Mass., at 218, 47 N.E.2d, at 32.
17. 345 Mass. 342, 187 N.E.2d 383 (1963).
18. Keenan, *supra* note 21, 314 Mass., at 548-549, 50 N.E.2d, at 788.
19. 353 U.S. 232 (1957).
20. 353 U.S. 252 (1957).
21. 271 Md. 196 (1974).

Part IV

Special Perspectives

The Washington Lawyer:
Some Musings

Max M. Kampelman

A prominent Washington attorney and active Democrat was recently warned by a Department of Justice official that his "superiors" in the Department were planning to bring a civil fraud action against him—and that the decision to do so was based on political rather than legal considerations. Last year, a prominent law firm whose members are oriented toward the Democratic Party was publicly embarrassed by being threatened on flimsy pretext with a grand jury investigation and possible criminal prosecution. There were stage whispers of a similar nature emanating from the Nixon Administration about other attorneys. These instances are perhaps understandable during the initial period of a new Administration, which comes into office filled with suspicions of the old, suspicions that are fed by campaign oratory. Fortunately, however, most Washington attorneys are generally not adversely affected by political changes in the White House and Congress despite their private partisan activities.

Politics is inescapably related to the practice of law. And Washington lawyers are even more preoccupied with the political process than are lawyers in other communities, including those in state capitals. It takes politics to make laws, and this requires an interaction between lawyers and politicians.

A century ago, Alexis de Tocqueville generalized that "[i]n all free governments, of whatsoever form they may be, members of the legal profession will be found at the head of all parties."[1] Of the fifty-six signers of the Declaration of Independence, thirty-three were lawyers; of the fifty-five participants in the Constitutional Convention, thirty-four were lawyers. Only in Sir Thomas More's irrelevant Utopia was society free of both government and lawyers. (A society free of government, according to its advocates, has no fear of tyranny and is not troubled by the refrain that: "Where law ends, tyranny begins.")

But simply to state that the interrelationship of law and politics is traditional—or that such a relationship is necessary for a stable and free society—by no means assures the Washington lawyer's good reputation in society. The symbiosis of lawyer and politician creates a major problem for the practicing attorney, for there exists a strong puritanical strain in the American body politic which mistrusts the political process and most of those associated with it. Rhode Island, while a colony, experimented with prohibiting lawyers from membership in its legislature. George Washington, who had good reason to be wary of politicians and lawyers, provided in his will that any dispute over its contents was to be resolved by a panel of three abitrators who would not hear lawyers. A nineteenth century dictionary explained that the "lake-lawyer" fish got its name from its "ferocious look and voracious habits." The Constitution of the Illinois Grange in 1872 provided that anyone could be a member, except actors, gamblers and lawyers.[2] And the American muckraking tradition in journalism nurtured an unhealthy cynicism about "politics" and the lawyers and politicians associated with it.

Illustrative of the problem is that many lawyers still find too many clients or potential clients seeking not advice, wisdom or legal assistance, but rather "influence."[3] Obviously, this is the clients' measure of the profession whose aid they seek. John Kenneth Galbraith recently wrote: "In a democracy, one should scrupulously avoid using influence except when it is needed."[4] But even a tolerant attitude toward the word or the practice (and it has many manifestations) still implies a special advantage.

It is difficult to know why "influence" plays such an important role in the minds of so many businessmen who seek professional guidance through the maze of government bureaucracy. Many of them may have found this to be the currency that counts in the business world or in solving their problems with state or local authorities. Perhaps they receive this impression of how Washington works from colorful press accounts of real or imagined misconduct. Be that as it may, even though the Federal Government is in the main incorruptible and influence has limited utility, the contrary impression is a prevalent one, particularly among clients inexperienced or unsophisticated in the ways of Washington.

How does a lawyer handle this problem when it appears? If the client's approach is a direct one, our firm's policy is to be just as direct, stating that we offer legal services, experience, knowledge, judgment—not influence, whatever that means. But if the possibility of influence is not openly raised, we make it a practice to engage potential clients in a general discussion of Washington decision-making, debunking the widely held and frequently unshakable but mistaken impression that the Federal Government functions primarily by favoritism. We point out that many who seek Washington legal representation erroneously seek to build their influence rather than their case; that it may indeed be that some government officials are corrupt, but that this is rare; that a government official or lawyer who agrees to be part of a corrupt practice is unworthy of trust, to say nothing of foolishly endangering his reputation and his livelihood. By now, the potential client probably has the point, and we either have a good client or nearly had a bad one.

Large fees, particularly large initial retainers, nurture the impression that the lawyer is offering more than legal services or advice. A number of years ago, shortly after I left Capitol Hill and entered private practice, a large corporation asked us for advice on a particularly sensitive problem with a congressional committee. The assignment required endless conferences with company officials, intensive search of the company's files and extensive legal research, at the conclusion of which we advised the corporation president that he should obtain personal legal counsel of his own in light of a possible, albeit remote, conflict of interest between the corporation and himself. A prominent Washington attorney was retained. The issue was resolved within a few days, whereupon the newly arrived attorney submitted a statement for $25,000 to cover a day or two of time, including two hours sitting next to his client during the latter's uncomfortable grilling by the committee. The huge fee was paid, and there was no doubt in my mind that the client believed he paid largely for whatever good he might have derived from the friendship of his new attorney with the committee chairman.

Congress, of course, is the center of the conflicting pressures within society and lawyers properly have a vital role to play in the law-making process. But it would be a mistake to assume that most Washington lawyers work with the Congress. The reverse is true. Out of Washington's estimated 7,500 private attorneys, only half deal with a federal government practice and only a handful of those with the Congress. The other half does the "bread and butter" business of any community of comparable size— real estate, zoning, negligence, banking, commercial, estates and trusts, and criminal matters. The lawyers are a part of Washington every bit as much as the attorney whose only interests are national and who may not even have joined the Bar Association of the District of Columbia until he was shamed into doing so a decade ago by a colleague who pointed out that his vote was needed to eliminate racial discrimination within the organization.

Some firms, like our own, try to combine a local and national practice. We developed a local commercial and real estate practice, with accompanying tax and estate planning services, because most of us preferred to maintain that legal expertise. The main thrust of our practice, however, remains a national one. Our firm was established in Washington by Felix Cohen, the architect of modern legislation benefiting the American Indian. It specialized in representing Indian tribes. This in itself meant counseling tribes with respect to their own local problems, as well as representing them before the Bureau of Indian Affairs, related government agencies and the Congress. My own experience as counsel to a senator for six and half years attracted clients who value a familiarity with legislative and administrative intricacies.

The lawyer with relationships to Congress does run into delicate problems. Some personal examples follow:

Very early in my practice, a friend introduced me to representatives of a trade association interested in advancing legislation to tax farmer's cooperatives. The potential client was wealthy and willing to pay. But it was clear that the association's interest in me was less for my skill than for what the client hoped could be provided by my friendship and previous association with the farmer's champion, Senator Hubert H. Humphrey. I turned it down.

Some time later, a congressional friend introduced me to a representative of a Latin American dictatorship interested in engaging my services at an attractive annual retainer—and could I persuade my good friend, the senator, to visit that country as its guest for a few days and see for himself that the charges of dictatorship were highly exaggerated and even irrelevant? I rejected that too.

Then there was the mining representative, who learned that I had made a personal investment in a mining venture. Why not represent the industry in an effort to persuade my senator to maintain, if not extend, its depletion allowance benefits in the tax laws? Again, I said no.

Am I trying to say that lawyers should represent only those causes or client interests consistent with their own personal values? Not at all. Recently, a few law students demonstrated against one of Washington's most prestigious law firms. The picketers claimed that the objectives the firm was pursuing for its clients were hostile to the public interest. This was condemned as moral arrogance. But, more important, it betrayed an inadequate appreciation of our adversary system of jurisprudence.

Ours is an adversary system of law that assumes every interest is effectively represented by an advocate. In most cases, the assumption is accurate and from the clash of interests and the resultant decisions or compromises, the "truth" emerges and justice is approximated. A law firm performs an advocate's role in our system pursuant to that assumption, and should not be faulted for not at the same time playing judge. Clearly, the system can be faulted when significant interests are in fact not adequately represented, particularly when the public interest is only feebly advanced, if at all. The Department of Justice or other public agencies may on occasion view their role as public representatives too narrowly, or may be performing their responsibilities inadequately. In certain areas, perhaps the Congress should provide for the participation of independent public representatives within the adversary system.[5] But to criticize an attorney for representing his client is to misdirect the effort. Our legal system may require some modification to bring within its adversarial framework representatives of interests previously neglected, but the adversary system need not be abandoned in order to better meet the needs of society. I hope that students will come to understand it rather than undermine it in their efforts to right the wrongs they perceive.

The student protest also quite improperly imputed to the attorney the real or imagined economic sins of the client. This, of course, is neither a new problem nor one unique to the Washington lawyer. It is common to criminal lawyers and those who from time to time represent political causes. Here again, however, the important values of our system require an understanding that the attorney does not assume the disabilities, if any, of the client. The independence of attorneys is essential to the viability of the adversary system and to the energetic fulfillment of the public obligations of the Bar. To alter this vital understanding is to undermine the adversary system by making it difficult for unpopular clients to obtain adequate legal representation and by making lawyers more conscious of public relations than of traditional legal skills and principles.

Judgments as to how we adjust our personal values to our professional responsibilities are for each of us to decide, guided by our own conscience. And there is no question but that conscience is more precise and rationalization less necessary as the requirement to earn a livelihood becomes removed from the decision. Some of our colleagues benefit from this fact. Obviously, for most, it is simpler to carry out personal ideological commitments and fulfill community responsibilities during the hours that clients are not being served.

This too presents difficulties. An example from my earlier Washington career might be helpful. Senator Humphrey had been persuaded to lead a legislative drive to close tax loopholes. To assist him to prepare for the legislative effort, an immense task given the complexity of the subject and the power of the opposition, we gathered a group of young tax experts, including lawyers in private practice. In our group was a Treasury Department attorney, acting without knowledge of his superiors, who feared to irritate the ranking members of the Senate Finance Committee. A preliminary meeting of the experts was scheduled for our office one evening. I noticed that the Treasury man left the room as the group assembled. The phone rang and it was my secretary asking me to step out for a moment. I saw an ashen-faced government attorney convinced that there were spies in our group and that his own role would be exposed, because he saw in our group two attorneys whose working hours were spent opening tax loopholes for their clients! None was more steadfast or earnest in their assistance in the days that ensued than these private practitioners. But the ethical problems raised by their participation, vis-a-vis the relation of attorney to client are obviously serious ones. Should they disclose their activities to their clients?

We were not so very long ago presented by clients with two problems that strained our personal view of the public interest. Mrs. Lyndon Johnson's highway beautification program presented a serious threat to junkyard and automotive parts dealers with yards adjacent to federal highways. However, it did not take much effort to persuade our clients that their best economic interest rested with their ability to convince their local communities and the Congress that they, too, were interested in beautifying the perimeters of their land and in shielding the ugliness of their inventory. The cooperative effort to find a practical method of attaining a community objective proved most satisfying to the clients and to us as well.

Then there was the problem of how to assist clients who felt that the administration's flammable fabric legislation could adversely affect their economic self-interest. To oppose an essentially useful piece of consumer legislation, as some advised, would not only be foolhardy, but self-defeating. Why not, therefore, lend the energies of the industry to helping the congress enact legislation which would serve the public interest and, at the same time, recognize that safety standards were to be established under the procedural and jurisdictional safeguards of the Administrative Procedure Act?[6] That is what we did.

For most Washington lawyers, a national practice does not mean congressional lobbying or bill drafting, but rather appearances in behalf of clients before executive departments and specialized administrative agencies. It is the congressional part of the work, however, which frequently draws most public attention (although attorneys for sugar quota-seeking clients, or with oil import interests, have their own tales of unwanted publicity to tell). For one thing, the registration provisions of the lobbying law, however inadequate they may be, require public disclosure.[6] Furthermore, lobbying itself is imprecise, and codes regulating congressional ethics are either nonexistent or so vague as to lend themselves easily to abuse and resultant notoriety.

Legislative strategy and tactics offer intellectual challenge, and the analysis of legislation has its obvious appeal to anyone who likes law. Lobbying, however, goes far beyond these areas. It requires endless hours and days of patient attention to and communication with busy members of Congress who find it difficult to keep appointments on time and have little opportunity to study. I have personally always found it distasteful to importune congressmen, no matter how valid or bona fide the cause of our clients, and I, therefore, appear on Capitol Hill only rarely. Fortunately for our firm and clients, my partners do not share this reticence and bring to their clients extraordinary zeal. When we do assume a legislative responsibility, our approach is not much different than it would be in any administrative proceeding. We marshal the facts and the evidence, prepare the best justification we can for our client's position, and do our best to make certain that the appropriate members of Congress are as well informed as possible as to the merits of the issue.

We find in legislative work that it is often necessary to educate the client, as well as the Congress, about the realities of the situation. Most legislative proposals that receive serious consideration are designed to deal with some real problem or abuse, and the client must be made aware of this fact. Very often the issue is not whether there is a problem requiring legislative action, but what that action should be. An industry which is prepared to offer practical and constructive alternatives or amendments is much more likely to be successful than one which insists on fighting every proposal, regardless of its merit. Frequently, therefore, a lawyer working on a legislative matter can do much to obtain results which are consistent with his view of the public interest and are in the interest of his client as well. If through blind zeal or excessive timidity the legislative lawyer neglects these alternatives, he is not serving his client effectively.

No discussion of the Washington lawyer's relationship to Congress can escape the question of ethics. It is imprudent to approach any discussion of ethics with anything other than humility. Which one of us has not on hindsight, by design or accident, acted at some time in a manner vulnerable to ethical criticism from some more detached observer? The subject, however, cries out for attention if public confidence in the integrity of our democratic system is to escape further deterioration.

It is not adequate to recognize that ethical standards in Washington are as high as and perhaps higher than those elsewhere in the country or the world. It is also inadequate to note that the morality of official conduct is deeply interwoven with public morality in general. (For instance, the policeman who accepts a bribe to fix a ticket has to be first offered it by an equally unethical motorist.) The ethical standards of lawyers and of government officials must be and *are* higher than those in the rest of society.

There are criminal laws to protect society from the rare instances of bribery and other clear violations of proper behavior. The more difficult area is one where the color is gray, the lines blurred between the proper and the improper, the ethical sensitivity dulled because of the encroachment of usage. With but few exceptions, men in Congress and elsewhere in government desire to obey the law, live with their consciences and avoid situations that could lead to their embarrassment. The desire to "do right," however, is not sufficient if it becomes difficult to define "right." It is this lack of clarity, coupled with the permissiveness and absence of supervision characteristic of the institution, which has made the Congress and its staff so vulnerable to ethical charges over the years.

If the statutes do not specifically prohibit an act, is it "right?" If it has become a common practice, is it necessarily "right?" It was once "right" for a federal judge to serve as a corporate director and collect a fee for that service, but today it is being questioned whether it is even "right" for a judge to accept a fee for a lecture or royalties for a book or to have private investments. Conditions, institutions and ideas change. So far, it has been considered "right" for a member of Congress to be a partner in a law firm, but will it continue to be "right" for him to do so? It is accepted that a congressman may recieve campaign contributions from lawyers and their noncorporate clients or from officers of their corporate clients with legislative interests. It is also "right" for him to accept fees for lecturing. But is it "right" for him to accept fees for lecturing before a group seeking legislative favors? Does it depend on the amount of the fee? Obviously, ethical standards in this area must depend not only on an evaluation of the intrinsic substance of the deed itself, but on the appearance of the deed and how it is likely to be interpreted.

My first exposure to this complex problem came early in my Washington experience, shortly after Senator Humphrey's election in 1948. A liberal Minneapolis shirt manufacturer sent him a few monogrammed shirts. The constituent's liberalism also led him to admire Paul Douglas, and he wanted to send the newly elected Illinois senator a similar gift. He asked us to forward the senator's shirt size. I telephoned the senator's administrative assistant who said firmly that "Paul won't accept anything more expensive than the value of a five pound ham." It appeared to me then to be an arbitrary standard, but with time, I have come to see the need for an arbitrary standard.

In a recent proceeding, a Department of Justice official thought it improper for a senator to have strenuously injected himself into an administrative determination. But the senator insisted that by writing letters to the agency, he was being of assistance to a constituent and was not usurping in any way the authority of the administrative decision-makers. And a recent article on congressional ethics in *The New York Times* asserted: "[F]ew would question that it is legitimate for a member to exert what influence he can with executive departments to further what he believes to be the economic interests of his constituency." [7]

A congressman's drive in writing letters or telephoning in behalf of a constituent can be directly traced to his interest in political survival. By satisfying a constituent or by bringing business or prestige to his district or state, he is making friends, and this is translatable into votes. Where questions of legislation are involved, he faces the obvious dilemma of conforming his constituent's interests to the national interest. Where a decision is not a legislative one, however, but is rather one for a member of the Executive Branch or an administrative agency to make, the dilemma is less evident. Most congressmen look upon their responsibility in this latter area as being one of representing the constituent rather than being judicial in nature, on the assumption that it is the administrator's responsibility to judge the conflicting demands and preserve the national interest. Intervention is not ipso facto undue influence. A congressional communication requires the bureaucracy to take a closer look, perhaps at a higher level of government, but it by no means should be allowed to be or construed to be a form of intimidation. More often than not, in fact, the congressman's communication will have the protective statement: "Of course, I am not in a position to appraise all the facts, but. . . ." The intensity of the "but" and of the representation will bear some relationship to the congressman's evaluation of the constituent's cause and the impact upon the welfare of the district; but the intensity has much less relationship than one might imagine to the identity of the constituent. Highly politically conscious congressmen are aware that assisting a constituent who is identified with the opposition may produce added political dividends. And the congressman who ignores the needs of his constituents does so at his own peril.

From my own experiences as a legislative aide, I can point to many examples where a congressman's vigorous intervention with an executive agency prevented an injustice. The injustice might be a human one, such as correcting a rigid bureaucratic ruling preventing a serviceman and his wife from bringing home their newly adopted Korean children. Or it might be an economic one. A group of small independent businessmen came to our office a few years ago complaining that as a result of a congressional hearing stimulated by one of the largest industrial companies, at which they had not been invited to testify, the Department of Commerce had adopted rules that prevented them from importing for sale American surplus property purchased by them overseas. Interesting a congressman to persuade the subcommittee to hold new hearings provided additional facts and perspectives, which, in turn, eventually led to a modification of the administrative regulation, thus permitting the group to survive in business.

On another occasion, one of our clients learned from reading a news report that the army was going to cease purchasing a product the company had been supplying for a number of years and would instead purchase another competing product from one of the giants of American business. Intensive inquiries by us could produce no facts to justify the change, no serious complaints about our client's products, and absolutely every indication that our carefully prepared documentation was falling on deaf ears. Only the intervention of a congressman acting for his constituent, presenting the case against the army decision to the Department of Defense, produced a reconsideration at a higher level by people who did not have a stake in defending the earlier decision.

Providing these services to constituents has been deprecated by some as a form of "errand running" and the motivation of political survival has been condemned as selfishness. It is my belief, however, that the process can be defended as essential to the preservation of our democratic system. It is healthy that elected representatives are interested in satisfying voters. Furthermore, one of the serious problems facing our society, as our population increases and as public issues become more complicated, is the growing disassociation between the governed and those who govern. This disassociation produces a political anomie which is one of the great problems of twentieth century democracy. The extent to which congressmen work to narrow that disassociation and relate government to their constituents helps reduce the dimensions of the problem. I welcome the trend by which the congressman is becoming an "ombudsman" in American government, attempting to ameliorate the occasional harshness and arbitrariness of the administrative process.

If it is proper for a congressman to aid a constituent in this manner, is it not equally proper for the constituent's lawyer to play a role in the process by presenting to that congressman the client's case, preparing memoranda and even drafts of bills or congressional communications to agencies?

Many believe there is virtue in a lack of precision as to what is proper or improper for a congressman, in that it permits standards to change imperceptibly and without resistance. It is this very ambiguity, however, which lends itself to misinterpretation, if not abuse. Lawyers who deal with the Congress have a stake in the development of a clear and precise standard by which to judge proper behavior, if for no other reason than to protect themselves in their own professional relationships with the Congress.

It makes sense to establish a Joint Congressional Committee on Ethics. Its first task would be to codify and amend, where necessary and possible, all existing legislation dealing with the behavior of congressmen while in office. In addition, it should adopt a set of broad Standards of Behavior, somewhat like the Code of Professional Responsibility of the American Bar Association. The Joint Committee should have a continuing responsibility similar to that of the American Bar Association Committee on Professional Ethics, even if its only sanction is the issuance of a public report. Congressmen should have the right to submit questions of ethical propriety to the Joint Committee for Advisory Opinions. These could be formal or informal, and in either event should be published in the *Congressional Record*. These "opinions" need never be discussed or voted upon by the Congress, unless a congressman takes issue with a conclusion of the committee, in which event he may request that an opinion or standard be debated and voted upon by his house.

From a practical point of view, it is essential that there be no opprobrium for a practice engaged in prior to the codification or publication of a standard or opinion. In this way, resistance to the establishment of new principles of propriety may disappear or be minimized. I find it difficult to believe that congressmen would not endorse and welcome the clarity that would then emerge as to proprieties in regard to lecture fees, legislative oversight, gifts, campaign fund raising, use of the postal franking privilege, use of staff during campaigning, expense reimbursement, personal investments, constituent services and scores of other questions that arise to plague an office-holder. The ultimate decision as to how he behaves, of course, rests with the individual congressman and his constituents, except in those areas where Congress has legislated or set firm standards of behavior. But at least the rest of us, including the Washington lawyers who deal with Capitol Hill, would have a publicly agreed-upon yardstick, in addition to private criteria, by which to guide our relations with the Congress.

Much the same problem exists in the executive and administrative areas of government. Newspapers recently reported that a group of lawyers who practiced before the Interstate Commerce Commission arranged an expense-paid trip for some of the commissioners. They obviously thought it was proper to do so—after all, it had been done before. Did the fact that a reporter for *The New York Times* made the trip public for the first time make it suddenly improper?

Should a lawyer pay for the lunch of a government attorney with whom he is discussing a problem, since he has an expense account and the government attorney does not? Does it matter if he charges the client for both lunches? Can anyone say that any government lawyer will compromise himself for the price of one lunch—or even two? Will he do so for a dinner at the Shoreham Hotel? How about dinner at the lawyer's home? A weekend at the beach with the family? What if the two lawyers are close personal friends or classmates and there are no official matters between them? Ralph Nader suggests that those who regulate industry and those who are regulated should not be social friends at all.[8] How realistic is this proposal?

Once again, what is needed is a Committee on Executive Branch Ethics, whose members are appointed by the president and whose task it is to recommend legislation to the Congress and, equally important, interpret existing codes of behavior by publishing standards and issuing opinions on specific issues that are presented to it for advice. Here, since we do not face the same political questions that exist where congressional ethics are involved, the opinions themselves and the standards could become hard and fast rules of behavior until changed, and should be backed by the power to recommend sanctions.

Ethical considerations are obviously not easily definable, but considerations of public policy and the maintenance of public confidence in government require a continuing serious effort to do so. There is the story of a little old lady who was given a small lovable calf. She loved it so much that she carried it to her second floor bedroom each night. At some point, this little old lady was carrying a cow. When did the calf become a cow? When does the innocent friendly gift of sentiment become a "thing of value" and thus a bribe? There is nothing immoral about driving forty miles an hour, but it is illegal to do so if the police post a thirty mile an hour warning in the zone. Instead of permitting our behavior to be rationalized, it is time to define the zones of what is proper and improper and to do so in an atmosphere less interested in finding moral fault and more interested in establishing guidelines that function to preserve the best interest of our society as a whole.

There is a corollary, if not a moral, to all of this. For the Washington lawyer, there is no substitute for the use of legal skills in the marshaling of facts, law and declarations of public policy. These and the experience that comes from a thorough familiarity with the court, the agency or the specialty of law are much more important than personal contacts. Familiarity with people in the decision-making process can be important in helping to obtain information quickly or easily to identify a problem. But this is a far cry from "influence" in the sense of obtaining an improper decision or information.

Yet, however great or complex the task, and however subject to misunderstanding and spiced by occasional criticism, the satisfactions and rewards are great. Those of us who are Washington lawyers must believe this, for there are so many of us and our number keeps growing.

Notes

1. A. DE TOCQUEVILLE, DEMOCRACY IN AMERICA 279 (15 The World's Great Classics 1900).
2. MAYER, THE LAWYERS 7 (1967).
3. A word such as "influence" means one thing to "a man of influence" and still another when used in "influence peddler." Similarly, a "wheeler-dealer" to one's enemies may be a "mover and shaker" to ones friends.
4. GALBRAITH, AMBASSADOR'S JOURNAL 4 (1969).
5. On February 10, 1970, Senator Edward Kennedy (D-Mass.) introduced S. 3434 to establish a public counsel corporation to speak for the "unrepresented public" before the agencies of the Federal Government. 116 CONG. REC. S1529 (daily ed. Feb. 10, 1970). For a discussion of this and related bills, see Appendix III *infra.*
6. 2 U.S.C. § 267 (1964).
7. *Speaker: Where Do You Draw the Ethical Line?,* New York Times, Jan. 18, 1970, § 4, at 3, col. 7.
8. Washington Post, Sept. 20, 1969, § A7, col. 7.

The International Lawyer:
Extra-territorial Application of
Professional Responsibility Standards

Milton Gwirtzman

The subject of this paper is inspired by a series of events which have shaken both the business and legal communities, and raised questions among the public at large. In recent years, lawyers for many American multinational companies have participated in the creation of a variety of devices by which business profits earned abroad were returned to the United States without the required payment of taxes, and later illegally contributed to American political parties. Some of these lawyers created or approved schemes by which bribes were paid to foreign officials to obtain business contracts. Some·participated in tax fraud by allowing such payments to be taken as deductions from gross income, in violation of the Internal Revenue Code. Furthermore, by failing to reveal information about these payments to stockholders, the lawyers violated the materiality sections of the Securities and Exchange Act. It is doubtful that such activities were engaged in, or approved, by the great majority of lawyers in international practice. However, these practices were common enough and publicized enough to create a substantial problem of legal ethics, and of faltering public confidence in the bar.

Perhaps I can put these problems in focus by briefly summarizing the growth of international law practice. For a long time in this country, international law was something like the law of the sea or the law of space. Much was written about it, but there was very little actual practice on the part of private lawyers, except in the area of trade. Only a few lawyers specialized in international transactions while in private practice. However, beginning in the 1960's—with American corporations' growing interest in foreign markets, with the strength of the American dollar as the reserve currency for international transactions, and with the establishment of the "Eurodollar" market—the field of international law grew very rapidly. There are now probably over two hundred billion dollars worth of American assets invested in foreign countries. International trade makes up fifteen percent of the gross national product of the United States.

Accordingly, there are many American lawyers in private practice, representing American companies, who find themselves dealing with the laws and customs of foreign countries on behalf of clients who are doing business abroad.

One might wonder why an American firm doing business in a particular country does not seek advice from a foreign attorney, who is a resident of that country and knows its laws. This is done in some instances. But there is a significant difference between the role of the American private lawyer and the role of his counterpart in most other countries. There, the lawyer is looked upon solely as a specialist in drafting legal papers, litigation, taxation, or some other technical field. The concept of a lawyer as a business consultant, so prevalent here, is unknown. The idea of a lawyer sitting in with company officers and learning about all the affairs of a company is almost inconceivable. Thus, American companies rely upon American lawyers for these broader purposes of consultation.

There are three types of lawyers in the international field. The most common type are outside counsel, who represent several different companies. Second, there are house counsel employed solely by one company. Third, there are a small number of attorneys who live and practice abroad, but are members of American bars. They are neither citizens nor nationals of the countries in which they reside, and are therefore ineligible for admission to foreign bars.

Much of the discussion of improper payments assumes there is a different standard of ethics for an American lawyer when he is in another country. Some attribute this difference to the fact that the standards of legal ethics in foreign countries are somewhat lower than those of the United States. This is not necessarily the case. In some respects, ethical standards abroad are higher. For example, foreign lawyers are never allowed to advertise in any way. There are no contingency fees in other countries. The idea of a lawyer taking a portion of the recovery as his fee in unknown. It is also unheard of for a lawyer to sue for a fee.

In other respects, ethical standards abroad are lower. In some nations of continental Europe, for reasons that lie deep in the history, culture, and political attitudes of those nations, tax evasion is an accepted way of life. Partly because of the traditional political instability of those countries, many wealthy people routinely transfer their income out of the country so it will not be taxed. The economies of Switzerland, Liechtenstein, and to a lesser extent the Baleares, are to a surprising extent based upon the receipt (for safekeeping) of large amounts of foreign funds—most of which, according to disinterested observers, is sent there to evade taxes. Because nonpayment of personal income tax is a way of life in many countries of Europe, the governments of these countries collect only ten to twenty percent of their total revenue from income taxes, compared with approximately sixty to sixty-five percent in the United States. In order to make up for revenues lost through the evasion of income taxes, these countries impose a sales tax of up to twenty-seven percent on each step in the process of manufacturing, wholesaling, and retailing goods. Insofar as local lawyers assist their clients in evading taxes, there does exist a lower standard of ethics for attorneys. But it corresponds to a lower societal standard of social responsibility.

Now, if an American lawyer is working abroad, and a client asks his or her opinion about whether a given course of action in the tax field or some other field violates the laws of some European country, the attorney must decide whether to say (a) yes, but the client can go ahead because no one is going to do anything about it, or (b) yes, but the client should not go ahead even though the law is unenforced. If the attorney gives the former advice, technically he or she is telling the client that they can violate the law. This would be an unethical practice if done in the United States. If the latter advice is given, the lawyer is, in effect, restricting the client's freedom of action much more than a local attorney and local custom would.

For purposes of this discussion, let us assume that the general counsel of an American multinational corporation, a member of an American bar, is asked to review a contract establishing a Swiss corporation, which is to receive two percent of the gross on all sales of a certain type of aircraft the corporation is selling abroad. The general counsel knows that the only real purpose of the emerging corporation is to serve as a funnel for bribes to officials of the purchasing countries, to induce them to purchase aircraft from that company, rather than from an American or European competitor. As an American lawyer, what does one do in this situation, in this ethical matter? Suppose, further, that these bribes, which amount to millions of dollars, have been made, and counsel is asked to approve the company's deduction of them for corporate income tax purposes, or to justify the company's application for their reimbursement under government contract regulations. Is it ethical for an American lawyer to approve either the dummy corporation, the deduction, or the reimbursement application?

Suppose that a lower-ranking member of a company's legal staff comes across the company's so-called "private" file, which indicates that bribes have been made or deductions have been taken in violation of the Internal Revenue Code. Does he or she have an ethical duty, as an associate counsel of the company, to inform the local bureau of Internal Revenue Service that these illegal acts have occurred? If so, how does one reconcile that duty with the duty of loyalty to the company?

Assume that a lawyer in private practice is asked by his or her client, an American corporation, to set up a corporation in the Bahamas which would act as a tax haven. It would receive revenues from its parent, and then transfer them to a Swiss bank, instead of repatriating them to the United States where they would be subject to taxation. Is it ethical for the attorney to participate in the creation of a corporation for this purpose?

Suppose an American lawyer, residing in Italy, has as one of his or her clients a large American corporation. An Italian citizen who is the president of the Italian subsidiary of that company seeks the attorney's tax advice. The attorney is pleased that the Italian seeks his advice, rather than that of an Italian lawyer—it shows he has won the confidence of his client's chief Italian operative. Were the Italian to go to almost any Italian lawyer, he would receive advice which probably would result in the evasion of Italian taxes—no more or less than any wealthy Italian citizen evades in what seems like the standard practice of that country. Should the American lawyer refuse to give advice, in light of the fact that the prospective client heads the local subsidiary of his American client? What would his American client think of that?

Suppose, finally, that an American lawyer residing in Europe is asked, in his or her capacity as a business advisor, to undertake an investigation of whether or not a certain request for a bribe will in fact find its way to the intended recipient. His client-company may be trying to sell a product to the Soviet Union. The company's agent for the sale says that the Soviet Union will purchase the product only if a certain Soviet official is assured that $50,000 will be placed in his numbered account in Geneva. The lawyer doubts this story, since he is certain that a Soviet official caught taking a bribe would be sent to Siberia. Accordingly, it could be that the company's agent is actually trying to get the $50,000 put into his *own* numbered account in Geneva. The company would never know. Should the lawyer refuse to make inquiry (as to whether or not this illegal payment will reach the intended beneficiary) because the scheme violates our code of legal ethics?

What if the client wants the attorney to act as a middleman in such a transaction? An article from the *New York Times* indicates that the managing partner of the Paris office of the prestigious law firm of Coudert Brothers was charged with serving as middleman for European payments for the Lockheed Aircraft Corporation:

> The senior partner in the firm's Paris office, Charles Toren, denied in a recent telephone interview that the concern had ever handled money for Lockheed. However, according to sworn testimony before a Senate sub-committee by a former Lockheed vice president. Coudert paid $100,000 in 1972 out of a special fund it managed for Lockheed, to an intermediary, who passed it on to Prince Bernhard, of the Netherlands. Whether Coudert made payments to Lockheed or not, the allegations about the firm's role, say legal experts, raises issues that have so far received little attention. Coudert was alleged to have managed a special trust account for Lockheed to pay money at the

direction of Lockheed officials in California to third persons in Europe. Professor Hazard of Yale Law School, who was a draftsman of the ABA code of professional conduct, says it certainly should not be improper *per se* for a law firm to establish a trust account.

The problem here, he says, is the fact that they may have been couriers for payments which may have been illegal, because "I would think a law firm has an obligation to avoid participation in the commission of a corrupt act. The canons say you can't assist your client in perpetrating a fraud. And this would have been a fraud if the purpose was to induce the foreign government to make a decision it would not have otherwise made.

What would we think of an English solicitor who gave money to one of our congressmen to vote a certain way? The question is really how circumspect a lawyer should be when a client is undertaking a course of conduct that may be doubtful." However, Professor Sutton of the University of Texas Law School says that even so "there might be a problem in disciplining the firm when you are dealing with overseas activities. Does that authorize any jurisdiction which they happen to be licensed here to take disciplinary action against him?

These are interesting and important questions. When an American lawyer practicing abroad commits an act which would be a violation of the code of legal ethics here, the foreign country does not have jurisdiction over him because he is not a lawyer in that country; he is not admitted to its bar. In order for his American state bar to take jurisdiction and institute a disciplinary proceeding, it would need evidence it probably could not obtain, because American disciplinary boards do not have subpoena powers that are enforceable in foreign countries. Consequently, there would be no way of proving that illegal acts had been perpetrated.

Suppose a lawyer is a member of the legal counsel's office of the United States State Department, and he or she learns that certain illegal payments have been made by an American government official to insure that officials of foreign countries vote a certain way in the United Nations, or take other actions beneficial to the United States. Does the lawyer have an ethical responsibility, as a lawyer, to bring these facts to the attention of the Secretary of State or to the official's own bar association? If the lawyer does nothing, can he be disciplined by *his* own bar association for not disclosing the information?

This hypothetical situation reveals the double standard which exists today with respect to bribery in the private sector as distinguished from bribery in the public sector. If a general counsel for the Central Intelligence Agency (hereafter CIA) was asked whether a CIA agent could pass bribes to Italian officials in order to influence the Italian elections, he or she would probably reason that the agent would be acting as a servant of the state in furthering American public policy, and that bribery was necessary to get the pro-American party in Italy elected and the Communist party defeated. Accordingly, he would probably conclude the action was not improper. But what if, instead of being an agent of the CIA, the person making the bribe was a *former* agent of the CIA now working for Exxon, passing a bribe to the same Italian officials so that the Italian government would allow Exxon to built a refinery in Italy. One could argue that in the case where the American government is passing the bribe, it is permissible for "reasons of state." However, are not American multinational companies, in many foreign countries, in practice (if not in fact) agents of the American government, pursuing the same policies, interested in the same results? Surely, American foreign policy encourages their successful operation as one of the ways to cement ties between that country and ours. If a CIA agent can employ bribery for valid American public purposes, certainly the former CIA agent should be able to bribe the same person for an American multinational firm for a purpose that strengthens the American presence there. And if he should not be able to do it as the representative of a private company, why should he be able to do it as a representative of our government? Why should there be a double standard of ethics controlling what a government servant may do and what a lawyer for a private company may do? Are not their roles essentially the same?

Significantly, the argument that the client has a "right" to legal assistance does not apply here. These clients are not like a suspect in a criminal case who asks a lawyer to represent him. There, even though the lawyer thinks the client is guilty, he represents him anyway, because all clients have the right to effective assistance of counsel and may not be deprived of their liberty without due process of the law. I would not think this "right" to counsel exists in a purely commercial matter. if someone wants to enhance his company's business by engaging in activities abroad that would be possibly illegal and certainly improper here, and if in addition he wants to perpetrate a fraud on the Internal Revenue Service, he has no "right" to a lawyer's assistance in carrying out his plans.

The decision one has to make in all these problems—whether he or she is a corporate house counsel, an American lawyer practicing abroad, or a corporate lawyer in private practice in America—is not much different from the decisions that legal practitioners have to make every day. Are you going to "go along" and "help out" with questionable practices, or are you going to refuse to participate, and by doing so lose some income, possibly a client, and perhaps even your job? An attorney in private practice can always tell a client "no." If he does so, however, he may lose that business, and might even lose the client. If the attorney is house counsel to a corporation, he might very well lose his job, because in corporations the house counsel is considered part of the company's "team." The other executives of the corporation often look to him for the means to accomplish their ends, especially if those means do not violate the law. A practice may not be illegal, but the real question is whether it is unethical. If an attorney advises, "You cannot do that," and management says "it is the only way we can get the business," a lawyer whose personal standards of legal ethics prevent him from participating may well find himself looking for another job. Corporations prefer their counsel to act as part of the "team." An attorney employed full-time by a corporation is not in as comfortable a position as a lawyer in private practice who has many clients and may be able to afford to lose a few. He is utterly dependent upon the corporation for his livelihood, and for a recommendation if he seeks another job.

The American lawyer who lives abroad is similarly vulnerable. He may be competing for business with a group of local lawyers who tell their clients to pay bribes because it's the only way to get business in many countries. If the American advises his clients not to pay the bribes, he may not keep the clients for long. Clients want a lawyer, not a confessor.

However, there is a solution for an American lawyer residing abroad. He does not really have to continue in the legal profession. He does not have to be a member of an American bar to advise American business firms abroad. He cannot be a member of the bar of the nation in which he lives because he is not a citizen. If someone is in that position, and they want to go along with the national ethics of a country, they should abandon the pretense that they are acting as an American lawyer; otherwise they will be violating their legal and ethical obligations almost every day.

The kind of matters I have discussed here have not yet come up before any of the disciplinary committees. One find no footnotes in the Code of Professional Responsibility on the subject. I have looked through the index to legal periodicals for the last twenty years and have found no articles on international legal ethics. I am reminded of a passage from *Profiles in Courage,* in which (regarding the lives he wrote about) John Kennedy remarked: "These examples of past courage provide inspiration; they can give help; but they cannot provide courage itself. For that, each man must look into his own soul." In this area, too, one has to look into one's own soul. A lawyer can do all these things and make good money at them without getting disbarred. If, however, he or she refuses to participate, and others do too, if enough American lawyers use their powers of persuasion and the respect in which they are held to convince enough American businessmen to stop international bribery, tax dodging, and other antisocial, unethical acts, we might then be able to convince other countries to do likewise, and eliminate the competitive advantage they would otherwise gain. Other nations are, on balance, no more or less ethical than we are. It is a crude sort of cultural chauvinism to assume that their standards are lower, or that the press attention and public discussion that enforce a degree of business morality here do not exist there.

This is the only solution I see to the problem. But I do not really think the private sector should be required to do this by law, unless the public sector does so too. I do not think we are going to get other nations to go along if our multinational corporations end bribery and our government continues it. But if we can abandon this double standard as a nation, other countries will do likewise. It will not be the first time American activities have influenced other countries. Certainly the Watergate affair, in which we almost impeached a president for acts that would be considered quite proper in many other countries, was a healthy precedent. America set a new standard of morality and acted on it, and I think we were glad we did. In some ways, we may have helped to elevate the standards of political behavior and governmental action of other countries with regard to wiretapping, eavesdropping, secrecy in government, campaign financing, and the like.

I have outlined the broad public policy issue. The personal issue is one lawyers have to face, whether they go into international law or any other field.

Very few law students choose to specialize in international law. However, the basic choice between practicing ethical principles and risking the loss of a client or a retainer is a decision almost every lawyer will have to make. The business world, like other parts of the community, has plenty of people with lower standards, people who want to cut corners to gain their ends, and who seek the assistance of lawyers to do so. The attorney who cuts his own corners to help these people, either because he wants to build up a practice or because he feels everyone else does it, will—almost without knowing it—cross the line between ethical and unethical practice. He will become the kind of lawyer who puts the economic rewards of practice above his responsibility to society. There are a lot of lawyers like that. Some are very successful. They are rarely disciplined by the bar because they operate in grey areas, and usually no one ever knows what they do, except for themselves and their clients. The worst of these are the lawyers who do this sort of thing without even realizing they are acting unethically, because they crossed the line so long ago they do not know what side of it they are on.

It is difficult to practice law with impeccable ethics; there are many inducements to do otherwise. But the canons are a useful guide. They are based on long experience. And one's own moral principles are an even more certain guide if we think about them and apply them vigorously to each new situation.

Ethics in Medicine and Law: Standards and Conflicts

Martin L. Norton

The sword comes upon the world on account of
the delay of justice and the perversion of justice . . .

Ethics of the Fathers (Pirke Avoth)
Chap. 5, Sect. 11, Talmud, Judah HaNassi

To understand the professions one must recognize the thought processes guiding each discipline and the conflicts produced thereby. The legal profession, steeped in the concepts of advocacy, pursues the logic of the possible. Words are the tools and the weapons. One's client bears the standard assumption of "truth," be it in civil or criminal law, and it is incumbent on society to demonstrate the contrary. On the other hand, the medical profession—pursuing the logic of the probable, the most likely, using Koch's scientific method of observation, hypothesis, testing, and confirmation—finds the questioning process of advocacy an anathema. Both professions claim dedication to the interests of the patient/client; both wear a second hat of dedication to societal interests. While both disciplines pursue their interests, until recently, neither has given more than lip service and token obeisance to the long-term societal implications of their actions.

It is the purpose of this presentation to point out some specific areas of these professions in which similarities and conflicts arise in the practical application of ideologic principles to the realities of life. While it is not possible to discuss the entire field of professional responsibility (sometimes called ethics), it is this author's hope that constructive thought and action, arising out of controversy, will result from this discussion.

The use of the language of the profession has come to be the hallmark of that learned group. This is also true in this intellectual exercise.[1] "Professional ethics" has been defined as the rules or principles governing professional conduct, vis-a-vis client or patient.[2] In essence, it is a consensus of expert opinion about the moral questions which arise in the day-to-day conduct of our endeavors. While no single rules apply, there still remains

an accumulation of practical wisdom and experience based on the handling and results of analogous situations—the case method of the legal
profession. Yet this is not enough, for philosophers all too frequently
become lost in sophisticated discussion of the trivia of the language of morals, avoiding the problems of the historical situation and the most concrete
dilemmas of individuals. While our colleagues in sociology (as well as psy-
chologists and academic philosophers) inevitably are involved and may
contribute, they rarely bear the responsibilities of their pontification.

> The example of academic moral philosophers is not very helpful here. For,
> instead of concerning themselves with the nature of day-to-day decision
> making in moral situations, they have tended to focus attention on the con-
> flicts which arise when there is a clash between different value systems, and
> the rare and somewhat exceptional circumstances when we feel compelled to
> choose between them. Related to this has been the tendency to be preoccu-
> pied with the extremely abstract problems involved in the ultimate justifica-
> tion of a value system as a whole, and the various reductionist theories which
> have been adduced to meet this demand. The modern tendency to be con-
> cerned with the meta-ethical analysis of the "language of morals," with a
> view to characterizing its "logic" and "semantics," might appear to be closer
> to our demand were it not for the fact that such philosophers should be con-
> cerned with such issues. In addition, their concern with the "logic of moral
> discourse" involves too often the attempt to force moral discourse onto the
> procrustean bed of an extensional logic which is ill adapted to the needs of
> discourse about values, rather than any serious attempt to characterize its
> own inherent logic . . . . The very urgency of decisions in clinical practice
> makes much of this irrelevant. The proper identification of the concrete com-
> ponents and factors in clinical situations requiring some kind of moral deci-
> sion is an urgent practical requirement for clear-headed and balanced
> judgment. The theoretical analysis of moral judgments as such, abstracted
> from the real life context in which the judgment is made, ignores the struc-
> ture of relations which give the judgment its significance. The coordinates of
> the judgment are the basis for its reliability as a judgment of value, and the
> values, if they are to be discovered in the fabric of relationships which make
> up the situation.[3]

The clinician must therefore follow the tradition of Hippocrates, who
insisted that "every physician should be a philosopher," in that he should
constantly be engaged in the critical appraisal of the attitudes and values
on which his professional practice is based.

Confidentiality

There is no area of interrelationship more sensitive than that of the confidentiality of the professional-client relationship. No physician, or attorney, could serve his client in a truly fiduciary relationship without this
assurance. The relationship depends on both a duty on the part of the pro-

fessional and a level of confidence in privacy manifested in no other area of secular endeavor.

The patient or client must be frank, ready, and willing to expose his innermost thoughts and motivations. Similarly, he must be convinced that his confidence will not be used against him, directly or indirectly—even only to the point of giving the appearance of such misuse.[4]

The issue of confidentiality is one which obsesses the legal profession at the present time. Lawyers are faced with what Dean Freedman of Hofstra Law School calls the tri-lemma in this area. Lawyers are bound by Canon Seven to be zealous advocates. They are also bound as officers of the court. Finally (though this *should* be first), they have a primary obligation to truth and justice. The conflicts in this area, particularly where a defendant may desire to commit perjury and a lawyer is aware of this intention, are obvious.

The dichotomy arises when we accept the concept that the professional serves more than one master. The lawyer serves "as an officer of the court."[5] He has a duty to society. He has a duty to his client—often in conflict with society. The physician similarly wears two or more hats. Responsibility to the patient is obviously primary. However, his duty extends to the family and to the public. A recent case held a physician negligent for not informing the proper authorities of the potential homicidal tendencies of his patient, tendencies sadly proven all too true.[6] Justice Tobriner's imposition upon doctors, psychotherapists, and police—who have reason to believe that a mentally ill patient may harm someone—to notify the potential victim, his family, friends, or the authorities, has implications and ramifications that are only beginning to be realized.[7-9]

Perhaps the solution, at least in part, is the differentiation of retrospective from prospective situations.[10] Yet, we must face the question of potential risk in contradistinction to real hazards to society. Perhaps the solution is to develop a lay-professional board to consider the ethical (moral), legal, and other aspects of especially problematic circumstances.

We recognize that the suggestion that regulatory agencies of each profession be structured on an interdisciplinary basis is one which is quite properly in current vogue. All too often, we are blocked by concern for the mechanics of such structuring, when we should be involved in the functions, duties, and answerable responsibilities of such groups. In this era, qualified laymen can be found in paramedical or paralegal organizations, academic institutions, religious centers of learning, citizens' advocate groups, and many other sources. The real problem lies in making the group members collectively and individually responsible for their functions. Roadblocks are primarily presented by the "political realities" involved; this is only another way of pursuing our inability or unwillingness to open our inventive thought processes to new concepts and approaches.

In the search for solutions to problems, peer review committees, interdisciplinary reviewers, medical society ethics and disciplinary and bar review committees have each been presented as the answer sine qua non. However, the committees and review boards that have been developed have their own inherent dangers; these review bodies are usually not held responsible (and thus liable) for the products of their deliberations, or, just as significant, their failure to deliberate and act within a reasonable time.[11] This aspect of their functioning is further alluded to in the next section.

Conspiracy of Silence/Discipline

After three years of studying . . . discipline throughout the country, this Committee must report the existence of a scandalous situation that requires the immediate attention of the profession. With few exceptions, the prevailing attitude of . . . [professionals] toward disciplinary enforcement ranges from apathy to outright hostility. Disciplinary action is practically nonexistent in many jurisdictions; . . . that [professionals] will not appear to cooperate in proceedings against each other . . . but instead will exert their influence to stymie the proceedings; . . . the members of the disciplinary agency simply will not make findings against those with whom they are professionally and socially well acquainted; . . .[I]n states with a small . . . [professional] population or in which disciplinary jurisdiction is vested in small local units, prominent [professionals] . . . guilty of misconduct received an unofficial immunity from disciplinary action because of the reluctance of the disciplinary agency to proceed against them . . . [T]he disciplinary process is stymied, public confidence in the profession is destroyed and continued depredations upon the public are made possible.[12]

The medical profession has for years been charged, harassed, vilified, and degraded by charges of attorneys, the courts, and legislators of a "conspiracy of silence."[13][14] The first thing that a law student hears about when discussing "medical malpractice" is this dastardly practice of the medical profession in protecting "their own."[15]

The quotation at the beginning of this section comes from the ABA Special Committee on Evaluation of Disciplinary Enforcement.[16] It highlights the importance of *every* profession's obligation to look within itself, to policy itself. The constant and current conflict between the medical and legal profession is agitated and certainly not alleviated by "holier than thou" attitudes and by hiding, within intraprofessional secrecy, the failures and deficits of our professions. No one learned profession, no single trade or business has a monopoly on either virtuosity or immorality.

The foregoing quotation further supports the argument that no institution or profession can serve as its own peer reviewer. The failure of the learned professions to adequately control the ethical, moral, and professional conduct of their constituencies has led to a progressive loss of confidence by the public. Backbiting by one profession against its confrere hastens this destructive process. Long overdue is the need for professions, jointly and severally, to face the realities and frailties of man. It is high time for the professional organizations to recognize that they must join in truly interdisciplinary bodies to consider the problems of ethical judgments—each contributing its experience to the problems of the other. It is also imperative that such bodies be composed of members drawn from many disciplines. They must be freed from the politics of institutions and professional organizations, and likewise freed from the corrosive influences of governmental agencies (as exemplified by Watergate and subsequent revelations about the FBI, CIA, and others) be they legislative, judicial, or executive. The ethics review boards must, of necessity, be developed through the support and encouragement of professional organizations and the educational establishment as a whole.

Availability

The current cry that professionals are not available to the poor, the disadvantaged, and the general public, with exceptions, is all too true. However, attention has only been given to minorities and ethnic groups, when in fact, the professionals have progressively made themselves *generally* unavailable—to an extent usually related to degree of economic success. This phenomenon is found at all levels of society. The allergist who is away at his country farm when his patient suffers a severe, hyperallergic bee sting is the classic example. A call to his office meets the response of the newly ubiquitous answerphone, telling the patient to wait till the sound of the beep, leave name, phone number, and any message—and the doctor will call back as soon as the office opens Monday morning! What happened to the sense of responsibility mandating proper coverage—arranging for a colleague to cover emergency calls during vacations, weekends off, and illness of the physician? Indeed, it is unfortunate to report that in a number of states the medical society no longer feels a sense of responsibility to provide emergency referral physicians. The reply, in answer to questioning, is that the patient can always go to the hospital emergency room. The sense of individual and collective responsibility is just not there. The effect that this has on hospital maintenance of emergency facilities, and the increased cost to the health provider organizations, third party payers and ultimately the public are ignored. The problem could be approached by making it the responsibility of every physician under the age of sixty to serve one day per year on an emergency listing in general practice, or in the area of his specialization.

Similarly, could not the bar association see to an emergency referral service in both civil and criminal practice? Certainly, this would prove to be a phenomenal public relations endeavor at the least! It is true that the attorney doesn't seem as acutely needed, until there is a problem requiring legal advice on how to protect one's job security, or how to get the son of the local businessman out of the jail where he has just been taken on a charge of possession of narcotics for sale. It should be apparent that this problem is in no way related to those who are not economically or socially "disadvantaged."

The responsibility to be "available" means more than sitting in the office by the phone. It means the "ability to communicate with or be accessible." It means providing a substitute or agent when the principal must be elsewhere. It also means responding when messages are transmitted, or at least providing a surrogate.

Under Canon Two of the Code of Professional Responsibility, lawyers are required to make legal counsel available to the public. How many adhere—unless directed to do so by the court—in criminal cases? With respect to both the legal profession and the medical profession, it is not the quantum of service, but its quality that bears significance.[17][18] It should be noted, though parenthetically, that the system of criminal justice usually does provide attorneys for criminal matters on an emergency basis. Again, the real question in issue is the quality of service provided, in sharp contradistinction to the quantity of available services.

What ethical or moral concept are we discussing? The moral responsibility to serve those who, in their despair, seek our aid—not our responsibility to our profession, or to our personal convenience or aggrandizement. This does not imply self-deprivation, but rather a return to idealism, to that truly fiduciary relationship which places the client/patient first and foremost in the time-honored traditions of service, duty, and honor.

Specialization and Qualifications

Since the Carnegie Foundation sponsored the Flexner Report, the medical profession has progressively developed the specialist category. This was promulgated under (1) the concept that the further development of medicine involved ever-increasing technology and both a basic and advanced information explosion, and (2) a recognition that it was impossible for the average general practitioner to have all the requisite knowledge and fulfill all the needs of his patients. Evidence supporting the validity of this philosophy is manifest in the progressive developments in medicine to date. Subsequently, there has been a feeling of patient-doctor alienation, and related problems in the technologic and information explosion. This has been spurred on by opportunistic and often politically motivated expressions of concern generally regarding the health care delivery system.

This led to the Himmler and Budd reports[20] suggesting a need for a modified slowdown in the specialization trend in medicine, with more emphasis on the interpersonal relationships of the old-time general practitioner (now euphemistically called the family physician). Thus, the pendulum has once again deviated from its extreme, and a restraining influence suggestive of a more balanced approach has returned.

There can be no question that the specialist has been able to contribute to progress in health care in a way that his counterpart, the familiar, traditional, romanticized "family doctor," could not. There also is no question that many influences, other than professional specialization, have led to these advances, and similarly to the breakdown of the patient-doctor relationship.

The legal profession, traditionally even more conservative than the medical, now faces a situation analogous to the days leading up to the Flexner Report. Prestigious practitioners, including our Chief Justice of the Supreme Court of the United States, have decried the competency of some of our legal practitioners and suggested a revamping of legal education with an eye to specialization.[21] Justice Burger's analogy of a situation of "Piper Cub advocates trying to handle the controls of Boeing 747 litigation" is certainly a case in point. Though characteristically slow to effectuate change, the legal profession is giving ever-increasing attention to this trend, manifested currently in California in the areas of criminal law, workmen's compensation, taxation, and the traditional patent law and admiralty law specialties. Mr. Burger suggested a program in every way analogous to Flexner:

> We should first recognize three implicit and basic assumptions about legal training that permeate their system. First, lawyers, like people in other professions, cannot be equally competent for all tasks in our increasingly complex society and increasingly complex legal system in particular; second, legal educators can and should develop some system whereby students or new graduates who have selected, even tentatively, specialization in trial work can learn its essence under the tutelage of experts, not by trial and error at client's expense; and third, ethics, manners and civility in the courtroom are essential ingredients and the lubricants of the inherently contentious adversary system of justice, and they must be understood and developed by law students beginning in law school . . . . Indeed our failure to do so has helped bring about the low state of American trial advocacy and a consequent diminution in the quality of our entire system of justice. The high purposes of the Criminal Justice Act will be frustrated unless qualified advocates are appointed to represent . . . .

The members of the legal profession, as yet, have not truly met the challenge and the example of their medical colleagues, in developing specialty training programs, standards, and examination for certification. The public at large, therefore, must rely on the intrinsic conscience of the attorney relative to his knowledge in very specific areas of legal practice. We must consider how this affects the confidence and reliance factor in the attorney-client relationship. There can be no doubt that such reliance is often without foundation. Certainly, the client cannot truly give an informed consent to his lawyer's suggestions, if this basic understanding of the lawyer's qualifications are not clarified. This leads us to the second aspect of this problem, namely, prelaw preparation for specialization.

As an individual with a modicum of training in three of the learned professions (engineering, medicine, and law), this author has been shocked by the total lack of understanding of basic scientific principles by legal practitioners. For example, the courts have fallen back on the legal fiction of the "reasonable man" when basic application of provable concepts in physics would more rationally meet the situation (for example, concepts of riparian rights as applied to air currents in issues related to environmental law). Another example is the use of dicta attempting to make law in the image of what the judiciary think it should be, or as Justice Black has phrased it, "promising what none but God can fulfill."[22] Can it possibly be that there is more to social interrelationships than vaguely defined and verbose sociologic and psychologic conceptual figures? Perhaps an interdisciplinary interdigitation, exposing the law student to the basic sciences of the armamentarium, might contribute to both a better understanding of and respect for the law, not heretofore seen. What this author is suggesting is that law schools require at least the basics of physics, chemistry, and biology, and at least an understanding of the principles of logic and scientific method[23] as exemplified and embodied in Koch's postulates.[24] The ability to apply these to everyday situations should be required as much as communication skills.

So, too, must we relate the practice of medicine to the premedical curriculum. The total lack of preparation of the average medical student and physician in the skills of communication is a notable case in point. One has but to read a patient's medical record, or request a summary of a patient's illness and hospitalization records, or, worse still, read the articles submitted for publication in scientific journals, to verify this atrocious lack. Even the laboratory researcher cannot and does not escape the requirement of communication in journals and meetings. Knowledge gained by the professional which he cannot communicate to both his colleagues and his patients is largely wasted, and constitutes a void in this era of informed consent, reliance, and patient/client participation in decision making. Furthermore, the physician must be introduced to psychologic and sociologic aspects of the health care delivery system, and their implications for society—ever recognizing the fact that the learned professions exist only to serve the public.

Informed Consent: Advising the Client

Questions about professional responsibility, ethics, and morality often start with platitudes—perhaps more to salve the conscience than to guide. It is only when this verbiage is translated into concrete practices that it has any significance. Thus, when the professional informs his client about the responsibilities he will assume in his representation or care, he assumes that many factors can be left unsaid. The surgeon is obligated to make clear the extent to which he himself will be performing the operation, the extent to which others (such as residents, interns, medical students) will participate, and even the fact that a partner will actually do the procedure. We know very well that informing the patient adequately in this regard is not standard practice in most of our institutions (despite vociferous denials). Indeed, all too often when the anesthesiologist makes his preanesthetic rounds the night before surgery, he has to answer the questions, "Am I going to surgery tomorrow? Who is going to operate?"

The practice of allowing the resident or other assistant to initiate surgery prior to the attending surgeon's arrival is somewhat prevalent. But even more prevalent is the practice of an operating surgeon leaving the operating room after the definitive surgery is completed, telling his assistant to "check for bleeders" and "close up." Commonly, it is the most junior person in the room (medical student, intern, or junior resident) who completes the procedure in as much time as it took to perform the definitive procedure, or an even longer period. Just as probably and frequently, this takes place despite the protest of the anesthesiologist, who has been struggling to keep the poor-risk patient viable. Another aspect to be considered is that the prolongation of the procedure leads to increased costs for time in the operating room and anesthesia management. The cost implication for health providers and third-party payers is self-evident, but by no means a current concern of the surgical practitioner (unless it affects his fee).

Similarly, the attorney must be strongly constrained to advise his client as to his responsibilities and duties.[25] Associates and clerks will be active in the research, brief writing, and conduct of the legal processes and office activities; the new junior associate may, in fact, be so deeply involved in presentation of the law suit that the predominant influence in the conduct of the action will not be exerted by the prestigious frontman on the letterhead of the firm. Again, despite the profession's protestation to the contrary, these circumstances are borne out by the experience of any law student, clerk, or junior member of the firm. To the client, the conduct of the case is just as important as his visit to his physician. One has only to review the cases and materials in our law school texts to find flagrant examples of ineptitude and borderline incompetence on the part of the various firms handling the cases.

The judgments made by the professional, his influence on the client, and, indeed, the client's own ability in decision making further complicate the matter. The courts have stated that the patient must have "whatever information may be required in order to make an informed understanding judgment."[26] [27] The applicability of this concept to the legal profession is obvious, yet carrying this requirement to the extreme is itself hazardous. The fallacy may be found in a recent report on informed consent.[28] In the study, preoperative patients were interviewed, and the preoperative visit and discussion was tape-recorded with the full knowledge and approval of the patient. Postoperatively, the patients were again interviewed, and asked to recall what they were told before the operation. This recounting was then compared to the preoperative tape-recording. The results indicated a complete breakdown in the recall, understanding, and consent procedure. In fact, the patients who were most emphatic in insisting on their full recollection had the lowest recall scores. We shall not try to analyze here the multitude of factors entering into this failure, although there is no doubt that such a breakdown exists, rendering the realities of the concept of "informed consent" open to serious question.

Contingent Fees

For many years the contingent fee concept has been accepted in this country. The ABA EC 2-20 lists the historical bases as follows:

(1) they often and in a variety of circumstances, provide the only practical means by which one having a claim against another can economically afford, finance, and obtain the services of a competent lawyer to prosecute his claim . . .

(2) a successful prosecution of the claim produces a res out of which the fee can be paid.

Here we find both implicit and explicit admission of the failure of the legal profession to provide services to the economically deprived, despite programs such as the Legal Aid Society, and others.

These situations demonstrate most dramatically the schism in logic between the medical and legal professions. The medical profession has, for many years, forbidden contingency fees on the basis of the duty of the physician to provide "medical service to all, whether able to pay or not,"[29] and admonishes that "a physician should not dispose of his services under terms or conditions which tend to interfere with or impair the free and complete exercise of his medical judgment and skill."[30] The legal-medical professional dichotomy is thus twofold. Consider the emphasis of the medical profession that each and every physician has a duty to provide services "to all, whether able to pay or not." In contrast, Canon One, EC 1-1 states: "A basic tenet of the professional responsibility of lawyers is that every person in our society should have ready access to the independent professional services of a lawyer . . . . " The absence of emphasis is self-evident in principle as well as in practice, despite EC 2-25.[31]

The accceptance by the legal profession of such a fee system permits, indeed encourages advocacy wherein the attorney has a personal and vested interest in the outcome. The dual role of the client advocate and officer of the court (and therefore of society) thus becomes an adverse burden, fraught with conflicts of interest. The medical profession has recognized and firmly acted against the hazards of permitting the professional a vested interest in the process and outcome of his attention to his patient—to influence his fiduciary relationship.[32]

A recent development, declaring unconstitutional an ABA prohibition against using expert witnesses on a contingent fee basis (DR 7-109[c] of the Code of Professional Responsibility) is another aspect of this problem.

A partial but significant provision of ABA DR 5-103(A)(2) is that "a lawyer shall not acquire a proprietary interest in the cause of action or subject matter of litigation he is conducting for a client . . . ." This would appear, superficially, to remedy the situation. However, it specifically exempts contingency fees! Nevertheless, this contradictory, double-standard type of reasoning does represent an admission of the very hazards of a vested interest as discussed above. (*Also see* EC 2-25, standards versus practice). In England, contingency fees are outlawed for many of the reasons suggested herein. A particular laissez-faire attitude prevails in this country with respect to agreements.

Expert Witness: The Consultant

The legal system relies to a great extent on the expert witness in matters of an "esoteric" nature. What is meant by this in essence is a consultant who has extensive knowledge and experience in an area of expertise. In practice, it means going out and scouting around till you find someone who will testify in favor or in support of the views to be presented by the plaintiff. As the physician sees it, the consultant brings additional intellectual skills to the care of the patient. His opinion contributes in an advisory capacity, but is not controlling or definitive of the "standard of care." Unfortunately, the concept of expert witness in law has acquired a pervading reputation of disrepute, based on financial influence. The courts have similarly degraded his status by accepting as "experts" individuals of lesser qualification (for example, substituting the qualifications of a nurse anesthetist for those of a board certified anesthesiologist, or the opinion of an optometrist for that of the ophthalmologist). The legal practitioner often shops around seeking the expert who will support him on his particular theory, rather than accept one who can and does speak for the mainstream of medicine. Some experts become professional testifiers, even advertising such availability in the classified section of the *Journal of the Association of Trial Lawyers of America*. Recently, a further refinement has brought added question to the current concept and use of the expert witness. In the matter of Attorney *Carl E. Person* v. *Association of the Bar of the City of New York, et al.*, the ABA Disciplinary Rule 7-109(c) prohibiting using expert witnesses on a contingent fee basis has been declared unconstitutional.[33] This retrogressive opinion can only serve to further the adverse reputation of the "expert witness" and make the unbiased expert more unwilling to participate.

The ethical concept of the expert witness has been challenged repeatedly. Nowhere has this concept been abused more than in litigation in the field of psychiatry. What Szasz has called "mercenary psychiatry" exemplifies the degree of disrepute.[34] The alternative to the problem is simple, and as presented most recently, is readily available: the use of the consultant concept by the judiciary. The court merely appoints individuals or a panel of specialists to study the problem and report as unbiased witnesses (amicus curiae by invitation or Master's appointment). Certainly this concept is no stranger to the legal profession, whose members are mandated as agents of the court. This is a common practice in labor law as well as many other fields. Cost to the plaintiff is minimized, thus negating the claim that specialized services are denied to the poor. Surely, the opportunity to obtain justice based on truth is more readily assured without the retributive greed extant under our current system. The objective is justice, not merely winning the case—an old-fashioned concept at best! Principles of ethics as published by both professions recognize, at least in writings, the quest for truth, justice and *societal peace*. This writer, at least, cannot conceive of the expert witness's (or the attorney's) vested interest in the outcome of the case as measured by his possible windfall of money contributing to that social justice.[35]

Summary

What we have presented here has been a comparative review of principles and practices. While we have specifically discussed confidentiality, conspiracy of silence, discipline, availability, specialization and qualifications, informed consent, and fees, as well as the expert witness, the reader should not infer that this encompasses the entire area of ethics. The ethics or morality of right and wrong pervade all areas of endeavor. We have not previously commented on teaching methods—

the manner of increasing the awareness of such problems. No technique of teaching has yet been devised for instant ethics or instant morality. The examples of teachers, colleagues, and one's peers serve more effectively than all the textual material in our libraries. Still, it is possible to analyze situations or cases to demonstrate the types of circumstances one faces. Even with this, the author believes that right and wrong and principles and ethics are rooted in the entire moral development of the individual; they are rooted in the family at home, and are expressed in the larger family away from home—the profession.

Notes

1. HARE, THE LANGUAGE OF MORALS (1952).
2. For the purposes of this paper the terms *patient* and *client* will be used interchangeably.
3. Thompson, the Implications of Medical Ethics, 2 J. Med. Ethics 74 (1976).
4. The discussion herein relates to ethical confidentiality rather than evidentiary rules alone.
5. Vanderbilt, *The Five Functions of the Lawyer: Service to Clients and the Public,* 40 Am. Bar Assoc. J. 31 (1954).
6. Tarasoff v. Regents of the University of California, et al., 529 P.2d 533 (Cal. 1974).
7. 18 A.T.L.A. News Lett. 49-51 (February 1975).
8. 19 A.T.L.A. News Lett. 6,244 (August 1976).
9. Ayres, *Law, Psychotherapy and the Duty to Warn: a Tragic Trilogy?* 27 *Baylor L. Rev.* 677 (Fall 1975).
10. *See* ABA Canons of Ethics, DR 4-101(C)(3); ABA Opinion 314 (1965); ABA Opinion 155 (1936); ABA Canon 37 and Opinion 202 (1940).
11. Norton, *When Does an Experimental/Innovative Procedure Become an Accepted Procedure?* 38 Pharos A.O.A. 4,161 (October 1975).
12. ABA Special Committee on Evaluations of Disciplinary Enforcement: Problems and Recommendations in Disciplinary Enforcement, Section I, The Present Status of Disciplinary Enforcement, at 1-9 (Final Draft 1970).
13. CURRAN, LAW, MEDICINE AND FORENSIC SCIENCE 581-82,589,590 (2d ed., Shapiro Ed. 1970).
14. Beli, *An Ancient Therapy Still Applied: the Silent Medical Treatment,* 1 Vill. L. Rev. 250 (1956).
15. Personal experience of the author in three law schools.
16. ABA Special Committee on Evaluations of Disciplinary Enforcement (1970).
17. Morrison, *Bar Ethics: Barrier to the Consumer,* Trial Magazine 14 (March-April 1975).
18. Marks, et al. *The Lawyer, the Public and Professional Responsibility.* In MORGAN AND ROTUNDA, PROBLEMS AND MATERIALS ON PROFESSIONAL RESPONSIBILITY 80-81 (1976).
19. Flexner, *Medical Education in the United States and Canada,* Carnegie Found. Bull. 4 (1910).
20. AMA House of Delegates, Report of the Committee on Planning and

Development, Minority Report of the Committee, Delivered at Clinical Convention, Denver, Col., November 30-December 3, 1969.

21. Burger, Fourth Annual John F. Sonnett Lecture, in 60 Am. Bar Assoc. J. 171 (1974).

22. Guillmet v. Campbell, 385 Mich. 57 (1971), V. Black dissenting.

23. See COHEN AND NAGEL, AN INTRODUCTION TO LOGIC AND SCIENTIFIC METHOD (1934). (*Compare* Section 3, at 1, *with* Section 7, at 347-351 [scientific method contrasted with legal reasoning]).

24. Koch's postulates, paraphrased: (1) Observation of the phenomenon or circumstance with all similar situations, (2) the situation as well as surrounding circumstances must be isolated or capable of isolation. (3) Reproduction of the phenomenon must produce the original type of situation (4) The phenomenon or circumstance must be again capable of isolation or specific delineation. (Robert Koch, German bacteriologist, Nobel Laureate of 1905, 1843-1910).

25. ROSENTHAL, LAWYER AND CLIENT: WHO'S IN CHARGE: (1974).

26. Cobbs v. Grant, 104 Cal. Rptr. 505, 502 P.2d 1 (1972).

27. Canterbury v. Spence, 464 P.2d 772 (1972). *See* 235 J. Am. Med. Assoc. 10,993 (1976) regarding Robinson, George, Montefiore Hospital, New York.

29. AMA Judicial Council, Opinions and Reports, at 2-5 (1971).

30. AMA Principles of Medical Ethics, Section 6 (elaborated in Section 7-15).

31. EC 2-25 admits that the legal profession has not does not meet this obligation.

32. The definition of "fiduciary" should and must be taken literally as "a person having duty, created by his undertaking, to act primarily for another's benefit in matters connected with such undertaking" (Black's Law Dictionary).

33. Person v. Association of the Bar of the City of New York, et al., 75C1473, USCD, EDNY, June 25, 1976.

34. Szasz, *Mercenary Psychiatry,* 174 New Republic 10 (March 13, 1976).

35. Wise, *Expert Medical Testimony,* 235 J. Am. Med. Assoc. 1425 (1976).

Contributors' Acknowledgments

Alexis de Tocqueville is the author of *Democracy in America* (1835) from which his brilliant and classic essay about the American legal profession is excerpted.

Samuel J. Ervin, Jr. is a former U.S. Senator from North Carolina and was chairman of the Senate Watergate Investigation Committee. Senator Ervin's article is adapted from a speech delivered at the Sixth Annual Law Day Dinner held by the New England School of Law on May 1, 1975. It initially appeared in 2 *New England Law Review* 1 (1976).

Jimmy Carter is the thirty-ninth president of the United States. President Carter's article is taken from the text of an address presented at the One Hundredth Anniversary Luncheon of the Los Angeles County Bar Association on May 4, 1978.

William B. Spann, Jr. is the former president of the American Bar Association. Mr. Spann's article is reprinted from 640 *American Bar Association Journal* 845 (1978).

Robert J. Lipshutz is the former Counsel to President Jimmy Carter. Mr. Lipshutz's article is reprinted from the *Washington Post,* May 15, 1978.

Jerold S. Auerbach is Professor of History, Wellesley College, and author of *Unequal Justice: Lawyers and Social Change in Modern America* (1976).

Joseph W. Bishop, Jr. is Richard Ely Professor of Law, Yale Law School. Professor Bishop's essay is adapted from an article in *Commentary* (August 1976).

Alan Dershowitz is Professor of Law, Harvard University. Professor Alan Dershowitz's article initially appeared in the *New York Times Book Review* (January 25, 1976).

Jerome Frank is a former renowned federal judge, and author of *Courts on Trial: Myths and Realities* (1949), from which his essay is adapted.

273

John J. Sirica is the former Chief Judge, U.S. District Court, for the District of Columbia. Judge Sirica's article is based on a speech delivered at the Seventh Annual Law Day Dinner of the New England School of Law on May 1, 1975.

Monroe H. Freedman is Professor of Law, Hofstra University. Professor Freedman's article, "The Lawyer as a Hired Gun," is adapted from an address delivered as the Annual Pope John XXIII Lecture at Catholic University, Washington, D.C., on October 28, 1977. The full text of this address appears in 27 *Catholic Law Review* (Spring 1978). His article on Judge Frankel's views appeared initially in 123 *University of Pennsylvania Law Review* 75 (1975).

Stuart Nagel is Professor of Political Science and a member of the Illinois bar. *Marian Neef* is a Ph.D. candidate in political science at the University of illinois. Their essay is adapted from an article published in 20 *New York Law Forum* 123 (1974).

Marvin E. Frankel is a former District Judge, U.S. District Court for the Southern District of New York. Judge Frankel's article is adapted from a lecture presented as the Thirty-first Annual Benjamin N. Cardozo Lecture, delivered before the Association of the Bar of the City of New York on December 16, 1974 and published in 123 *University of Pennsylvania Law Review* 1031 (1975).

H. Richard Uviller is Professor of Law, Columbia University. Professor Uviller's article is reprinted from 123 *University of Pennsylvania Law Review* 82 (1975).

Thomas Hobin, David J. Jensen, Michael S. Callahan, and *Hal. C. Pitkow* are attorneys and formerly students at the New England School of Law.

John A. Pino is an attorney practicing in Boston, Massachusetts.

Neil Pickett is a National Law Journal staff reporter. Mr. Pickett's article first appeared in 1 *National Law Journal* 5 (January 22, 1979).

John F. Groden, Harold Rosenwald, and *John M. Reed* are attorneys practicing in Boston, Massachusetts.

Barry Brown is Professor of Law, Suffolk University, and formerly Associate Counsel of the Massachusetts Bar Grievance Committee.

Max. M. Kampelman is an attorney in Washington, D.C. Mr. Kampelman's essay is reprinted from 38 *George Washington Law Review* 589 (1970).

Milton Gwirtzman is an attorney based in Washington, D.C.

Martin L Norton is a practicing physician in Boston, Massachusetts. Dr. Norton's essay first appeared in *Legal Medicine Annual* (1977).

"Judgment of the Massachusetts Supreme Judicial Court" is reprinted from 333 *North Eastern Reporter,* 2nd. 429 (1975).

Index

Administrative Procedure Act, 244

Adversary ideal, modifying the, 113

Aliens, 21; harassment of, 27

American Bar Association, viii, 7, 24, 38, 40, 187, 188; admission to, 41-42; *ABA Journal,* 25; deficiencies of trial bar, 109; antitrust proceedings against, 37

Antitrust suit, 17-18, 37

Appellate advocacy, 111

Aristocracy, 32; habits of, 4-6

Arnold, Thurman, 64

Attorney-client: relation, 45; privilege, 146-53

Auerbach, Jerold S., viii, 38, 41, 273

Availability of lawyers, 263-64

Bell, Griffin, 23

Bentham, Jeremy, 151

Bill of Rights, 159

Bishop, Joseph W., viii, 273

Board of Bar Overseers, 209

Brandeis, Louis, 42

Bribery, 245

Burger, Warren, 24, 109-11, 265

Canons of Ethics, 33-35

Carnegie Foundation, 264

Carter, Jimmy, vii, 24-25, 26-28, 273

Case system, 47

Centennial History of Harvard Law School, The, 46

Character, of lawyers, 4-6

Circuit Court Nominating Commission, 27

"Client control," 64

Client obligation, 172-73

Code of Professional Responsibility, vii, 33, 36, 44, 152, 170, 183, 257

Colson, Charles, 226

Combat system, 85-87

Comment on the Commentaries, 53

Committee on Executive Branch Ethics, 249

Concentration of lawyers, 18

Conduct, limits of permissible, 183

Confidentiality, 260

Congressional Record, 248

Conspiracy of silence, 262-63

Constitutions, national and state, 11

277